Žižek

Žižek

Beyond Foucault

Fabio Vighi and Heiko Feldner

First published 2007 by
PALGRAVE MACMILLAN
Houndmills, Basingstoke, Hampshire RG21 6XS and
175 Fifth Avenue, New York, N. Y. 10010
Companies and representatives throughout the world

PALGRAVE MACMILLAN is the global academic imprint of the Palgrave Macmillan division of St. Martin's Press, LLC and of Palgrave Macmillan Ltd. Macmillan® is a registered trademark in the United States, United Kingdom and other countries. Palgrave is a registered trademark in the European Union and other countries.

ISBN-13: 978–0–230–00151–0   hardback
ISBN-10: 0–230–00151–3   hardback

This book is printed on paper suitable for recycling and made from fully managed and sustained forest sources. Logging, pulping and manufacturing processes are expected to conform to the environmental regulations of the country of origin.

A catalogue record for this book is available from the British Library.

Library of Congress Cataloging-in-Publication Data

Vighi, Fabio, 1969
    Žižek: beyond Foucault / Fabio Vighi and Heiko Feldner.
        p. cm.
    Includes bibliographical references and index.
    ISBN-13: 978–0–230–00151–0
    ISBN-10: 0–230–00151–3
        1. Žižek , Slavoj. 2. Foucault, Michel. I. Vighi, Feldner. II. Title.

    B4879.594V54 2007
    199'.4973–dc22   2006049327

10   9   8   7   6   5   4   3   2   1
16   15   14   13   12   11   10   09   08   07

Printed and bound in Great Britain by
Antony Rowe Ltd, Chippenham and Eastbourne

Contents

Prologue

In Slavoj Žižek and Michel Foucault, this book brings together two of the most intriguing intellectuals of the last half-century, whose influence on contemporary critical theory is immense. Today few conferences in the humanities and social sciences can do without a touch of Foucault. Indeed, his thoughts on discourse, knowledge and power have passed into common sense to an extent comparable to the widespread literacy in Marxist and psychoanalytic idioms. If in the wake of his 1966 best-seller *The Order of Things* Foucault rose to the status of an intellectual pop star, Žižek can now lay claim to this title too. Since *The Sublime Object of Ideology* in 1989, he has attracted an ever-growing readership across a vast range of disciplines. Though no-one has yet dubbed him a 'fucking saint' (Halperin, 1995, 6), his work has generated a riveting corpus of secondary literature which is rapidly expanding.[1] While to some he is 'the most formidably brilliant exponent of psychoanalysis, indeed of cultural theory in general, to have emerged in Europe for some decades' (Eagleton, 2005, 200), others see in him 'an excitable Slovenian philosopher' (Boynton, 1998) who prefers to 'enjoy his symptom rather than question it' (Resch, 2001, 18).

This book does not try to steer a middle course clear of Scylla and Charybdis. We fully endorse Eagleton's assessment of Žižek, and one of the reasons for writing the book was to show why. Starting from a critical assessment of Foucault's paradigm of discourse analysis, we explore the theoretical scope and political consequences of Žižek's blend of Lacanian psychoanalysis, Hegelian philosophy and Marxist politics. Contrasting the two thinkers throws into relief the commonalities and irreconcilable differences of their respective brands of critical theory. By unmasking reality as a contingent discursive fiction, we will argue, Foucauldian criticism has only deconstructed the world in different ways; the point, however, is to discern the Real in what seems to be a mere discursive construct, and to change it.

The book, then, is not an analysis of Žižek's views on Foucault, although we will take them into account, but an exploration of

Žižek's work against the background of Foucault's. While the writings of both Žižek and Foucault have been subjected to close scrutiny from a variety of perspectives, there is no study mapping the psychoanalytically informed theory of the former against the poststructuralist theory of the latter. There are two good reasons to approach Žižek through Foucault. For one thing, the Foucauldian oeuvre is one of the most enlightening reference points for an exploration of Žižek's political philosophy, which is in many respects a 'post-poststructuralist' theory. Moreover, Foucault's writings have come to satisfy a widespread demand among leftist critics for a cogent theory for the now unipolar world at history's deplorable, yet inevitable end. Foucault-euphoria is symptomatic of a political constellation and an intellectual outlook which have been the primary targets of Žižek's criticism since the fall of Soviet Communism. They form the foil to his endeavour to reinstate critical theory in the field of radical politics. Three questions underlie our enquiry: What consequences do Foucault's and Žižek's theorisations have for emancipatory politics today? How do they affect the way in which we experience social reality? To what extent do they help us to imagine, account for and effect political change?

The book has a tripartite structure. Part I maps Žižek's notion of ideology critique against Foucault's theory of discourse. We take a closer look at how the Žižekian battle-cry 'Discourse analysts of all countries, get Real!' has given the withering paradigm of ideology critique a new lease of life, and explore the implications of this for our understanding of historical change. Part II continues this exploration by contrasting Foucault's account of power and resistance with Žižek's notion of the political act. We pursue Žižek's attempt to conceive a political intervention that breaks free of the vicious circle whereby regimes of power reproduce themselves by continuously creating and obliterating their own, potentially transformative, excess. The theoretical analysis in part II is complemented by a brief excursus addressing Žižek's take on the future of Europe. Part III expands our argument that it is essential to move beyond the exposure of reality as a contingent discursive fiction, by exploring Žižek's appropriation of the Lacanian notion of the Real as that which resists our symbolic representations, but whose very absence throws them out of kilter. We conclude with some timely meditations on Diego Maradona's 'Hand of God' and the universal applicability of Žižekian thought.

The book is intended for students, teachers, fellow academics in the arts and social sciences, and the general reader with an interest in critical theory beyond the confines of academia. It would be an added bonus if it also proved useful to specialists on Žižek and Foucault.

Note

1. Among the recent literature, see R. Butler and Stephens (2006) on Žižek's politics; Resch (2005), Pfaller (2005) and Robert Porter (2006, 52–85) on his theory of ideology; R. Butler (2005) on the notion of the act; and for a wide-ranging assessment of Žižek's work, see Boucher, Glynos and Sharpe (2005) and Vighi and Feldner (2007). For a recent introduction to Foucault, see O'Farrell (2005) and Sarasin (2005); for a critical overview of key themes, see Gutting (2005b); on his late lectures and subjective turn, see Gros (2006) and Paras (2006) and on Foucault and historical reason, see Flynn (2005a). For current debates, see the journal *Foucault Studies* (www.foucault-studies.com), and the *International Journal of Žižek Studies* (http://ics.leeds.ac.uk/zizek/home.cfm). Since we finished this book, Jodi Dean's *Žižek's Politics* has appeared, which lays out the underlying system of Žižek's political thought (Dean, 2006).

Part I
Discourse Analysis or Ideology Critique?

If Foucault's multi-dimensional work has left an indelible mark on the landscape of the humanities and social sciences, one of his most inspiring contributions was unquestionably the concept of discourse analysis. Only six years after his death in 1984, the anthropologists Lila Abu-Lughod and Catherine Lutz observed that '(d)iscourse has become ... one of the most popular ... terms in the vocabulary of Anglo-American academics' (Abu-Lughod and Lutz, 1990, 9). Seventeen years on, Foucauldian discourse analyses are at home in practically all fields of critical inquiry. Their ubiquity coincides with the belief that they provide compelling alternatives to the discredited Marxist paradigm of ideology critique. It is precisely here that Žižek disagrees.

Taking the customary degree of leftist Foucault-critique to new heights, Žižek brands Foucault 'a perverse philosopher' and 'anti-dialectician *par excellence*' who 'liked to present himself as a detached positivist' and lacked 'the appropriate notion of the subject' (Žižek, 2000a, 174, 251, 253, 257). The 'fatal weakness of Foucault's theory', he argues, is his 'abandoning of the problematic of ideology' (Žižek, 1994b, 13). This is compounded by the fact that the now pandemic repudiation of ideology critique has lent currency to an attitude which 'translates antagonism into difference' and extols the 'horizontal logic [of] mutual recognition among different identities' without due attention to existing power relations and the antagonistic 'logic of class struggle' (Žižek, 2004b, p. 20). Against the overwhelming trend towards the depoliticization of social relations in the name of identity politics and a number of theories of globalisation, Žižek emphasizes the importance of 'keep[ing] the *critique* of ideology alive' (Žižek, 1994b, 17). But does the Žižekian renaissance of ideology critique deliver more than new wine in old bottles?

The following seven chapters will shed some light on this. To start with, we take a closer look at the astonishing career of the Foucauldian notion of discourse and his historicist brand of discourse analysis, understood here in the wider sense of the term, as an intrinsic feature of Foucault's entire work (Chapters 1–2).[1] In a second step, we will examine the implications of Foucault's failure to theorise the generative principle of socio-symbolic formations (Chapters 3–4), and then explore how by conceptualising the Real of class antagonism as the disavowed core of ideological fantasy, Žižek tries to achieve exactly this (Chapters 5–6). Finally, we will consider the usefulness of Žižek's critique of Foucault by examining the politics of his model of ideology critique (Chapter 7).

1
Why Discourse?

It is worth recalling how the current Foucault euphoria originated. Paul Rabinow and Nikolas Rose evoke vivid memories of the intensity of the impact Foucault has had on many intellectuals:

> Foucault 'rendered visible' certain aspects of our experience *in profoundly new ways* for a whole generation of thinkers. Prisons, schools, and asylums now appeared as less than obvious responses to the need of crime control, the treatment of mental illness, or the requirements of mass education ... The belief that our psyche and our desires lie at the very heart of our existence as experiencing human creatures now turned out to be, not a foundational point that can ground and justify our demands for emancipation, but the fulcrum of a more profound subjectification (Rabinow and Rose, 2003, viii.).

It is no surprise that theorists especially were quickly fascinated by Foucault. After all, the persuasiveness of his ventures did not emanate primarily from their empirical outcome but from the particular way in which he approached and developed his themes. From *Madness and Civilization* to *The Care of the Self*, what proved most compelling was the way in which he re-arranged traditional lines of reasoning and turned blind alleys of research into intriguing *problématiques*. The following excerpts from volume one of *The History of Sexuality* illustrate this attitude perfectly:

> (M)y aim is to examine the case of a society which has been loudly castigating itself for its hypocrisy for more than a century,

which speaks verbosely of its own silence, takes great pains to relate in detail the things it does not say, denounces the powers it exercises, and promises to liberate itself from the very laws that have made it function (Foucault, 1990, 8).

The departure from the methodical pursuit of common sense could hardly have been more radical:

The central issue, then ... is ... to account for the fact that it [sex] is spoken about, to discover who does the speaking, the positions and viewpoints from which they speak, the institutions which prompt people to speak about it and which store and distribute the things that are said (Foucault, 1990, 11).

Methodological instructions like these from the often-quoted passage on Victorian repressed sex have long since been adapted and put to good use in a wide range of fields. It was, of course, not only the discourses of commonsensical empiricism and Whiggish progressivism which were meant to be disrupted by Foucauldian discourse analyses; nor were phenomenological accounts of the history of the sciences in themselves, or the hermeneutic project of uncovering authentic meanings of texts as such, the strategic targets of Foucault's critique. His criticism was levelled above all at Marxism and, increasingly, psychoanalysis insofar as they (1) championed reductionist and juridical conceptions of power (economism, repression); (2) seemed to adhere to humanist precepts and did not share Foucault's prophesy that, soon, the modern subject ('man') 'would be erased, like a face drawn in the sand at the edge of the sea' (Foucault, 1970, 387); and (3) appeared to identify power effects with the distortion of truth (false-consciousness and privileged-viewpoint theories).[2] The term that was meant to (and did most effectively) function as both a conceptual roadblock and an analytical catalyst was 'discourse'. In the course of the 1980s two of the key concepts of critical theory, *ideology* and *culture*, were indeed superseded by this rather indistinct term, which reflected intellectual-political needs that reached far beyond the compounds of academia. What, though, did the concept of discourse offer that transformed it into a kind of 'master signifier', while also elevating Foucauldian discourse analysis into a privileged paradigm? There was a whole range of circumstances which, from the late 1960s, lent 'discourse' a competitive edge over 'ideology' and 'culture'. The following aspects are of particular relevance to our enquiry.[3]

To begin with, Althusserian Marxism and structuralist anthropology, both highly influential in the 1960s and 1970s, were understood to employ concepts of ideology and culture that were universalist, synchronist and ahistorical. In contrast, Foucault's brand of discourse analysis – 'genealogical in its design and archaeological in its method' (Foucault, 2003a, 53) – offered specifically historicist frameworks which conceptualised epistemic practices and technologies of power as historically situated and contingent. With postmodern relativism on the rise, Foucauldian historicism seemed better equipped for analyses into what constitutes knowledge claims and power relations and how they change over time.

Second, the concept of culture was traditionally associated with the realm of ideas, meanings and symbolic structures, as distinct from material social reality. The concept of discourse, by contrast, offered an approach to culture that drew attention to the specific materiality of symbolic practices and was thus beyond the suspicion of idealism, which proved attractive to a range of intellectuals who were inspired by Marxist ideas but less than enthused by the dualistic orthodoxy of dialectical materialism.

Third, while received notions of culture accentuated consciousness, meanings and values, Foucauldian discourse analysis promised 'to reveal a positive unconscious of knowledge: a level that eludes the consciousness ... and yet is part of ... discourse', i.e. an implicit 'stratum of knowledge' which materially restricts what it is possible to think in a given domain and period. It promised, in other words, to reveal the 'historical apriori' of ideas, rationalities and knowledge systems, their 'mute ground' or unconscious condition of possibility (Foucault, 1970, xi, xvii, xxii; 2000g, 261f.). We will come back to this in Chapter 3.

Fourth, Althusser's theory of ideology had triggered great interest insofar as it did not centre on the content of ideas or systems of belief but on the unconscious categories by which the material circumstances were represented and interpreted. Far less convincing, however, was Althusser's endeavour to exonerate (Marxist) science from the charge of ideology. Foucault's theory of discourse, in comparison, seemed to offer what was required for a thorough criticism of scientific reason to the extent that it was structured around the 'microphysics of power' and its attendant discursive practices. 'Ideology is not exclusive of scientificity', Foucault argued in *The Archaeology of Knowledge*, and cannot simply be opposed to scientific discourse; its role 'does not diminish as rigour increases and error is dissipated' (Foucault, 2002a, 205). Later, Foucault distanced himself from the concept of ideology itself, which 'cannot be used without circumspection', inasmuch as it 'always stands in virtual opposition to something else that is supposed to count as truth'. The latter, as he famously put it, 'isn't outside power or lacking in power'. All forms of thought are inescapably caught up in the interplay of power and knowledge, and the regimes of truth sustained by it (Foucault, 2002c, 119 and 131; see also 1991, 26–8).

Fifth, the concept of ideology was also associated with the Marxist theory of base and superstructure, a sociological model which, after a century of battering, was considered obsolete even among Marxists. Foucault rejected the notion of ideology not only on the grounds that it was masquerading as the opposite of truth, but also insofar as it stood 'in a secondary position relative to something that functions as its infrastructure, as its material, economic determinant' (Foucault, 2002c, 119). The horizontal notion of discourse and the Foucauldian paradigm of discourse analysis, by contrast, seemed to offer a persuasive alternative to ideology critique while, at the same time, retaining many of its analytically valuable functions. By denaturalising terms such as illness, madness and sexuality, all of Foucault's major works were pointing to the possibility of thinking about these topics and others in radically different ways. His concept of discursive formations as introduced in *The Archaeology of Knowledge* (Foucault, 2002a, 34–43) could even serve as a potential framework for the analysis of ideologies that avoided the crude determinist implications of the base-superstructure model. Yet it is Foucault's genealogical works that provide the most striking examples of the degree to which his strategy of bypassing the problematic of ideology via discourse analysis fulfilled vital functions of traditional ideology critique. By highlighting the contingency of historical processes, *Discipline and Punish* and volume one of *The History of Sexuality* exposed the eternalisation of historically specific modes of power and subjectivation as untenable, and raised by implication the question of potential, yet not actualised, historical alternatives (see also Foucault, 2003a, 53f.).

Sixth, the concept of ideology seemed to be inextricably linked with the Marxist concept of class struggle, whereas discourse appeared to reflect also, or more adequately, the conflicts of gender and race, which became paramount topics for the fast growing fields of feminist, post-colonial and cultural studies.

Seventh, the collapse of Marxism as a geopolitical presence since 1989 has been accompanied by a mass exodus from 'ideology' as a critical framework for cultural and political analysis by leftist Western critics.[4] Many cultural and political theorists have turned to one or another spin on Gramsci's notion of hegemony and even more so to Foucault, as in much queer theory. It is striking how the acceptance in academia of Foucauldian approaches surged during the 1990s, with even more tradition-bound empiricist disciplines such as History opening to Foucauldian strategies as a matter of normality.[5] 'The theory wars are over', as Michael S. Roth puts it, 'Jenkins's *Refiguring History* is a Routledge classic, Hayden White is required reading' (Roth, 2004, 378) and, one might add, a Foucault industry has finally been established.

Of all the aspects enumerated above, the single most important one to elevate 'discourse' into a privileged paradigm was its historicism: Foucault's uncompromising historicism was the trademark of his brand of discourse analysis. It was this historicist stance more than anything else, after all, which earned him the unsolicited title of '*post*-structuralist'.

2
Foucault's Critical Historicism

The nature of Foucault's historicism, however, can hardly be taken for granted. What Jürgen Habermas rejected as 'presentistic, relativist and crypto-normative pseudo-science' (Habermas, 1985, 324) was hailed by Paul Veyne as a 'Copernican reversal' and revolution in the writing of history (Veyne, 1997, 150; 2003). Gilles Deleuze praised Foucault as a pioneer of a 'properly philosophical form of interrogation which is itself new and which revives History' (Deleuze, 1999, 42), Oswyn Murray saw in him the 'greatest modern philosophical historian' (Murray, 1992, viii) and Mitchell Dean 'a kind of touchstone for many ... in the humanities and social sciences' (Dean, 1994, 2). Indeed, to a growing number of historical theorists today Foucault epitomises the idea of 'history writing as critique' which 'opens up new ways of imagining the future' (Scott, 2006). In one of the most meticulous studies of Foucault in recent years, Ulrich Brieler embraces the 'relentless historicity' of his work as the most radical attempt in contemporary historical thought to overcome the ostensible objectivity of history and its multifarious rationalisations. By practicing history without transcendental certainties, Brieler argues, Foucault has stretched the limits of traditional historicist positions to breaking point, which makes him 'a *historian par excellence*' (Brieler, 1998, 4f., 627). Paul Hamilton, by comparison, is more sceptical. He contends that far from effecting a radical break with tradition, Foucault's engagement with history winds up in 'yet another variant on the [hermeneutic] historicism with which he always tried to break' (Hamilton, 2003, 124). At the hands of historical practitioners Foucault fared usually worse. More often than not, his historical explorations were dismissed as 'self-consciously opaque pyrotechnics' (Scull, 1981, 5), 'simplistic and over-generalized' (Porter, Roy, 2003, 93) and thus of limited use (Evans, 2001, 82 and 195).[1] It was left to Hans-Ulrich Wehler, however, to issue Foucault the *testimonium paupertatis*. Wehler's Foucault is 'an intellectually dishonest, empirically absolutely unreliable, crypto-normative "snake charmer" at postmodernity's service' (Wehler, 1998, 91), which brings us back to Habermas and his rejection of Foucault's 'radical historicism' (Habermas, 1985, 324).[2] If Foucault's writing as a whole has polarised his readership from the beginning, his historicist stance is no exception. But what exactly are we referring to when we call Foucault a 'historicist'?

Without delving into the infinite story of the controversy 'What is historicism?', the term can be attributed to positions which subscribe to one or more of the following propositions.[3] First, the view that nothing in the social world is eternal and immutable: everything has a history and is subject to change, our institutions and practices as well as our aesthetic preferences and ethical maxims. Second, the conviction that historical development is the most basic aspect of human existence, and the attendant belief that the study of the evolution of a given phenomenon holds the key for an adequate understanding of its nature and identity. Third, the assumption criticised by Popper (1957) that historical evolution is governed by law-like patterns, the discovery of which allows to predict future developments with scientific precision. Fourth, the notion that human practices, institutions and beliefs are historically situated and defined by their specific context and thus have to be explained in terms of the contingent factors which gave rise to them. Where, then, does Foucault stand on this?

While it is often difficult to locate Foucault intellectually as he remained notoriously cryptic on the coordinates of his ventures, if we search for a concise account of Foucauldian historicism we quickly find what we are looking for. Like no other text before and after, Foucault's 1971 essay *Nietzsche, Genealogy, History* spells out clearly and uncompromisingly his relativistic notion of history as an object of study and epistemic practice. The quintessence of this is captured in the following passage on genealogical or 'effective' history.

We believe that feelings are immutable, but every sentiment, particularly the noblest and most disinterested, has a history. We believe in the dull constancy of instinctual life and imagine that it continues to exert its force indiscriminately in the present as it did in the past. But historical knowledge easily disintegrates this unity....We believe, in any event, that the body obeys the exclusive laws of physiology, and that it escapes the influence of history, but this too is false. The body is moulded by a great many distinct regimes; it is broken down by the rhythms of work, rest, and holidays; it is poisoned by food or values, through eating habits or moral laws (Foucault, 2003c, 360).

Foucault concludes this passage by stressing that:

'Effective' history differs from the history of historians in being without constants. Nothing in man – not even his body – is sufficiently stable to serve as the basis for self-recognition or for understanding other men' (Foucault, 2003c, 360).

In other words, by refusing the 'certainties of absolutes', effective history in the Nietzschean sense of *wirkliche Geschichte* (i.e. proper and effectual historiography) promises to avoid the pitfalls of 'traditional history in its dependence on metaphysics'. Genealogical historiography becomes effective historiography inasmuch as it 'reintroduces into the realm of becoming everything considered immortal in man' (2003c, 360f.). Yet Foucault is far from being an evolutionary historicist. On the contrary, his genealogical historiography

does not pretend to go back in time to restore an unbroken continuity that operates beyond the dispersion of oblivion; its task is not to demonstrate that the past actively exists in the present, that it continues secretly to animate the present, having imposed a predetermined form on all its vicissitudes. Genealogy does not resemble the evolution of a species and does not map the destiny of a people (Foucault, 2003c, 355).

Foucault then is first of all a historicist in the first sense of the term historicism: everything has a history and is in this precise sense historical. But unlike evolutionary historiography with its predilection 'for retracing the past as a patient and continuous development', Foucault's genealogical historiography is meant to 'uproot [the] traditional foundations' of history and 'relentlessly disrupt its pretended continuity' (2003c, 360). This conforms to his notion of archaeological historiography as developed in the 1960s. In *The Birth of the Clinic, The Order of Things* and, more systematically, *The Archaeology of Knowledge*, Foucault was keen to prove how the most striking continuity of history consisted in its radical discontinuity.[4] In the 'run-up' to his notion of genealogical historiography – which was meant to explore the discontinuous redeployment of power in different discursive regimes – Foucault then, in a review essay from 1970, aligns himself with Deleuze's reading of Nietzsche's notion of Eternal Return and now emphasises that what recurs eternally is difference (while 'the analogous, the similar, and the identical' do not return): 'Being is a Return freed from the curvature of the circle'; it is 'the recurrence of difference' as the force which over and over again produces the New. Still in the same essay he casts the emphatic relativism of his concept of history in a memorable formula: 'the present is a throw of the dice ... in the same stroke, both the dice and the rules are thrown' (2000c, 360 and 366).

This implies that, against an 'entire historical tradition' which tries to dissolve the singularity of events into the ideal continuity of a 'theological movement or natural process' (Foucault, 2000c, 360 and 366).

> The forces operating in history do not obey destiny or regulative mechanisms, but the luck of the battle. They do not manifest the successive forms of a primordial intention and their attention is not that of a conclusion, for they always appear through the singular randomness of events (2003c, 361).

In other words, Foucault not only expresses great reservations vis-à-vis the progressive evolutionism inherent in historicism number two, he also rejects the teleology and finalism of number three. Rather than presuming 'that the present rests upon profound intentions and immutable necessities', genealogical history 'confirms our existence among countless lost events, without a landmark or a

point of reference' (2003c, 361). Its mission is to show us how successive historical configurations emerged as a consequence of contingent turns of history rather than as the result of inevitable trends.

Foucault, of course, is in important respects also a historicist in
the fourth of the meanings cited above. For Foucault, human practices, institutions and beliefs have to be explored in their distinctive
historical contexts without imposing anachronistic categories of
recognition and evaluation. 'What Foucault takes from History', as
Deleuze has pointed out, 'is that determination of visible and articulable features unique to each age which goes beyond any behaviour,
mentality or set of ideas, since it makes these things possible'; any
new regime of knowledge – which in Foucault 'is defined by the
combinations of visible and articulable that are unique to each ...
historical formation' – engenders its own, specific objects rather than
progressing to a fuller knowledge of the previous ones (Deleuze, 1999,
42, 44). Whether on reason and madness, the medical gaze, the formation of the human sciences, the birth of the prison or the history
of sexuality, all his major writings show how our most firmly held
beliefs about our selves, our bodies and social relations are embedded in contingent historical systems of discursive representation.

Yet the angle of Foucault's historicism remains distinctive. Not
only does he reject the leitmotif of classical Rankean *historism* by
refusing to take the past on its own (conscious) terms,[5] his genealogical historiography is, moreover, radically *presentistic*. Its task is to
write 'the history of the present', albeit not in the meaning of a
'history of the past in terms of the present' (Foucault, 1991, 31), but
as a historiographic practice which takes as its point of departure a
particular problematic in the present, exploring former intensities
of power recognisable now in different disciplines and settings.
What ultimately propels Foucault's historicist project is not so much
(a) the aspiration to set the story straight and tell us how it really
was (although there clearly is a positivist streak in Foucault), nor (b)
the ambition to develop a general historical methodology (although
this, too, is clearly present in his writings), but rather (c) the endeavour to subvert the historical narratives which organize the way in
which we experience our present reality (an endeavour for which a
good dose of (a) and (b) proved very instrumental). Yet in order to
expose the mechanisms of intellectual socialisation through victorious accounts of the past, it was vital to understand how the history

of the West was intertwined with the way in which *truth* was produced. The history of the West, Foucault argued in an interview with Bernard-Henri Levy in 1977, could not be dissociated from the history of the making of truth and the inherent power of discourses which have been accepted as true (Foucault, 1988, 112). Against entrenched notions of power, freedom and knowledge, one would have to demonstrate 'that truth is not by nature free – nor error servile – but that its production is thoroughly imbued with relations of power' (Foucault, 1990, 60). At the heart of Foucault's historicism, then, we find a 'political history of truth' (ibid.), where archaeological method and genealogical design combine to form a Nietzschean variant of ideology critique.[6]

Foucault did not adopt a supra-historical position to exempt himself from such a history of truth. Far from it, his presentism was coupled with a thoroughgoing *perspectivism* which, in his genealogical historiography, explicitly extended to his own position of enunciation.[7] Against 'these lustful eunuchs of history' who 'take unusual pains to erase the elements in their work which reveal their grounding in a particular time and place', as Nietzsche (2000, pt. 3, sec. 25) put it. Foucault's historicist project of a political history of truth was meant to be a 'vertical projection of its position', which would allow knowledge, ultimately, 'to create its own genealogy in the act of cognition' (Foucault, 2003c, 362f.).[8] – What, then, is 'wrong' with Foucault?

3
The *Positive Unconscious*: in Search of the Matrix

In a self-interview, Žižek once posed the question whether 'from Foucauldian historicist premises' it would not be justified to criticise his own writing as eternalizing 'a historically specific, limited logic of symbolization'. He rejected the reproach of ahistoricity by drawing a line between 'historicity proper' and historicism. Historicity proper, he argued, was predicated on a dialectical relationship with the Real as the unhistorical traumatic kernel that returns as the Same through all historical epochs, albeit 'not as an underlying Essence but as a rock that trips up every attempt to integrate it into the symbolic order'. The Real, in its unhistoricity, would be constitutive of the very order of symbolic historicity, setting 'in motion one new symbolization after another' (Žižek, 1994a, 199). In this context, Žižek came up with a concise definition: 'historicism', he suggested, equals 'historicity *minus* the unhistorical kernel of the Real', the latter being the 'blind spot of historicism' (Žižek, 2001a, 81). Did Foucault "overlook" the dimension of the Real? Not at all. On the contrary, Foucault was well aware that 'there, in the midst of [discourse] is an essential void: the necessary disappearance of that which is its foundation' (Foucault, 1970, 16); 'a void, a moment of silence, a question without answer, ... a breach without reconciliation where the world is forced to question itself' (Foucault, 1965, 288). How can we account for such obvious discrepancy?

To begin with, the relationship between Žižek and Foucault is not so straightforward as it might appear at this stage. There is no symmetry of opposites which can neatly be recounted, as Žižek's allusion to the 'blind spot' of historicism might suggest. Foucault did

18

not simply overlook the dimension marked out by the Real. Between the meticulous historian of the present with positivist leanings on the one hand, and the theorist of power/knowledge with his nominalistic bias on the other, there lurks another Foucault who homes in on the notion of a presence which 'is there and yet is hidden', which 'exists with the mute solidity of a thing' like 'a text closed in upon itself'; who explores the void from which language speak, a region which is 'by definition inaccessible to any theoretical knowledge of man', a region 'where representation remains in suspense'; who is by no means surprised at the fact that the human sciences, while advancing towards the unconscious 'with their back to it, waiting for it to unveil itself as fast as consciousness is analysed', dismiss it as 'Freudian mythology', for 'to a knowledge situated within the representable, all that frames and defines, on the outside, the very possibility of representation can be nothing other than mythology' (Foucault, 1970, 374f.; 1963, 207f.). This 'third' Foucault, as it were, is a close relative of Žižek's.

Charles Shepherdson has mapped this side of Foucault's work with unrivalled mastery (Shepherdson, 2000, 153–86). Joan Copjec even hinted at the existence of a 'Lacanian Foucault' who knew full well of an 'existence without predicate' yet turned away from this insight in his influential analyses of power in *Discipline and Punish* and volume one of *The History of Sexuality* (Copjec, 1994, 2–4).[1] To be sure, Foucault did not entertain the concept of the Real. He developed, however, parallel concepts which vied for the same epistemological terrain. The crucial question, then, is how, from what angle and to what end did Foucault theorize the dimension marked out by the notion of the Real? As we shall see, Foucault's theorization of the conceptual space marked out by the 'Real' does not outrun the analytic framework of his historicist position but betrays its precise limits. Perhaps at this point we can hazard the following hypothesis: Foucault's brand of historicism hinges on his anti-Freudian concept of the 'positive unconscious' on the one hand, and his Nietzschean refusal of the notion of self-relating negativity on the other. Both the persuasive force and the critical weakness of Foucault's historicism flow from his categorical rejection of the Hegel-Lacanian assumption that positivization of being is only possible through a dialectical logic of negativity. We want to illustrate this briefly with an example from Foucault's masterpiece *The Order of Things*.

In her seminal book *Foucault's Critical Project*, Béatrice Han (2000) has interpreted Foucault's philosophical journey in the light of his enduring preoccupation with the Kantian question of the conditions of possibility for knowledge, as a string of successive endeavours to historicise the transcendental. Indeed, Foucault's aim was to reveal a particular layer of discourse which would identify precisely these conditions while avoiding the pitfalls of ahistorical, subject-centred approaches for one thing, and reductionist perspectives for another. The paradoxical term he employed to signify this level was the 'historical *a priori*', which expresses perfectly his endeavour to historicise the transcendental.[2]

We want to highlight another, related motif which runs through Foucault's entire work. This motif is his quest for the 'positive unconscious', a notion which captures very well his love-hate relationship with the Freudian-Lacanian tradition of psychoanalysis. While the term 'historical *a priori*' hints at the thrust and inherent tension of his endeavour to historicise the transcendental, the concept of the 'positive unconscious' illuminates the way in which he intended to achieve this. Although Foucault deploys the term only once, namely in the foreword to *The Order of Things*, the quest for the 'positive unconscious' can be seen as emblematic of his work as a whole. It will give us some important clues about the relationship between Foucault and Žižek.

In a structuralist vein *The Order of Things* was shifting the agenda from the Imaginary to the Symbolic, calling attention to a non-subjective symbolic dimension of discourse which escaped the subject's imaginary self-understanding and of which it was but an effect. But more than this, Foucault revealed a *specific* dimension of the "unthought" of discourse, a 'middle region' between (a) the reflexive knowledge of 'scientific theories and philosophical interpretations', and (b) the 'fundamental ordering codes of a culture – those governing its language, its schemas of perception, and exchanges'. Foucault called this 'middle region' the 'positive unconscious of knowledge', defining it as 'a level that eludes the consciousness of the scientist and yet is part of scientific discourse' (Foucault, 1970, xi). It was a provisional expression which functioned as a stand-in for other terms used simultaneously, such as 'archaeological level', 'historical a priori' and '*épistémè*'. In the *Archaeology of Knowledge* it was replaced by more concrete terms such as 'archive' and in his later works by notions like 'dispositif' and 'regime of truth', which all signified exactly the same distinctive level of Foucauldian analysis (Foucault, 1970, xi, xx-xxii; 2002a, 145–48; 1990, 7, and 2002c, 131f.). But what level is this?

When in *The Order of Things* Foucault refers to 'a positive unconscious of knowledge' which he wants to uncover, he sets it apart from 'the scientific consciousness' on the one hand, and 'the unconscious of science' on the other. He distinguishes it from the unconscious of science insofar as the latter is 'always the negative side of science – that which resists it, deflects it, or disturbs it'. Foucault discards the negative unconscious of Freudian psychoanalysis, since the object of his archaeological enterprise is a positive unconscious of reason which constitutes 'the positive basis of knowledge' in a given period and domain (Foucault, 1970, xi, xxi). In other words, modelled on Bachelard's idea of a non-Freudian '"psychoanalysis" of reason' (Gutting, 1989, 17), Foucault's discourse-analytic notion of the positive unconscious is not a 'censored chapter' in the history of reason, nor by any stretch of the imagination predicated on the notion of repression.[3] While tapping the reservoir of psychoanalytic criticism – after all, Lacanian psychoanalysis figures prominently in *The Order of Things* as one of the counter-sciences (see Foucault, 1970, 373–86) – Foucault purges the unconscious from its Freudian 'negative' implications.[4] The proximity to Lacan is here as striking as it is deceptive. To be sure, Foucault's 'positive unconscious' is a kind of 'unknown' symbolic knowledge (*savoir*); yet, at the same time, as an historical a priori it must be seen as a 'purely empirical figure' designating a historical set of discursive rules defining the conditions one has 'to fulfil, not to make [one's] discourse coherent and true in general, but to give it, at the time when it was written and accepted, value and practical application' (Foucault, 2002a, 144, and 1970, xiv).[5] The true kinship of the positive unconscious is not with Lacan – certainly not with the late Lacan – but with the transcendental empiricism of Deleuze.

In his 1976 preface to Deleuze's and Guattari's *Anti-Oedipus*, Foucault finds a memorable formulation for his rejection of the negative unconscious of the Freudian–Lacanian tradition.

Withdraw allegiance from the old categories of the Negative (law, limit, castration, lack, lacuna), which Western thought has so long held sacred as a form of power and an access to reality. Prefer what is positive and multiple, difference over uniformity, flows over unities, mobile arrangements over systems. Believe that what is productive is not sedentary but nomadic (Foucault, 2002d, 109)[6]

This has to be seen in conjunction with Foucault's utter dislike of Hegelian dialectics. One of his most scathing attacks on Hegel can be found in another piece on Deleuze. In his 1970 review essay of *Difference et Répétition* and *Logique du Sens*, Foucault pronounced that 'now, it is necessary to free ourselves from Hegel – from the opposition of predicates, from contradiction and negation, from all of dialectics.'[7] To Foucault, dialectics was tantamount to 'the fakery of prepared answers' (Foucault, 2000c, 358f.). Its original sin consisted in its pretence of liberating difference when it did not. Quite the contrary, Foucault argued, rather than liberating differences, dialectics guarantees

> that they can always be recaptured. For difference to have a place, it was necessary to divide the 'same' through contradiction, to limit its infinite identity through nonbeing, to *transform its indeterminate positivity through the negative*. Given the priority of the same, difference could only arise through these mediations. ... The dialectical sovereignty of the same consists in *permitting differences to exist but always under the rule of the negative, as an instance of nonbeing*. They may appear to be the successful subversion of the Other, but contradiction secretly assists in the salvation of identities (Foucault, 2000c, 358; our italics).

What would be required in order that difference could be freed was 'thought without contradiction, without dialectics, without negation'; that is, 'affirmative thought' which 'accepts divergence' and 'whose instrument is disjunction'. What was needed, then, was 'thought of the multiple' that was not 'confined by constraints of the same', i.e. thought that 'attacks insoluble problems' (Foucault, 2000c, 358f.).

> Far from being the still incomplete and blurred image of an idea that would, from on high and for all time, hold the answer, the

problem lies in the idea itself, or rather, the idea exists only in the form of a problem ... in which the question ceaselessly stirs. What is the answer to the question? The problem. How is the problem resolved? By displacing the question. *The problem ... disobeys the Hegelian negative because it is a multiple affirmation*; it is not subjected to the contradiction of being and nonbeing, since it is being. *We must think problematically rather than question and answer dialectically* (Foucault, 2000c, 359; our italics).[8]

This has important implications, as Copjec has shown. Foucault's dismissal of the negative, repressed, resisting and disturbing surplus of discourse, does more than remove the Real from the radar of discourse analysis. The fact that Foucault dismissed the notion of a cause that is never present in the field of its effects, had important consequences especially for his analyses of power. While in *The Order of Things* it had still been possible to evade the question of how to account for historical change – Foucault acknowledged that for the time being he was incapable of offering a satisfactory explanation (Foucault, 1970, xiii) – this was no longer an option in his genealogical studies of the 1970s which were explicitly designed to overcome these shortcomings and to account for the (trans)formation of regimes of power and knowledge. However, in his endeavour to put an end to historical meta-narratives, Foucault eventually abandoned *any* explanation based on principles that would exceed the regimes under scrutiny. He plumped instead for the principle of *absolute immanence,* i.e. the notion of a positive cause which is immanent within the field of its effects. What he 'overlooked' was the gap between the discursive space and the positive content that fills it out, a weakness that he shares with the tradition of metaphysical materialism from Newton to Luhmann. Foucault's failure to distinguish between the *positivity* of a given formation and the *negativity* of its generative principle which does not appear among the elements of that formation, renders social reality 'realtight'; it obfuscates the question of desire – which registers itself negatively in cultural statements – and makes historical change ultimately inexplicable (see Copjec, 1994, 1–14).

  This is why Žižek is right to define historicism as a deficit enterprise: *Historicism = Historicity – the Real.* Foucault is a historicist first and foremost insofar as he gives in to the temptation to reduce society 'to its indwelling network of relations of power and knowledge', 'refuses to believe in repression and proudly professes to be *illiterate in desire'* (Copjec, 1994, 6 and 14). Put differently, Foucault is a historicist first and foremost insofar as he does not contemplate the notion of an immanent exception hinting at the indiscernible wherefrom (vanishing mediator) and the im/possible beyond (the Real of an act) of a socio-symbolic regime whose constitutive 'black hole' (ex-timate core) it is. As a result, he remains blind to the entire economy of enjoyment (*jouissance*) which is at the heart of Žižek's understanding of ideology. But before turning to Žižek, we want to address another aspect of Foucauldian theory.

4
Suspending Ontological Questions

There can be no doubt that Foucauldian historicism achieved a great deal. It thoroughly de-naturalised and de-reified entrenched notions of the social. It de-idealized scientific thought by revealing its intrinsic discursive materiality. It historicized concepts which were thought to have no history, such as objectivity and truth, and relativized culture- and domain-specific experiences which were more often than not considered universally valid. In short, Foucauldianism has shown convincingly – and in a distinctly different way than Marxism and psychoanalysis – 'that reason has its reasons that reason knows not of' (Rée, 2004, 27).[1]

Yet it achieved this at the expense of ontological questions. Foucault himself preferred to explore the historical conditions of possibility on the basis of which we pass judgement on the morality and truth of actions and beliefs, rather than assessing whether actions and beliefs were, in fact, ethical or true.[2] By the same token, Foucauldian theory does not encourage us to ask 'What is power and where does it come from?', but instead 'How is it practised?', as Deleuze – alluding to the pragmatic streak in Foucault – put it (Deleuze, 1999, 60). But naïve and essentialist as 'what is' questions might appear, they remain indispensable.

Žižek has frequently criticised the historicist attitude with regard to the 'Cultural Studies prohibition of direct ontological questions'. To give an example: film theorists, he argues, 'no longer ask basic questions like: "What is the nature of cinematic perception?", they simply tend to reduce such questions to the historicist reflection upon conditions in which certain notions emerged as the result of

25

specific power relations'. By extension, the historicist stance jetti-
sons the problematic of 'the inherent "truth-value"' of a given
theory:

> when a typical Cultural Studies theorist deals with a philosophi-
> cal or psychoanalytical edifice, the analysis focuses exclusively on
> unearthing its hidden patriarchal, Eurocentric, identitarian, etc.,
> 'bias', without even asking the … question: OK, but what *is* the
> structure of the universe? How *does* the human psyche "really"
> work? (in Butler *et al.*, 2000, 230f. and 233)

Another example for the 'Foucault-effect' is the refusal of historical
epistemologists to address questions of existence and legitimacy. In
an instructive piece on the ascendance of the ideal of 'aperspectival
objectivity', for instance, Lorraine Daston delineates this approach
as follows:

> Insofar as objectivity has been a theme in recent science studies,
> it is questions of existence and legitimacy that have exercised dis-
> cussants, rather than those of history. Neither the question of
> whether objectivity exists or not …, nor that of whether it is a
> good or bad thing …, will concern me here (Daston, 1992, 598).

As in the case of cultural studies, it goes without saying that the aim
here cannot be to dispute the immense intellectual fruitfulness of
historical epistemology (see, for example, Daston, 2000 and Daston
and Park 1998). The distinctive advantages Foucauldian approaches
offer over ahistorical, essentialist or moralising perspectives are
obvious enough. However, the historicist suspension of ontological
questions has a range of problematic implications. The most important one is that we are left clueless as to how to get out of this
hermetic universe of self-enclosed discourses, powers and counter-
powers, which Foucault himself has depicted so compellingly. To be
sure, the political *pointe* of Foucault's critique of evolutionary
historiography with its 'old idea of continuity' which denied
'human history … the potential for a violent revolution', was to
provide the theoretical instruments which would enable us to 'really
grasp both the discontinuity of events and the transformation of
societies'. Time and the past were no longer meant to be the funda-

mental categories of historical thought but change and the event (Foucault, 2000e, 431, 423).[3] But in the Foucauldian universe there are no cracks, no extra-discursive loopholes from where the new could enter. With the surplus dimension of the Real missing, all we can do, if we do not want to fall prey to the lures of ideology as a privileged-viewpoint theory, is to describe the workings of discourse and power-knowledge, and feel encouraged by the fact that what we are facing is merely a historically contingent setting which might have been, and thus could be, utterly different.

> [H]istory serves to show how that-which-is has not always been; i.e., that the things which seem most evident to us are always formed in the confluence of encounters and chances, during the course of a precarious and fragile history ...; and that since these things have been made, they can be unmade, as long as we know how it was that they were made (Foucault, 2000e, 428).

What about Žižek? Rather than removing the Real from the radar and thus constructing the social as 'realtight' (Copjec), Žižek conceptualises social reality as fissured and self-external, his wager being that reality itself is always-already based on some exclusion or inconsistency – reality, as we know it, is 'not all'. And it is here, in these very gaps and interstices in the social edifice, that Žižek believes critical thought has its proper place.

While for the historicist everything is historical, for Žižek, as it were, nothing is unhistorical, although – or rather because – history is 'not all'. Historicism, Žižek argues, functions as a domestication of historicity proper insofar as it does not take into account the Real of historical representation. It lacks a truly historical dimension in that it ignores the traumatic, non-symbolizable kernel of historical change. The concept of historicity, by contrast, is anchored in the Real as that which stands outside the temporal sequence of the symbolic order: rather than being defined by historical time, the Real is the constitutive outside defining it. It is the inherent antagonism of the Real, Žižek avers, which 'again and again sets in motion the movements of history, propelling it to ever new historicizations/symbolizations'. While historicism gentrifies such antagonism, the concept of historicity fully acknowledges its disruptive potential. Ultimately, Žižek claims, 'the historicist theme of the endless open play of substitutions is the very form of ahistorical ideological closure' and as such the worst form of collusion with the status quo (in Butler *et al.*, 2000, 232). What is more, Žižek insists that the Real itself can be 'touched' and that 'the true act is precisely, as Lacan puts it, that which changes the Real itself' (in Beaumont and Jenkins, 2000, 7). Paraphrasing Marx, the step from Foucault to Žižek thus could be summarized as follows: by unmasking reality as contingent discursive fiction, poststructuralist criticism has only deconstructed the world in different ways. The point, however, is to identify the Real of what seems to be mere discursive fiction, and to change it.

5
Matrix Reloaded: Žižek's Ideology Critique

At the outset of his essay 'The Spectre of Ideology', which would probably qualify as his most consistent piece of writing on the subject,[1] Žižek defines the term in question as the 'generative matrix that regulates the relationship between visible and non-visible, between imaginable and non-imaginable' (Žižek, 1994b, 1). Such a definition introduces us to Žižek's psychoanalytic conceptualisation of ideology as a radically split domain, or rather an elusive kind of knowledge divided between its explicit manifestation (a rationally constructed and linguistically transparent set of ideas) and its uncanny 'appearance beyond appearance' (an unthinkable, unrepresentable and unmediatable nucleus of disavowed enjoyment). By claiming that ideology regulates the dialectical relationship between the above two orders (in Lacanian terms, between the order of the Symbolic and the order of the Real), Žižek also undermines the parameters of critical theory 'as we know it', for he shifts the object of critical analysis onto what has hitherto been regarded as *the* non-ideological field *par excellence*: the obscure realm of enjoyment – which, however, is not to be mistaken with mere pleasure, as it stands for the excessive and fundamentally disturbing dimension of libido that Lacanian psychoanalysis knows as *jouissance*.

The seemingly paradoxical move towards 'ideological enjoyment' undoubtedly represents Žižek's most original and fecund contribution to critical theory, one that characterises his writing since the publication of his groundbreaking volume *The Sublime Object of Ideology*, in 1989. Let us take, for instance, the often-rehearsed Žižekian argument that in their different guises all totalitarian systems rely on an instance of fetishistic disavowal. Particularly in his early production, Žižek tackles the question of ideological efficacy in both Nazi-Fascism and Communism, frequently resorting to Octave Mannoni's formula on the contradictory nature of belief: 'Je sais bien, mais quand-même ...' [I know very well, but nevertheless ...] (see Mannoni, 1969). Žižek maintains that in totalitarian societies the power of ideology is, as a rule, reflected in the cynical attitude of the subjects, who know full well that the official ideological line ('the Jews are responsible for all evils'; 'the Communist Party represents the people') is false, and yet they stick to it as a matter of belief – since, as both Pascal and Althusser knew very well, belief has less to do with reason and knowledge than with habit and senseless (from Žižek's standpoint: unconscious/traumatic) enjoyment.[2]

The same principle of 'totalitarian disavowal', Žižek frequently argues, is also in place in liberal Western societies, where the cynical distance we are encouraged to take from any form of traditional ideological belief effectively suggests that we are being caught in the system's ideological loop. The more we pride ourselves on being 'free thinkers in a free world', Žižek argues, the more we blindly submit ourselves to the merciless superegoic command ('Enjoy!') which binds us to the logic of the market. As with Hegel's 'Beautiful Soul', the display of purity turns out to be the measure of impurity, innocence the measure of evil. From this angle, the very notion of 'free will' (extensively exploited, for example, by modern advertising) might be said to function, today, as a supremely ideological formula, since it binds the subject precisely to that deterministic universe it seeks to escape. Žižek, however, does not deny the existence of free will. His understanding of the notion is predicated upon the German idealist account of the concept developed especially by Schelling. Against the philosophical cliché that there is no place for free will in German idealism, since the world operates according to laws that are ultimately inaccessible to us, Žižek argues that the idea of subjectivity constructed by the German idealists *does* endorse access to freedom of will – provided, however, that we conceive of this freedom as a traumatic encounter with an 'abyssal' choice that has no guarantee in the socio-symbolic order. Žižek's point is that free will implies the paradox of a frightful disconnection from the world, the horror of a psychotic confrontation with the radical negativity that ultimately defines the status of the subject.

Back to ideology. To convey the fundamental lure at work in ideological interpellation Žižek often draws on Hegelian dialectics, as when he contends that ideology 'resides in externalisation of the result of an inner necessity' (Žižek, 1994b, 4). The cunning significance of this movement of externalisation can be appreciated through a reference to contemporary politics. When, in 2005, Italian Prime Minister Silvio Berlusconi insisted that the reasons for former Italy's deepening economic crisis were to be ascribed to the 'international conjuncture' (from 9/11 to the effects of the introduction of the Euro, etc.), we could argue that he performed the ideological move *par excellence*, since his claim was aimed at displacing the internal and all-pervasive contradiction of contemporary capitalism onto an external and contingent event (or series of events). From Žižek's Hegelian angle, *'the stepping out of (what we experience as) ideology is the very form of our enslavement to it'* (Žižek, 1994b, 6).

One of Žižek's favourite examples here is that of 'canned laughter' – the idea developed in the early 1950s by Charles R. Douglass, who patented machines that reproduce live audience reactions to be used as sound effects on television programmes. What we get with artificial laughter on TV is precisely the externalisation of one of our most intimate and spontaneous feelings, a feeling normally associated with enjoyment. To what effect? The idea that someone else laughs in my place – or that I laugh by proxy, through another – reproduces the fundamental logic of ideological interpellation, insofar as by distancing myself from my innermost enjoyment (laughter, belief, etc.) I am all the more caught in the ideological predicament. Canned laughter brings to light the formal mechanism of displacement upon which ideology relies: we are truly controlled by ideology the moment we start displacing belief onto someone/something else: for instance when, within a given socio-symbolic order, we believe that someone else, and not us, is the poor idiot caught in the loop of ideology (the 'subject supposed to believe'); or, more radically, that belief belongs in the big Other *tout court*. As for canned laughter, its ultimate ideological effect is therefore not that it renders us passive and numb – as much conservative criticism would claim – but that, on the contrary, it 'deprive[s] us of our passivity, of our authentic passive experience, and thus prepare[s] us for mindless frenetic activity – for endless work' (Žižek, 2003a).

To Žižek, the central formal feature of ideology is therefore *distance*, the very dimension that is generally regarded as a defence against direct interpellation. Distance blinds us to the fact that, in ideology, belief is not necessarily a direct identification with a given set of ideas, but rather a reflexive mechanism that presupposes and foregrounds our choice not to believe (or, for that matter, to believe). In short: we believe that the big Other believes (not us), and therefore we contribute to the strengthening of the ideological machine. The point is that belief is the effect of (to put it with the title of one of Žižek's books) a parallax view: it is split between what we think we believe in and the disavowed belief that sustains this conscious belief. What counts for Žižek is this 'belief before belief', which essentially coincides with the belief that the big Other exists. The real question for critical theory, therefore, would be how to locate and disengage from this disavowed belief in belief.

Žižek is aware of the fact that, if on the one hand the status of ideology in our postmodern times is founded upon the displacement of belief (liberal multiculturalism), on the other hand it is also clearly linked to forms of direct belief (fundamentalist populism). The difference between the two modes of identification is that the cynical liberal multiculturalist mocks the very notion of 'direct knowledge', whereas the fundamentalist accepts it 'at face value'. The common feature that makes these two modalities two sides of the same coin is the fact that they neglect 'the "absurd" act of decision which installs every authentic belief, a decision which cannot be grounded in the chain o "reasons", in positive knowledge' (see Žižek, 2006a, 348). Put differently, what is foreclosed from the two postmodern applications of belief is the *tertium datur* of the abyssal choice deprived of any support in the big Other.

Problems inevitably emerge for Žižek the moment he has to specify the empirical nature of our relationship to this abyssal choice that grounds belief. Before dealing with such a question, it is worth noting how between multiculturalist liberalism and fundamentalist populism, Žižek (controversially) sees in the latter a higher potential towards a revolutionary intervention. The key paradox to which he refers here is the fact that, if we start from the Marxist

axiom of the primacy of class struggle over all other forms of antagonism, 'it is populist fundamentalism which retains this logic of
antagonism, while the liberal Left follows the logic of recognition of
differences, of 'defusing' antagonisms into coexisting differences'
(Žižek, 2006a, 362). Žižek in other words takes the old Marxist
slogan that 'every rise of Fascism is a sign of a failed revolution' very
seriously: his understanding of history is consistent with Walter
Benjamin's, in as much as it regards a given historical failure or even
catastrophe as indicative of the previous grounding 'openness' of a
given socio-political constellation. From this viewpoint, the liberal
leftist ideology of recognition of differences effectively works
towards concealing the gap between the symbolic order and its
founding inconsistency. This brings Žižek to conclude that we
should 'dare to look for an ally in what often looks like the ultimate
enemy of multi-culti liberalism: today's crucial "sites of resistance"
against global capitalism are often deeply marked by religious fundamentalism' (Žižek, 2006a, 365). The first thing to do apropos
such a potentially controversial statement is to fully integrate it in
the theoretical framework of Žižek's analysis. What it means is not
that we should simply side with fundamentalism against liberal
multiculturalism, but instead that we need to acknowledge how
fundamentalism allows us a clearer view of the crucial antagonism
that lies behind and structures today's global ideological enterprise,
where liberalism and fundamentalism become two sides of the
same coin.

If we go back to the notion of belief, Žižek's often repeats that full
identification with the ideological machine is guaranteed to at least
disturb its functioning. This logic is demonstrated very clearly in the
passage of *The Plague of Fantasies* where Žižek considers three films
about military life: *MASH*, *An Officer and a Gentleman*, and *Full Metal
Jacket* (see Žižek, 1997, 20–2). Žižek argues that contrary to standard
interpretations, *MASH* and *An Officer*, attempting to challenge the
logic of military life through either irony (*MASH*) or sentiment (*An
Officer*), actually end up legitimating its pressure, since they remain
blind to the fact that 'an ideological identification exerts a true hold
on us precisely when we maintain that we are not fully identical to
it, that there is a rich human person beneath it' (Žižek, 1997, 21).
Kubrick's *Full Metal Jacket*, on the other hand, resists the temptation
to 'humanise' or simply mock the military machine. While in the

first part of the film we are shown how mindless military drilling is accompanied by obscene enjoyment (hard discipline coupled with humiliating rituals), in the second part we get the truth about the attitude of ironic distance: the soldier who throughout the film had seemed humane and intelligent enough to dis-identify with military life, eventually shoots a wounded Vietcong girl, thus unwittingly demonstrating how, on him, military ideology has fully succeeded. Žižek often applies a similar reading to Francis Ford Coppola's *Apocalypse Now*, where Kurtz (Marlon Brando) is the perfect soldier who, through over-identification with the military system, turns into the excess that has to be eliminated: 'The ultimate horizon of Apocalypse Now is this insight into how Power generates its own excess, which it has to annihilate in an operation which has to imitate what it fights (Willard's mission to kill Kurtz is nonexistent for the official record – "It has never happened", as the general who briefs Willard points out' (Žižek, 2006a, 370).

In proposing his critical model, Žižek makes significant changes to the two standard critical theory approaches: traditional ideology critique (up to Habermas) and discourse analysis. In Žižek's view the problem with traditional ideology critique is that it thrives on the erroneous perception that ideology corresponds to a distorted representation of 'true' (or 'a truer') reality – a criticism, as we have seen, wholeheartedly shared by Foucault. However, Žižek's Lacanian insight takes us beyond this common ground. The classic opposition of the two terms illusion and reality can only sound hopelessly obsolete to a Lacanian ear, in as much as Lacan ultimately conceives of 'reality', the allegedly deeper level beyond ideological distortions, as 'Real', a dimension which, in its final configuration, is *more fictional* than a representational system of ideologically binding fictions. What lies beyond the smokescreen of ideological/symbolic illusions, in other words, is the viscous 'stuff' of the Real, whose precise function is to bind us to the explicit ideological text by making itself available as a secret/obscene mode of enjoyment. More precisely: while traditional ideology critique rightly aims to unravel the inconsistency of a given ideological structure, it does so in an ineffectual and ultimately powerless way, for it not only fails to acknowledge the fundamentally illusory status of reality, but it also ignores how the coercive power of ideology derives from ideology's duplicitous links with the Real *qua* disavowed modes of enjoyment.

We should be clear on a different point here: enjoyment does not need to be obscene, just as sexualisation does not necessarily have to possess overtly disturbing connotations. The dialectical link between ideology and illicit enjoyment, in other words, can work in both ways, as in the case of totalitarian systems: while the explicit content of Nazism and Stalinism in certain circumstances definitely takes on an obscene character, the implicit link that effectively interpellates individuals, manipulating (what appears to be) a trans-ideological kernel of enjoyment, can in those circumstances just as easily be filled with 'innocent' sentiments of solidarity and even idealised justice. Crucial is therefore the reference to form: more than the actual content of enjoyment, what matters in Žižek's thought is the formal mechanism that subtends to ideological formations. While the modes of enjoyment are likely to vary according to the different historical contexts in which they materialise, what remains the same is the reference to an external, trans-ideological core of enjoyment. The conclusion to draw is thus that ideology really lives up to its meaning in its trans-ideological core.

To Žižek, for example, the common mistake of the standard approach of traditional ideology critique to Fascism lies in considering its 'irrational' hubris as non-ideological. Rather, he claims that the opposite is true: what secures the consistency of Fascism as an ideological construct is always its (more or less clandestine) reliance on a kernel of enjoyment that is generally perceived by the people as a more authentic way to connect with reality. What Žižek has in mind here is

neither ideology *qua* explicit doctrine, articulated convictions on the nature of man, society and the universe, nor ideology in its material existence (institutions, rituals and practices that give body to it), but the elusive network of implicit, quasi-'spontaneous' presuppositions and attitudes that form an irreducible moment of the reproduction of 'non-ideological' (economic, legal, political, sexual...) practices'. Ideology taps into the Real insofar as it relies on those obscure presuppositions that 'structure our perception of reality in advance' (Žižek, 1994b, 15).

The key point, upon which we shall return at different stages in this book, is that these presuppositions are firmly anchored in *jouissance* –

which, following Žižek, we will continue to translate as enjoyment. The fact that Fascism does not rely on an explicit rational construct, therefore, works as the most compelling proof of its ideological force.

Let us now move on to Žižek's criticism of the second standard approach to ideology within contemporary critical theory, i.e. discourse analysis. With Žižek's understanding of discourse analysis the Habermasian 'Enlightenment critique of ideology' is turned on its head, as the focus shifts on the invasive presence of discourse: instead of ideology falsifying reality for the sake of pathological interests (power strategies), we start from the assumption that there is no way to access and conceptualise reality which is not already stained by discourse. The term ideology thus becomes redundant, Žižek argues, for what counts in critical analysis is that every ideological stance we assume is always-already parasitised by an intricate network of discursive devices whose function is to structure our point of view in advance, silently bestowing an appearance of necessity upon it. As with traditional ideology critique, Žižek duly acknowledges the diagnostic value of discourse analysis with its emphasis on how every ideological position emerges as the result of a complex interaction of discursive procedures. Ernesto Laclau, one of Žižek's regular interlocutors, is a perfect case in point here, since his claim that the veil of ideology conceals a relentless fight for hegemonic space, which articulates itself through a series of discursive appropriations, represents perhaps the most intriguing application of ideology–*critical* discourse analysis today.

Žižek's main concern with discourse, however, relates to the classic Foucauldian notion that the discursive battle for hegemonic space functions as a somewhat spontaneous event, that is to say, as an occurrence which is disengaged from the top-downward logic of ideological pressure: as Foucault himself repeatedly claimed, power operates first and foremost at the level of micro-power, i.e. through a plurality of discursive mechanisms that constitute themselves from below. Žižek is far from convinced by what he calls Foucault's 'suspect rhetoric of complexity', to the extent that he eventually discards it as 'a clear case of patching up, since one can never arrive at Power this way – the abyss that separates micro-procedures from the spectre of Power remains unbridgeable' (Žižek, 1994b, 13).

Along with its dubious emphasis on the political significance of micro-procedures, Foucauldian discourse analysis, according to

Žižek, is most importantly liable for doing away with any conceptualisation of radical externality, as we have seen in Chapters 3 and 4.
In discourse analysis one always starts from the presupposition that
it is impossible 'to draw a clear line of demarcation between ideology and actual reality', which in turn prompts the conclusion that
'the only non-ideological position is to renounce the very notion of
extra-ideological reality and accept that all we are dealing with are
symbolic fictions, the plurality of discursive universes, never
"reality"'. In Žižek's view, this boils down to nothing but a *'slick
"postmodern" solution'* (Žižek, 1994b, 17), a stratagem which, in fact,
ends up favouring the proliferation of ideology. Thus, key to his critique is the question of externality: while the traditional positing of
a conceptually viable space outside ideology is delusive, the negation of externality *tout court* is also defective, for it thwarts the artic-
ulation of radical political projects. Moving beyond traditional
critical theory (where ideology deforms 'true' reality) and discourse
analysis (where ideology is turned into an all-encompassing discursive practice), Žižek identifies a third model, whereby a place outside
ideology is possible, but *'it cannot be occupied by any positively determined reality'* (Žižek, 1994b, 17). What is situated beyond the ideological can never be retrieved as a rational paradigm, *and for this very
reason (because it relates to a non-discursive core) it is ideology at its
purest*. Again, we ought to insist on a fundamental point here,
which we shall develop in full in the following chapters. The excess
of ideology is not conceived by Žižek as a meta-narrative, or a trans-
epochal unchangeable feature (as many of his detractors, amongst
which for example Judith Butler, often complain). Rather, what he
emphasises against traditional historicism is that all historical/soci-
etal concretions are answers to the same formal deadlock or impossibility, which however manifests itself through different contents,
thus requiring different strategic interventions. If every society is
sustained by a secret reference to some excessive element, this
element is historically determined and necessarily mobilises radically heteronomous logics.

As previously anticipated, Žižek often describes the Althusserian
logic of ideological interpellation via a reference to the superego and
its covert injunction to enjoy, insofar as the superego's policing role
hinges on its shadowy double, a surplus of secret, disavowed or
illicit enjoyment. Every prohibition, in other words, is sustained by

a secret investment in *jouissance*. This stance proves vitally significant for a drastic reconfiguration of the political scope of subjectivity, for it generates the argument that the subject's full ideological potential is paradoxically realised in *jouissance*, in a senseless and unconditional injunction to enjoy. Consequently, since ideological interpellation 'is operative only in so far as it is not openly admitted' (Žižek, 2000a, 266), the best way to undermine its grip would be to assume its repressed libidinal core: if ideology functions 'by proxy', i.e. through its excessive and disavowed kernel, the subject's only chance to challenge the ubiquitous grip of ideology is via identification with this explosive kernel. This consideration brings us directly to the crucial notion of 'the act' and, with it, to a reflection on the question of agency; both these questions shall be developed fully in Part II.

Going back to Žižek's particular branch of ideology critique, we could maintain that the non-discursive excess of ideology effectively coincides with the non-discursive excess of subjectivity, in the sense that both supplements embody the Real substance around which the commonly understood notions of ideology and subjectivity are structured. (This, incidentally, can be regarded as the point in Žižek's critical model where Lacan meets Hegel: where the Lacanian notion of the Real overlaps with the key Hegelian thesis that 'subject is substance'). If, therefore, to truly comprehend the functioning of ideology we need to get in touch with its invisible centre, the first problem we are faced with is how to locate this centre. Since we are always-already controlled and moulded (interpellated) by ideology, the task clearly presents itself as an onerous one. Žižek's wager is that the core of ideology *can be reached via subjectivity*, that is to say, through a process of extraneation which culminates in our risking the assumption of 'what is in us more than ourselves': the libidinal content of our unconscious desires. One of the ways in which Žižek elaborates on the subversive potential inherent in the subject is by insisting on the Lacanian ethical injunction to 'traverse the fantasy' – a position that allows us to delve into the key question of the relationship between ideology and fantasy itself.

Amongst the series of terms regularly employed by Žižek to thematise the uncanny ideological function of enjoyment, none is more useful than the couple fantasy-spectre. When he defines the external excess of ideology as fantasy (see Žižek, 1997, 3–44), what he has in mind is not symbolic fantasy in its pacifying role, but the Lacanian fundamental fantasy, a pre-synthetic scenario whose traumatic content announces the Real *qua* fundamentally repressed antagonism (see Žižek, 2000a, 265–69). As anticipated, Žižek's use of the word enjoyment needs to be related to the Lacanian Real of *jouissance*, since only within such a framework does it lend itself to be conceptualised as *the kernel of ideology*. Ideology at its purest *is* a traumatic nucleus of primarily repressed (or foreclosed) substance, which, precisely through its being irreducibly 'other', opens up the space for the explicit ideological construct in its symbolic (linguistic, rational) allure. So when Žižek claims that in order to be ideologically effective fantasy has to be disavowed, he is referring to the Real of fantasy, a kernel of fantasmatic libido that eludes figuration. The line between fantasy as a protective (*explicitly* ideological) screen and fantasy as a disruptive (*implicitly* ideological) core is indeed very thin, yet crucial if we are to grasp Žižek's connection of ideology and enjoyment. Significantly, to emphasise the shattering dimension consubstantial with fantasy, Žižek has recently developed the notion of the 'imaginary Real', which he tends to privilege over the 'symbolic Real' (anonymous codes such as scientific formulae) and the 'real Real' (the monstrous traumatic abyss that swallows everything). The main feature of the imaginary Real is that it retains the traumatic character of the real Real but combines it with the thoroughly immanent fragility of the symbolic Real: in Žižek's words, it is 'not the illusion of the Real, but the Real in the illusion itself ... this elusive feature which is totally non-substantial, but it annoys you' (Zizek and Daly, 2004, 68–9).

The notion of spectre, on the other hand, can be seen as occupying what we might call 'the space between the two fantasies'. In referring to it, Žižek aims primarily at radicalising Derrida's version of this notion, i.e. that of spectre *qua* ethical Other, the incarnation of an impossible, never-to-be-fulfilled promise of ontological fullness.[3] From Žižek's psychoanalytic standpoint the spectre, far from representing the ultimate ethical horizon, should be conceived as a secondary, somewhat gentrified concretion of the Real. Consequently, the ethical significance of the spectre does not reside in its suggesting an infinite approximation to the impossible essence *qua* ontological fullness, but rather in demonstrating how this essence coincides with absolute negativity, with an incendiary freedom whose traumatic manifestation the spectre is there to delay. The point is that 'the spectre itself already emerges out of fear, out of our escape from something even more horrifying: freedom' (Žižek, 1994b, 27).

Ultimately, to comprehend Žižek's approach to ideology critique we need to come to terms with its Lacanian foundations, since the symbolic cogency of the ideological paradigm is brought to depend upon the trace of void which is both external to ideology (insofar as it cannot be rationalised and co-opted by language) and internal to it (insofar as ideological consistency hinges on the void at its core), thus producing the uncanny effect of *extimacy* (Lacan's neologism, indicating the paradox of a feature that is both internal and external to a given signifying system). Extimacy implies that the elusiveness of the excess at the heart of ideology can be experienced both as sense and as non-sense, both as a meaningful symbolic feature within our universe and as an alien formation we cannot recognise. The key point, however, is that the two dimensions overlap and are inseparable, they cannot be experienced as autonomous units. What deep down qualifies the Real is its uncanny ambiguity at the level of symbolic meaning: although it emerges from symbolisation, it is nothing but the measure of our failure to fully symbolise the world, and therefore remains, simultaneously, radically other. In ethical terms, this leads to the Žižekian thesis according to which the only true act of freedom available to the subject facing a repressive ideological predicament lies in the over-identification with this elusive/excessive gap of ideology itself, i.e. in the full assumption of the traumatic core of ideology. A true ethical stance, he argues paraphrasing Lacan, fulfils itself in the traumatic endorsement of the explosive kernel of ideology, which can only be confronted after the (*explicitly* ideological) fantasy has been traversed, after the spectre has been subsumed into the inconsistency from which it emanates.

As we will show in the next chapter, what is affirmed here is not the irrationalist 'mysticism of a sublime Subject', nor 'a Lacanian existential heroism' (Resch, 2001, 6, 18). Rather, by designating the moment when the principle of sufficient reason is suspended, Žižek's concept of freedom aims to re-inscribe a politically viable understanding of antagonism within today's increasingly saturated, self-enclosed and impenetrable ideological constellation.

6
Locating Antagonism: the Return of Class Struggle

On the 21 April 2005, the German weekly *Die Zeit* goaded its reader-ship with the headline 'The Return of Class Struggle?' accompanied by an entire section devoted to the question 'Do the Germans live in a class society?' Two months before, on 3 February, the British *Guardian* had revealed '(t)he third way's dirtiest secret: ministers have tried to cover up their dependence on forced labour'. The accusation was based on the discovery that the 'exploitation of migrant labour turns out to be at the core of our competitiveness'; if '(s)ocial justice for our own population turns out to depend on the importation of an under-class of foreigners to create our wealth', the report concluded, 'New Labour's whole narrative (of) the third way in which economic growth, based on global competitiveness, can be combined with tack-ling poverty and inequality', would be undermined.

Similar reports could be taken from other broadsheets from around the world. What they have in common is their indignation at something that is considered an intolerable exception to the norm. They tell us that class antagonism is not the founding princi-ple of modern society but a historical remnant of past developments to be overcome, or a recurring aberration to be dealt with. Thus con-ceived, class conflict can and ought to be avoided: there are always rational ways of negotiating differences of interest, opinion or belief, ways which maintain the social equilibrium and do not put civil peace in jeopardy. – Could there be a more clear-cut case of ideological fantasy?

However, what is, in concrete terms, ideological fantasy, and how exactly does it work? Commenting on the events that followed the violent impact of hurricane Katrina on New Orleans (summer 2005), Žižek aims precisely to unmask the workings of ideological fantasy (see Žižek, 2005b). He starts his analysis by considering the way in which the media dealt with the tragic natural occurrence and its aftermath. We all remember, he argues, how television and newspapers reported, in what seemed to be a legitimately indignated tone, the explosion of rape and looting allegedly perpetrated by gangs of blacks throughout the inundated city of New Orleans. However, later inquiries demonstrated that, in the large majority of cases, these 'orgies of violence' did not occur: non-verified rumours were simply reported as facts by the media (some looting did occur after the storm passed, but violence never reached the horrifying peaks broadcast by the media). The reality of poor blacks, abandoned and left without means to survive was thus transformed, as if by the imagination of a Hollywood scriptwriter, into the spectre of blacks exploding violently, of tourists robbed and killed on streets that had slid into anarchy, of the Superdome ruled by gangs raping women and children. The first point to make is that these reports were words that had a precise political effect: they generated fears. The second and most interesting point made by Žižek, however, takes the whole discussion on to a different level. Is it enough to blame the media because they exaggerated the evidence in order to create massive panic amongst the people, thus helping the cause of the neo-conservative and the populist right? Žižek argues that even if all the reports had proven to be factually true, the stories circulating about them would still be racist, since what deep down motivated these stories was not factual evidence, but a racist prejudice originating precisely in ideological fantasy: in the diabolical determination to displace social antagonism onto the question of race, thus fulfilling the repressed scenario that blacks are in truth violent barbarians unable to behave in a civilised way. In a similar manner, Žižek contends, even if some rich Jews in early 1930s Germany had really exploited German workers, seduced their daughters and dominated the popular press, Nazis' anti-Semitism would still have been an emphatically 'untrue', pathological ideological condition.

Here we have, therefore, a lucid exemplification of the role of ideological fantasy: not that of creating a false conflict out of some tragic event, but that of replacing the true source of conflictuality with a false one. Ultimately, the repressed truth of the events following hurricane Katrina is, according to Žižek, none other than class struggle, the fact that, to put it bluntly, the massive divide between the affluent and the ghettoized population in New Orleans (and by extension in most US cities) was masked as an utterly depoliticised antagonism invested by racial fantasies. What Žižek's ideology critique problematises, therefore, are these obscene fantasies accompanying the explicit message, for it is there that the message is secretly validated. The spectre (racist fantasy) conceals what is truly at stake (the fundamental, 'primordially repressed' fantasy of class division).

Žižek's relentless insistence on the importance of 'keeping the critique of ideology alive' results in the exposure of what he takes to be 'the ultimate ideological operation' of deconstructionist criticism, namely, 'the very elevation of something into impossibility as a means of postponing or avoiding encountering it' (Zizek and Daly, 2004, 70). This, he claims, is tantamount to occupying the position of the obsessional neurotic, for the structure of this form of neurosis implies that the real aim of our activity, whether mental or physical, is to avoid the confrontation with the potentially destructive kernel of our desire. It is worth recalling here that, repeating Lacan, Žižek sees no substantial difference between the normal and the neurotic subject, since normality itself is nothing but an imaginary ideal of wholeness that can only realise itself in a strictly speaking psychotic realm where we come face to face with the Real of enjoyment (the truth of normality is psychosis). The implications are that within the socio-symbolic (ideological) field, all subjects are in different degrees neurotics – what varies is not only the intensity of neurosis, but also its actual configuration, since neurosis materialises itself as either obsessional neurosis or hysteria. However, Žižek's wager is that this is not the whole truth. What is missing from this picture is precisely the analytic of how, despite the normality of neurosis, psychotic encounters with the Real *do happen*, and in a way *are happening all the time*, or else we would not be able to sustain our normal/neurotic position of relatively safe distance from the Real itself. What Žižek evokes, therefore, is the dialectical con-substantiality of the Symbolic and the Real, which we shall discuss in Part III.

From this angle, however, we can already see how, rather than discursively constructing social reality as a self-enclosed and fully immanent domain, Žižek conceptualises it as intrinsically per-forated, always-already penetrated by symptoms of its radical incon-sistency. The Lacanian subject he invokes is the name for these cracks in the social edifice. To clarify this we need to recall that the very process of subjectivization, as Žižek describes it from Lacan, is nothing but an answer to the uncanny otherness we experience in external reality, i.e. it is a thoroughly intersubjective affair. More precisely, we could say that what makes us subjects is the circulation of desire accompanied by its inseparable correlative, fantasy. How exactly? Lacan's favourite quip on this matter, often quoted by Žižek, is that 'desire is always the desire of the other'. To unravel the meaning of this enigmatic sentence we should go back to the ques-tion concerning the ideological role of fantasy: what sets our desire in motion, thus allowing us to construct those historically mediated fantasies that constitute what we perceive as our self, our unique identity, is always our radical indecision *vis-à-vis* the other's desire. The subject, in other words, constitutes itself against the back-ground of a troublesome question that constantly (secretly) under-mines the subject's relationship with external reality, inclusive of all its 'others'. This question is Lacan's famous *Che vuoi?* ('what do you want?'), which tells us that what is at stake in desire is not my fantasy ('what do I want?'), but the other's fantasy ('what does he/she want from me?'). It is this intersubjective modality of fantasy that, for example, defines the child's reaction to the caresses of the mother, the first other it encounters (a moment of pervasive confu-sion which is normally followed, during the so called 'mirror stage', by imaginary recognition, where for the first time the child is able to say 'this is me!'). Similarly, as in the famous case of Freud's little daughter's predilection for strawberry cakes, we can claim that our activity is a direct emanation of our desires only if we acknowledge that our desires are generally conceived as an answer to the bother-ing gaze of the other, a gaze invested by *jouissance*: in Freud's daugh-ter's case, 'the crucial feature is that while she was voraciously eating a strawberry cake, the little girl noticed how her parents were deeply satisfied by this spectacle, by seeing her fully enjoying it' (Žižek, 1997, 9).

Ultimately, therefore, if the subject *qua* desire and fantasy emerges as a (desperate) strategy to answer the other's desire, this means that if we strip our desire of its protective function, we get precisely what we seek to avoid: the radical inconsistency that marks the status of subjectivity proper. That is to say: if the process of subjectivization designates the space where we recognize ourselves through the other, the subject as such is the non-symbolisable fracture that compels us to construct our identity through the socio-symbolic network. It is at once the driving force and the limit of all forms of subjectivation, and thus correlative to the Real.

It is therefore only consequent that, as already pointed out, to Žižek the proper space for critical theory 'consists of these very gaps and interstices opened up by the "pathological" displacements in the social edifice' (Zizek and Daly, 2004, 53). And the most basic and underlying instance of ideological displacement is none other than class antagonism, together with its inseparable correlative, the commodity:

> (t)he class-and-commodity structure of capitalism is not just a phe-
> nomenon limited to the particular 'domain' of the economy, but
> the structuring principle that overdetermines the social totality,
> from politics to art and religion (Žižek in Butler *et al.*, 2000, 96).

One of the main consequences of this assertion is encapsulated in Žižek's attack on postmodern 'identity politics': when class struggle in its crucial structuring function is neglected, he argues following Wendy Brown's insight (see Brown, 1995), a whole series of differ-ent markers of social difference (gender, race, etc.) is suddenly allowed an inordinate weight, bearing 'the surplus-investment from the class struggle whose extent is not acknowledged' (Žižek in Butler *et al.*, 2000, 97).

Žižek is well-known for his firmly critical stance on multicultural-ism. However, put this way such a statement inevitably lends itself to dangerous misunderstandings, and therefore needs to be devel-oped beyond its crude meaning. First and foremost, we must stress that Žižek is not against the principle of multiculturalism *qua* nor-mative set of prescriptive measures; he is rather against what we might call 'the ideology of multiculturalism', insofar as this cultural ideology plays a dominant role in today's Western liberal–democra-tic order. The main line of Žižek's attack is easily summarised: multi-culturalism represents, in truth, the cultural backbone of Western (US *in primis*) upper-middle class capitalist ideology, and as such it should not be elevated into the ultimate horizon of our political engagement. Essentially, to him today's multiculturalism works as a blackmail. By accepting this blackmail and devoting excessive importance to questions involving sexuality, gender, race, cultural tolerance, etc. (as reflected in the academic fortunes of cultural studies), the left is effectively loosing sight of the real stakes of the struggle. Multiculturalism substantially implies the endorsement of the current framework of global capitalism with its political supplement (liberal democracy) as the *non plus ultra* of our social constellation. Against this persuasion, Žižek claims that one should simply break with the multiculturalist taboo by disturbing its mantra of political correctness, even though this may result in allegations of racism or chauvinism.

But there is a further twist to Žižek's analysis. Insofar as it plays a proper ideological role, the multiculturalist stance also necessarily relies upon its own dose of disavowed fantasy. Zizek never tires of repeating that, far from attaining universal validity, multiculturalism is a split domain where the very explicit message is sustained by a secret kernel of fundamentally obscene fantasies. The moment we, enlightened Western multiculturalists, defend the discourse of tolerance towards race and gender, for example, we cannot avoid generating, simultaneously, secret obscene fantasies that silently contradict the explicit message. According to Zizek there are crucial instances in which this core of disavowed enjoyment emerges in all its contradictory and disturbing nature. An example from his personal experience might help to clarify the question:

> One dimension of obscenity which always shocks me is how, at the level of libidinal economy, there is a certain way in which people can preach tolerance and anti-racism but in such a way that they remain racist at a second degree. I even have personal experience of this. When people in Western countries professed to be shocked about Balkan ethnic cleansing, intolerance, violence and so on, it was clear that, as a rule, their very repudiation was formulated in such a way as actually to bring them a certain racist pleasure. Sometimes this even explodes openly. For example, when I, as a relatively tasteless person, make some joke or vulgar remark which is considered unacceptable, it is incredible how often those people who pretend to be ultra-tolerant and

multiculturalist respond along lines of 'maybe this goes on in your primitive Balkan, but, sorry, here we are tolerant'. Their very identification of me in this way engenders a specific obscene enjoyment (Žižek and Daly, 2004, 130).

With regard to our tolerant times, it is this core of disavowed enjoyment that Zizek's psychoanalytic critique targets, well beyond the analysis of how the multiculturalist discourse feeds into the logic of late capitalism. The point is that once we have established the connection between multiculturalism and capitalism, we are still at a loss as to how to break out of this vicious circle. Much more productive is to insist on how today's discourse on tolerance is always accompanied, at a deeper libidinal level, by a fundamentally intolerant kernel of repressed enjoyment. Effectively, today's multiculturalism hinges on the following contradiction: 'We are tolerant, but if you are not tolerant like us (if you do not accept the normative structure of our discourse) you are a primitive ape who does not deserve to live in our world.' What should be emphasised is the libidinal investment accompanying the second, normally disavowed part of the sentence.

The argument that in his or her programmatic (but fundamentally hypocritical) insistence on tolerance the Western multiculturalist effectively mobilises a screen of implicitly racist fantasies brings us back to the ideological function of the spectre. This is actually a variation on the classic psychoanalytic theme of the return of the repress: in its uncompromising assertiveness, the explicit message engenders a spectral excess which implicitly transgresses the prohibition and is bound to return in violent fashion. The point, however, is not that we should simply say what we wish irrespective of the potentially racist or otherwise offensive content of our words; and even less, of course, that we should not tackle racism as a social evil. What Žižek suggests is that the ideology of multiculturalism will never manage to eliminate the plague of racism, since it itself remains racist at a different level – the level of spectrality. Put another way: what if the real aim of multiculturalism is not to get rid of racism but to resignify it as the ultimate manifestation of social evil that, as such, will never be completely eradicated? What if, for example, the anti-racist campaigns that increasingly tend to saturate the collective imaginary of the West actually aim at

reproducing the threat as a horrifying yet fundamentally inelim-
inable stain, as the pathological 'spectral' feature signalling the
metaphysical closure of our political horizon? The very redundancy
of depoliticised messages such as 'racism is stupid' or 'united we
stand against racism' in effect works against its declared target: it
simply tells us that, since idiots abound in this world, racism will
always be a problem. It is at this ideological level that Žižek intervenes. He is critical of the falsely emancipatory lure of the multiculturalist discourse, for he regards it as a profoundly ideological
intervention:

> Multiculturalism is a racism which empties its own position of all
> positive content (the multiculturalist is not a direct racist; he or
> she does not oppose to the Other the *particular* values of his or
> her culture); none the less he or she retains this position as the
> privileged *empty point of universality* from which one is able to
> appreciate (or depreciate) other particular cultures properly –
> multiculturalist respect for the Other's specificity is the very form
> of asserting one's own superiority (Žižek, 2000a, 216).

The conclusion Žižek draws from this analysis is that:

> The problematic of multiculturalism (the hybrid coexistence of
> diverse cultural life-worlds) which imposes itself today is the
> form of appearance of its very opposite, of the massive presence
> of capitalism as *global* world system: it bears witness to the
> unprecedented homogenisation of today's world. ... So we are
> fighting our PC battles for the rights of ethnic minorities, of gays
> and lesbians, of different lifestyles, and so forth, while capitalism
> pursues its triumphant march – and today's critical theory, in the
> guise of 'cultural studies', is performing the ultimate service for
> the unrestrained development of capitalism by actively partici-
> pating in the ideological effort to render its massive presence
> invisible (Žižek, 2000a, 218).

In short, multiculturalism as ideology obscures the only truly progressive position that the left should occupy: the politicisation of
class. The reference to class permits us to grasp the fundamental
dialectical nature of ideology, in as much as the explicit ideological

sphere hegemonised by conflicting discourses (say, today's liberal democratic consensus) is always-already sustained by the intractable Real of class struggle, *which therefore is, from a political angle, the very kernel of ideology,* i.e. *ideology at its purest.* What must not be missed in Žižek's account is that ideology functions as a dialectical device where its positive, historically changeable and describable content (Fascism, Socialism, Liberalism, etc., i.e. ideology in the plural) is always anchored in some disavowed kernel of traumatic negativity, a non-symbolisable and ultimately trans-historical notion of antagonism that Lacanian psychoanalysis defines as 'the Real of *jouissance*', i.e. non-discursive enjoyment. Strictly speaking, class struggle *is* political *jouissance*, and as such it remains 'impossible', which means – against the 'surrogate impossibility' of spectrality – that it can only emerge as a violent deflagration, an incendiary materialisation of the Real. Despite the strong emphasis on class, and the conviction that the anti-capitalist struggle should still play the central role in any leftist engagement, Žižek is careful not to turn the working class into a fetish. When he refers to class he does not necessarily mean proletariat, since he is aware that this term has undergone a radical transformation in today's socio-political constellation.

The linguistic dimension is more ambiguous and intrinsically important than it might seem: if on the one hand 'proletariat' has become obsolete, on the other hand Žižek pleads that we do not give in to the opposite, typically postmodern, fetish, i.e. the notion that in our globalised universe of shifting identities the working class is quickly disappearing from sight. Postmodern ideology forces upon us what Žižek calls a 'portfolio subjectivity' (Zizek and Daly, 2004, 148), whereby radical insecurity about job, salary and identity is sold as a new and exhilarating form of freedom, when instead it silently legitimises the exploitative potential within contemporary capitalism – the ultimate point being, of course, that our awareness of the trick played on us by postmodern ideology does not necessarily lead to our disenfranchising from it, since what ties us to the ideological injunction is nothing but 'blind enjoyment'. Žižek is therefore firm in advocating the centrality of anti-capitalist class struggle. However, although he rejects the old notion of proletariat as anachronistic, he also believes that the objective difficulties of defining the very terms of today's struggle should not prevent one

from striving towards a united and cohesive globalised anti-capitalist movement whose common aim would take priority over the
single demands voiced by the multitude of sites of resistance.[1]

Here, however, we need to add a crucial clarification, which
indeed should be taken as the distinguishing constituent in Žižek's
understanding of class struggle and political activism. Amongst all
his frequent and well-rehearsed Marxian allusions, perhaps the
strongest one is the insight that 'the only thing which can destroy
capitalism is capital itself. It must explode from within' (Zizek and
Daly, 2004, 152). This implies a significant relocation of the political
value of class struggle, which ties in neatly with his conceptualisation of ideology critique: according to him, class struggle is less the
militant political participation of the working class in the fight for
emancipation than the 'intractable' disavowed matrix of any socio-
political configuration. In today's global capitalist universe, class
struggle amounts to the explosive potential contained in capitalism's own self-destructive drive, which in Žižek's view is becoming
increasingly self-evident through new developments in such diverse
fields as biogenetics and digitalisation. In connection with these
developments, Žižek essentially questions the ability of capital to
contain its own excesses: has the digitalisation of the economy not
engendered a complex system of virtualisation – particularly manifest, for instance, in the ever-growing unmanageability of stock
exchange oscillations – whose irrational nature risks spinning out of
control? Is the very notion of private property not being progressively outmoded by the sheer complexity of today's virtualised
organisation of ownership? Is the progress of biogenetics not posing
serious and potentially explosive questions concerning the patent-
ing and ownership of human genes? Ultimately, Žižek's reference to
class struggle is predicated against the issue of capitalism's internal
and constitutive imbalance. This implies the awareness that the
struggle of (and/or on behalf of) the excluded and underprivileged
ought to dovetail with the ambition to take advantage of the
propensity for implosion displayed by the dominant ideology.

If we look at this argument from a Lacanian perspective, it is clear
that it concerns, once again, the consubstantiality of the Symbolic
and the Real: if on the one hand modern society exists only insofar
as the Real of class struggle remains disavowed, on the other hand a
given form of societal organisation can only express itself as *the*

failure to fully become itself, i.e. through its vital (and disavowed) reference to class struggle. Precisely as such, as a failure or distortion, society (the Symbolic) is consubstantial with the gravitational pull of class struggle (the Real). Another way of putting this is by stating that the Real is 'internally external' (ex-timate) with respect to the Symbolic, which implies that '(p)recisely because of this internality … it *is* possible to touch the Real through the Symbolic' (Žižek in Butler *et al.*, 2000, 121). To reiterate the central argument, if society ultimately coincides with a gesture of ideological gentrification, whereby the abyssal negativity of the Real is thoroughly negated – i.e. given a positive and empirical existence – the challenge faced by a radical critique of ideology

> is not to recognize fiction behind reality – i.e. you experience something as reality and through the work of deconstructive criticism you unmask it as mere symbolic fiction – but to recognize the Real in what appears to be mere symbolic fiction (Žižek and Daly, 2004, 102).

At the very heart of Žižek's critique of ideology, then, lies the invitation to traverse our ideological fantasies and to confront the Real that structures our desire.

7
Beyond Anti-capitalism and Liberal Democracy

We have concluded the previous chapter with the assertion that at the very heart of Žižek's critique of ideology lies the invitation to dispel ideological fantasies and confront the Real that structures desire. But how exactly, given the current political constellation, can such an intervention take place? In an attempt to unearth the interventionist kernel of Žižek's writing, which has so far been largely overlooked, in this chapter we seek to answer what is perhaps the most urgent question concerning Žižek's model.

Žižek's recurrent use of terms such as 'violence' and 'universality' alone is enough to explain the ambiguity of his position within today's left, best exemplified by the acrimonious confrontations with Judith Butler and Ernesto Laclau in *Contingency, Hegemony and Universality*. Particularly since the late 1990s, Žižek has progressively distanced himself from the official positions of contemporary leftist theory, both in their moderate and radical versions. On the one hand, he maintains that the moderates who endeavour to bring about a 'capitalism with a human face' (from Third Way leftists to supporters of multiculturalism and identity politics) engage in an empty battle which only reinforces the global hold of capital; on the other hand, he claims that those radicals who bemoan the triumph of global capitalism as today's supreme evil are generally too inhibited to invest their thinking in a project which legitimises the excess of the revolutionary intervention ('the pious desire to deprive the revolution of this excess is simply the desire to have a revolution without revolution', Žižek, 2002a, 261).

Within this framework, what remains absolutely unambiguous is that Žižek's theorisation of agency cannot be kept separated from his critique of late capitalism. In this sense, one can argue that his proposed solution is as extreme as the situation in which it intervenes. The originality of Žižek's anti-capitalism is rooted in his understanding of political struggle: 'politics is, in its very notion, the field of intractable antagonistic struggle' (Žižek, 2002a, 268). This means that a political intervention always and by definition 'disturbs' the demarcation line between the field of legitimate agonistic confrontation (say, the parliamentary logic of party confrontation in today's liberal democracies) and what from that point of view is considered illegitimate (say, positions of the extreme Left and Right). Such a vision clearly dismisses the liberal notion of politics as a neutral, all-encompassing field; instead, it draws on the psychoanalytic insight that the emergence of the socio-political field, insofar as it is symbolically ordered, hinges on an act of exclusion.

Once the political domain is defined as antagonised by its inherent exclusionary logic, Žižek can focus on his leftist critique of today's constellation. The main argument revolves around a classic Marxian insight which, Žižek laments, is ignored by both contemporary political theorists of the left (Laclau, Badiou, Ranciére and Balibar, mainly),[1] and the proponents of today's Cultural Studies.[2] What Žižek strives to incorporate into an authentically progressive notion of 'agency', is 'Marx's key insight into how the political struggle is a spectacle which, in order to be deciphered, has to be referred to the sphere of economics'. The problem, then, is that within the horizon of today's leftist engagement 'there is simply no room for the Marxian "critique of political economy": the structure of the universe of commodities and capital in Marx's *Capital* is not just that of a limited empirical space, but a kind of socio-transcendental a priori, the matrix which generates the totality of social and political relations' (Žižek, 2002a, 271). From this angle, the act proper comes to coincide with an intervention on capital itself, the disavowed background without which our symbolic existence, today, would be impossible to conceive: 'the only way effectively to bring about a society in which risky long-term decisions would ensue from public debate involving all concerned is some kind of radical limitation of Capital's freedom, the subordination of the process of production to social control – the radical *repoliticization of the economy'* (Žižek, 2000a, 351–2).

From Žižek's perspective, Marxism and psychoanalysis combine to give shape to a rather rigorous definition of the political act: 'because *the depoliticized economy is the disavowed "fundamental fantasy" of postmodern politics* – a proper political *act* would necessarily entail the repoliticization of the economy: within a given situation, a gesture counts as an *act* only in so far as it disturbs ("traverses") its fundamental fantasy' (Žižek, 2000a, 355). In psychoanalytic terms, the traversing (disturbing) of the fundamental fantasy is nothing less than 'the ultimate aim of psychoanalytic treatment' (Žižek, 2000a, 266), as it amounts to bringing to light the primordial attachment upon which the consistency of the subject ultimately hinges. As we shall develop further in Part II, this disavowed primordial attachment (excess) is 'none other than the primordial "masochist" scene in which the subject "makes/sees himself suffering", that is, assumes *la douleur d'exister*, and thus provides a minimum of support to his being' (Žižek, 2000a, 265). In this context, a Lacanian politicisation of the act[3] implies the undoing of the ultimate passionate attachment at work in today's social constellation: capital itself. Žižek's point is that, in a way, politics should be submitted to therapy, in as much as today's power is sustained by the fantasmatic core of capital as the disavowed kernel which effectively runs our lives. By submitting capital to strict social control, the repoliticisation of the economy would necessarily entail a radical, painful (masochistic) act of dis-attachment from our own ultimate fantasy.

Žižek's call for the repoliticisation of the economy, however, does not amount to a psychoanalytic reading of the old Marxian adagio on the supremacy of the economy. In his *Revolution at the Gates*, he has refined his position by stating that the domains of politics (liberal democracy) and economy (late capitalism) are inextricably intertwined. Their inseparability ultimately means that there can be no endorsement of anti-capitalism (no struggle aimed at undermining the economic base) without a political intervention which problematises the very concept of liberal democracy, insofar as 'liberal democracy a priori ... cannot survive without capitalist private property' (Žižek, 2002a, 273). In short, Žižek asserts that, today, parliamentary democracy constitutes nothing but the political form of late capitalism: attacking one (capitalism) without simultaneously intervening on the other (liberal democracy) is just a clever way to defy the very notion of agency.

Again, here we should bear in mind that Žižek's critique of ideology, far from accomplishing itself as a merely descriptive account of 'ideological processes', points us toward an intrinsically problematic theory of agency aimed at questioning the very symbolic framework that defines our subjectivity. He emphasises that

> [t]he perspective of the critique of ideology compels us to invert Wittgenstein's 'What one cannot speak about, thereof one should be silent' into 'What one should not speak about, thereof one cannot remain silent'. If you want to speak about a social system, you cannot remain silent about its repressed excess. The point is not to tell the whole Truth but, precisely, to append to the (official) Whole the uneasy supplement which denounces its falsity. As Max Horkheimer put it back in the 1930s: "If you don't want to talk about capitalism, then you should keep silent about Fascism." Fascism is the inherent 'symptom' (the return of the repressed) of capitalism, the key to its 'truth', not just an external contingent deviation of its 'normal' logic. And the same goes for today's situation: those who do not want to subject liberal democracy ... to critical analysis, should keep quiet about the new Rightist violence and intolerance (Žižek, 2002a, 168).

In pursuing the question of what is required of an effective critique of liberal democracy, Žižek points out that the term anti-capitalism has become an elusive misnomer within the discourse of today's radical Left (including the New Social Movements), the reason being that, at best, it stands for the emergence of 'sites of resistance' (Žižek, 2002a, 297), which lack authentic political incisiveness and ultimately serve the purpose of the radical Left's proud self-marginalisation. The logic is 'one which includes its own failure in advance, which considers its full success as its ultimate failure, which sticks to its marginal character as the ultimate sign of its authenticity' (Žižek, 2000a, 233), and in so doing it confirms the Foucauldian dictum that power and resistance secretly rely on each other. In view of this, Žižek grants that the only politically viable response of the Left to the onslaught of contemporary capitalism is represented by its two institutionalised positions. On the one hand, there is the 'opportunistic pragmatism' of the 'Third Way' Left, effectively trying to harness the global interests of capital by complying with its demands, and on the other hand the social-democratic instance of 'principled opportunism' (Žižek, 2004a, 71) which encourages us to stick to old, pre-1989 formulae such as the defence of the welfare state. As previously anticipated, Žižek's main point with regard to the Left's fidelity to traditional recipes is that it leads to a political cul-de-sac, insofar as the fall of the Berlin Wall has not only determined the demise of 'really existing socialism', but also, along with it, the end of the social-democratic project. All in all, given the ineffectual and fundamentally narcissistic stance of its most radical wing, the task of today's Left would be 'thoroughly to rethink the leftist project, beyond the alternative of "accommodating to new circumstances" and sticking with old slogans' (Žižek, 2004a, 73).

What has become clearer and clearer from Žižek's writings since his seminal book *The Ticklish Subject*, published in 1999, is that this 'rethinking the leftist project' does not simply imply 'questioning capitalism', but also, simultaneously, 'questioning liberal democracy', on the grounds that it is the reference to liberal democracy which, according to him, functions as a blackmail against radical political projects.[4] It is interesting therefore to note that Žižek's strategy is twofold: on the one hand he encourages us not to neglect the vital dimension of the economy, while on the other he reminds us that we should be fighting a political battle against a well-defined political actor. What effectively emerges is that the economic and political dimensions cannot be separated. However, Žižek tells us that despite their powerful alliance, they both require critical attention in separate investigative contexts. To the extent that, by attacking liberal democracy on an openly political ground, he seems determined to lend his psychoanalytic anti-capitalist strategy ('enjoying the symptom of capital *qua* Real') an unmistakable interventionist edge.

But what are the actual premises of Žižek's position? After reminding us that, owing to its supposed intrinsic openness, liberal democracy is hailed today as the only solution 'against the "totalitarian" temptation to close the gap, to (pretend to) act on behalf of the Thing itself' (Žižek, 2004a, 79), he proceeds to argue that rather than being situated *on the opposite side* of liberal democracy, the totalitarian temptation is its (inevitable) *other side*. By submitting the notion of liberal democracy to a Lacanian interrogation, Žižek denounces the strict complicity between today's post-political platforms (from the 'Third Way' to multiculturalism) and the 'totalitarian excess' which he regards both as their fantasmatic supplement and 'concealed true face' (Žižek, 2000a, 205): the more democracy is conceptualised as an abstract container purified of ideological divisions, the more it would reveal its disavowed and traumatic core by generating new forms of racism, outbursts of irrational/fundamentalist violence, and so on.[5] In a nutshell,

> the democratic empty place and the discourse of totalitarian fullness are strictly correlative, two sides of the same coin: it is meaningless to play one against the other, and advocate a 'radical' democracy which would avoid this unpleasant supplement. So when Laclau and Mouffe complain that only the Right has the requisite passion, is able to propose a new mobilizing Imaginary, while the Left merely administers, what they fail to see is the structural necessity of what they perceive as a mere tactical weakness of the Left (Žižek, 2004a, 112).

Žižek's contention is that if the Left continues to endorse the current democratic parameters (liberal democracy allied with global capitalism), it will face the same political deadlock *ad infinitum*: the Western Left will keep standing for a distributive justice that systematically fails to engender political passion, whereas the Right will keep mobilising various forms of obscene 'enjoyment' (racism, proto-Fascist nationalisms, etc.). The basic logic of this structural link could be appreciated by looking at today's hegemonic struggle over Europe, where 'all the leftist attempts to infuse the notion of united Europe with political passion (like the Habermas-Derrida initiative in summer 2003) fail to gain momentum' (Žižek, 2004a, 112).

It is here that Žižek's critique of ideology can be said to penetrate the disavowed (Real) kernel of contemporary Leftist politics: the only way to break out of the claustrophobic vicious circle of 'globalization-cum-particularism' would be to focus on the critique of (capitalist) political economy which simultaneously questions and undermines (liberal) democracy as today's Master-Signifier. Žižek puts this challenge in crude and unambiguous terms: 'why should the Left always and unconditionally respect the formal democratic "rules of the game"?' Along similar lines, he asserts that 'one should take the risk of radically questioning today's predominant attitude of anti-authoritarian tolerance' (Žižek, 2004a, 116–17), for what as a rule replaces legitimate authority is arbitrary power.[6] Paradoxically, then, the only chance of effectively challenging oppressive power relations would be through the acceptance of authority: 'the model of a free collective is not a group of libertines indulging their own pleasures, but an extremely disciplined revolutionary body' (Žižek, 2004a, 119). It is therefore arguable that the defence of the notion of legitimate authority, combined with the 'exhortation to dare', i.e. to move beyond the consensus of liberal democracy, represents the trademark of Žižek's political thought. This has often been criticised as a dangerous flirtation with those very totalitarian extremes that Žižek himself sets out to censure, and perhaps not without some justification (see for example J. Butler in Butler *et al.*, 2000, 268). However, before we jump to conclusions it is worth noting that Žižek is by no means advocating the abolition of democracy. From the following evidence from his own writings, could we not argue, instead, that his plea is about moving beyond (not behind) *liberal* democracy towards forms of 'direct democracy', or 'councils-democracy', which admittedly he holds to be superior?

> [D]irect democracy is not only still alive in many places like *favelas*, it is even being 'reinvented' and given a new boost by the rise of the 'postindustrial' digital culture (do the descriptions of the new 'tribal' communities of computer-hackers not often evoke the logic of councils-democracy?) (Žižek, 2005a, 148).

He specifies this as follows:

> [T]he awareness that politics is a complex game in which a certain level of institutional alienation is irreducible should not lead us to ignore the fact that there is still a line of separation which divides those who are 'in' from those who are 'out', excluded from the space of the *polis* – there are citizens, and there is the spectre of *homo sacer* haunting them all. In other words, even 'complex' contemporary societies still rely on the basic

divide between included and excluded. The fashionable notion of 'multitude' is insufficient precisely in so far as it cuts across this divide: there is a multitude *within* the system and the multitude of those *excluded*, and simply to encompass them within the scope of the same notion amounts the same obscenity as equating starvation with dieting to lose weight. And those excluded do not simply dwell in a psychotic non-structured Outside – they have (and are forced into) their own self-organization, one of the names (and practices) of which was precisely the 'council-democracy' (Žižek, 2005a, 148f.).

The key task here is to make sense of the relationship between the plea to move beyond liberal democracy and the notion of radical political intervention, which Žižek typically calls 'the act':

The point is not simply that, once we are thoroughly engaged in a political project, we are ready to put everything at stake for it, including our lives; but, more precisely, that *only such an 'impossible' gesture of pure expenditure can change the very co-ordinates of what is strategically possible within a historical constellation*. This is the key point: an act is neither a strategic intervention *in* the existing order, nor its 'crazy' destructive negation; an act is an 'excessive', trans-strategic intervention which redefines the rules and contours of the existing order (Žižek, 2004a, 81).

The Žižekian act would make it possible to dispense with the compulsive reference to liberal democracy by opening up a utopian space, by liberating territories akin to 'sites of eternity' (as opposed to mere 'sites of resistance'), for they would function as *'the Benjaminian other side of historical Progress, that of the vanquished'* (Žižek, 2004a, 82–3). To illustrate his point, Žižek enumerates cases of self-organised communities outside the law such as the Canudos in Brazil at the end of the 19th century, the Jesuit *reducciones* at the end of the 18th century in Paraguay, or more recently the territories occupied by 'Sendero Luminoso' in Perù (1990s). In *The Parallax View* he comes back to this question with renewed conviction, suggesting that we read the exponential growth of today's suburban slums as 'the crucial geopolitical event of our times'. Precisely as 'symptoms' of capitalist modernisation, extended shantytowns such as that of Lagos (Chad), with its 70 million people, tell us the truth about global capitalism, and simultaneously present us with authentic emancipatory opportunities. Moreover, Žižek argues that the slum-dwellers *qua* 'living dead' of capitalism are effectively out of power's grip, and as such they contradict 'the Foucauldian micropractices of discipline' (Žižek, 2006a, 268–9). With regard to these excluded sites, Žižek raises a series of crucial questions which lead him right to the heart of our Western topography:

> [I]s there in our 'postmodern' time, still a space for such communities? Are they limited to the underdeveloped outskirts (favelas, ghettos), or is a space for them emerging in the very heart of the 'post-industrial' landscape? Can one make a wild wager that the dynamics of capitalism, with its rise of new eccentric geek communities, provides a new opportunity here? That, perhaps for the first time in history, the logic of alternative communities can be grafted on to the latest stage of technology? (Žižek, 2004a, 83).

In *The Parallax View* he goes as far as conjecturing an alliance between the slum-dwellers and the progressive part of today's so-called 'symbolic class' (journalists, academics, artists, etc., see Žižek, 2006a, 269). Despite the tentative nature of such questions, which he does not relate to a truly practicable political project, Žižek hangs on to the notion of traumatic externality brought about by the act as an indispensable political gesture from which a desirable alternative to the practice of liberal democracy can emerge:

> The only adequate position is the one advocated by Lukács in *History and Class Consciousness*: democratic struggle should not be fetishized; it is one of the forms of struggle, and its choice should be determined by a global strategic assessment of circumstances, not by its ostensibly superior intrinsic value. Like the Lacanian analyst, a political agent has to engage in acts which can be authorized only by themselves, for which there is no external guarantee (Žižek, 2004a, 87).

This is to say that, to Žižek, an authentic political act opens up an emancipatory space beyond the prevalent definition of democracy which confines the meaning of the notion to the narrow limits of liberal democracy. This emancipatory space, he maintains, could be gained through 'elections or referenda'; but an 'authentic act of popular will can also occur in the form of a violent revolution [or] a progressive military dictatorship' (Žižek, 2005a, 149). More precisely, he argues that

> there is ... something inherently 'terroristic' in every authentic act, in its gesture of thoroughly redefining the 'rules of the game', inclusive of the very basic self-identity of its perpetrator – a proper political act unleashes the force of negativity that shatters the very foundations of our being. ... no, Liberal Democracy is not our ultimate horizon; uneasy as it may sound, the horrible experience of the Stalinist political terror should not lead us into abandoning the principle of terror itself – one should search even more stringently for the 'good terror' (Žižek, 2000a, 377–8).

The provocative character of Žižek's rhetoric is here thoroughly revealed; what should be underlined, however, is the strategic significance of this reference to terror. (We should bear in mind that, when in 1990 Žižek had the opportunity to side with terror in the crumbling Yugoslav federation, he chose to run for office as a Liberal Democrat candidate in order to defeat an alliance between nationalists and ex-communists). The important point to make is that Žižek mobilises all his theoretical and rhetorical resources in order to expose the 'untouchable' (and yet inevitably 'fantasised about') limit of contemporary political discourse, i.e. the 'Real' of the discursive platform of liberal politics where antagonistic positions are played out and tolerated *only* insofar as they do not question the platform itself. The Real of contemporary politics is what advocates of radical democratic politics such as Ernesto Laclau and Chantal Mouffe ultimately fail to disturb, for as Žižek often points out, their key notions of antagonism and hegemony can only be conceived of as inscribed in an endless struggle for democracy *qua* 'unfinished' project,[7] whose ultimate aim is not to engender radical change, but 'to solve a variety of partial problems' (Laclau in Butler *et al.*, 2000, 93). In other words, to Žižek, Laclau's and Mouffe's project of radical democracy is not radical and democratic enough. If antagonism and the hegemonic struggle are irreducible for Laclau and Mouffe, this irreducibility, Žižek argues, is nevertheless limited to agonistic confrontations within *liberal*–democratic parameters – whereas antagonism proper, he tells us, should expose the disavowed breaking point of these parameters. The difference between competing forces within a given symbolic field (liberal democracy) can be construed as the ultimate horizon of politics *only* if a more radical difference is disavowed, namely the difference between the field itself and what is excluded from it:

> The old narrative of postmodern politics was: from class essen-tialism to the multitude of struggles for identity; today, the trend is finally reversed. The first step is already accomplished: from the multitude of struggles for recognition to anti-capitalism; what lies ahead is the next, 'Leninist', step – towards politically orga-nized anti-capitalism (Žižek, 2004a, 98).

In Žižek's view all attempts to avoid the mediation of an agency that institutionalises the revolution by giving it direction, discipline and structure are doomed to fail. The final and definitive objective of Žižek's ideology critique is thus to be found in this exhumation of what has become one of the most ostracised notions of contempo-rary political thought, i.e. the party as the catalyst of revolutionary change. Despite the well-founded caution with which Žižek has started articulating the argument in his latest books, his invitation to reflect on the necessity of an avant-garde party is a logical conse-quence of his largely abstract and inherently problematic insistence on 'the act' and 'ethical violence': with this notion of the party, he finally spells out in concrete political terms what he believes to be required in order to 'intervene in the Real'. His argument is now anchored in a tangible political referent.

From this viewpoint, Žižek highlights what he considers the limits of an understanding of radical political practice as a politically unmediated immersion into the multiplicity of struggles for emanci-pation. He argues that

> one should have the courage to affirm that, in a situation like today's, the only way really to remain open to a revolutionary opportunity is to renounce facile calls to direct action, which

necessarily involve us in an activity where things change so that the totality remains the same. Today's predicament is that, if we succumb to the urge of directly 'doing something' (engage in the anti-globalist struggle, helping the poor...), we will certainly and undoubtedly contribute to the reproduction of the existing order. The only way to lay the foundations for a true, radical change is to withdraw from the compulsion to act, to 'do nothing' – thus opening up the space for a different kind of activity (Žižek, 2004a, 72).

Is this final injunction 'to do nothing' not in blatant contradiction with his previously mentioned recommendation to organise politically? That may appear to be the case. On the other hand, the above phrase could prove much more subtle than it may seem at first glance. For the proposal 'to withdraw from activity' could also be read as an invitation to 'practice nothingness', which in Žižek's terms – given his rhetorical predilection for hyperboles – is by no means a recipe for hopeless nihilism, but a necessary prerequisite for the emergence of an alternative socio-symbolic order. According to Žižek, then, 'practising nothingness' effectively means *to act*, since the act can only be understood in relation to the instance of absolute negativity that always-already structures the symbolic network (both at social and subjective level):

> For Lacan, negativity, a negative gesture of withdrawal, precedes any positive gesture of enthusiastic identification with a Cause: negativity functions as the condition of (im)possibility of the enthusiastic identification – that is to say, it lays the ground, opens up the space for it, but is simultaneously obfuscated by it and undermines it (Žižek, 2000a, 154).

As Žižek repeatedly emphasises, the enthusiastic identification with the Cause (e.g. anti-capitalism) is valid and effective only insofar as it is preceded by a crucial (and intrinsically violent/traumatic) act of dis-identification, whereby the revolutionary subject dies a symbolic death, i.e. detaches itself radically from its socio-symbolic predicament (the all-pervasive universe of liberal capitalism). Within the current political situation, this would imply, firstly, a thorough recognition of the fact that master-signifiers such us 'capitalism' and 'democracy' draw their seemingly unshakable strength precisely from their successful obfuscation of the bottomless negativity (antagonism) that sustains the point from which they enunciate their 'truths' ('capitalism is the only game in town'; '*liberal* democracy is the *non plus ultra* of political practice'). Secondly, in order to avoid the trap of the hysterical questioning of power, which ultimately sustains the logic of liberal democracy, the bedrock of negativity that makes capitalism and its political supplement possible would have to be fully *endorsed* (as opposed to merely located and described) – which is where, according to Žižek, politics proper comes into play.

Does this endorsement of a direct intervention into negativity entail a capitulation to, or a courting of, the 'terrorist temptation'? Not at all. Žižek is fully in line with the young Lenin when he regards violent factional extremism as an 'infantile disorder' of the Left, unequivocally dismissing it as a kind of 'acting out', 'as an index of its opposite, of a limitation, of a refusal actually to "go right to the end"' (Žižek, 2002a, 270). The point to be stressed, however, is that Žižek does not reject terrorism merely on moralistic grounds, but rather because of its refusal to submit its potentially subversive drive to a politically authoritative body; instead, this potential is thoroughly wasted on a reckless and indiscriminate use of violence. As Rex Butler puts it, '"terrorism" for Žižek is just this refusal to go all the (political) way: to avoid the necessity for Party organization, which is not at all a compromise but is the only form a true global revolution, any actual alternative to capitalism, can take' (Butler, 2005, 118). Žižek's fundamental wager is that the revolutionary act must emerge from within a highly-organised party that does not rule out the use of 'ethical violence' (which he opposes not only to terroristic violence, but also to the invisible violence of our epoch, where 'abstract humanitarian rejection of violence is accompanied by its obscene double, anonymous killing *without pietà*', 2004a, 122):

> [I]t effectively is the duty – *the* duty even – of a revolutionary party ... to bring about the transubstantiation of the 'old' opportunistic people (the inert 'crowd') into a revolutionary body aware of its historical task (Žižek, 2005a, 151).

Ultimately, the whole edifice of Žižek's ideology critique may be said to be driven towards one single question: is the Left ready to abandon the logic of hegemonic struggle within liberal democracy and embrace the idea that a true alternative to the current state of affairs requires a highly disciplined anti-capitalist party, i.e. a political avant-garde as the necessary catalyst for revolution? If capitalism will first have to implode, as Žižek believes, revolutionary political organisation will nevertheless be needed as a necessary constituent of such implosion, to the extent that the two (implosion and revolution) might be said to emerge and intervene coincidentally.

* * *

In his analysis of Žižek's concept of ideology critique, Robert Paul Resch comes to the conclusion that '[i]f he isn't simply a cynic lying in the guise of telling the truth, Žižek has, at the very least, chosen to enjoy his symptom rather than question it' (Resch, 2001, 18). We hope that our analysis goes some way to show how erroneous such an assessment is, not least for the simple reason that the aim of Žižek's critique of ideology is exactly that of encouraging us to enjoy the symptom, i.e. to identify with the repressed core of the ideological predicament. What Resch overlooks is the crucial dimension in Žižek: namely that the openness and radical undecidability that Žižek situates at the very heart of his psychoanalytic brand of ideology critique, with its emphasis on the potentially revolutionary status of *enjoyment* as a political factor, is conceived as the *sine qua non* of any progressive agenda for radical change. From a Žižekian angle, the subject's endorsement of its pathological attachment to a given socio-symbolic order is effectively the move that keeps the possibility of radical change alive, simultaneously suggesting how to break the deadlock in Foucault's historicist brand of discourse analysis which remains blind to the economy of enjoyment. If fully endorsed, in other words, attachment eventually turns into disattachment, producing a rift in the seemingly unbreakable consistency of ideological formations from which the radical rearticulation of the very ideological framework suddenly appears possible.

Žižek's path-breaking re-conceptualisation of the intrinsic features and aims of ideology critique has opened up a space from which to elaborate a leftist political vision that may actively oppose the onslaught of global capitalism. In the light of what is at stake in contemporary politics, and given the epochal paralysis of the Western Left, this is no small change. But rather than draw up a balance sheet of what is an ongoing discussion, we shall conclude with three questions concerning Žižek's politics.

1. Is there a difference between theory and practice? What price is it worth paying for the ideals of a political project to be realised?
2. Quite how far will we get with Lenin towards a society 'in which the free development of each is the condition for the free development of all' (Marx, 1977, 238), i.e. a society which aims to realise the full potential of open collective self-management? In the face of the experience of the 20th century, can we presuppose that the political avant-garde is compatible with the ideal of direct or councils-democracy?
3. If the critique of contemporary political economy holds the key to recognizing the Real (limits) of liberal democracy, what would an analogous critique reveal with regard to the political limits of a society which organises itself as councils democracy? What exactly can we say about the political economy of such a polity, and how in practice can it amount to more than a replica of etatist capitalism?

There is no such thing as a neutral question. The angle from which we raise these questions and from which we would prefer them to be considered is best captured in Brecht's poem *The Buddha's Parable of the Burning House*. In this poem Buddha tells his disciples of when he came across a house in flames; when the roof was already ablaze, the people inside, rather than act, kept asking him 'what it was like outside, whether it was raining/whether the wind wasn't blowing perhaps, whether there was/another house for them, and more of this kind'. In light of the fascist threat of his time, which the parable refers to, Brecht firmly rejected the collusive complicity of 'those/ who in face of the approaching bomber squadrons of Capital go on asking too long/how we propose to do this, and how we envisage that/and what will become of their savings and Sunday trousers after a revolution' (Brecht, 1967, 664).

Notes

1   Why Discourse?

1. We do not equate 'discourse analysis' with Foucault's archaeological writings in the 1960s. The former is a central aspect of Foucault's entire work, just as his preoccupation with power and subjectivation cannot be confined to his writings in the 1970s and 1980s but is an inherent feature of all his major works, albeit to a different degree. In his instructive account of Foucauldian discourse analysis, Niels Andersen distinguishes four interrelated strategies: the archaeology of knowledge, genealogy, self-technology analysis, and dispositive analysis. Rather than following the prevalent reading of Foucault, which suggests that the analytical strategies would replace one another successively, Andersen takes the view that, while Foucault's strategies develop 'parallel with the shift in his questioning', they do not replace each other but 'are constructed on top of one another' (Andersen, 2003, 1–32, quotes: p. 7f.).
2. On the relationship between Foucault, Marx and Marxism, see Smart (1983), Poster (1984), Balibar (1992) and Olssen (2004); on Foucault and psychoanalysis, see Lagrange (1990), Marques (1990), Rajchman (1991), Miller (1992), Shepherdson (2000, 153–86) and Whitebook (2005).
3. While the Foucauldian paradigm of discourse analysis has distinctive features, its success story was inextricably linked with the 'discursive turn' in the humanities and social sciences associated with the works of Emile Benveniste (1971), Michel Pêcheux (1975), Pêcheux *et al.* (1995) and many others. – The following draws on Macdonnell (1986), Laugstien (1995), Howarth (2000: 48–84), Saywer (2003), Andersen (2003, 1–32) and Mills (2004).
4. Exceptions confirm the rule. The Berlin *Projekt Ideologie Kritik* (PIT) associated with the name of Wolfgang Fritz Haug, for example, can be said to have continued their work in the new shape of the *Berliner Institut für Kritische Theorie* (InkriT), focussing on the encyclopaedic project of a *Historical–Critical Dictionary of Marxism* which has yielded six volumes so far. Another notable exception is the *Research and Graduate Programme in Ideology and Discourse Analysis* at the University of Essex which, set up in 1982 under the intellectual leadership of Ernesto Laclau, has initiated one of the most interesting developments in the field of ideology critique today, that is *The World Network in Ideology and Discourse Analysis*. Established in 2003, the *Network* encourages poststructuralist approaches to the humanities and social sciences, and seeks to appeal to researchers, students and activists alike. For details see http://www.essex.ac.uk/idaworld/. A third example is Terry Eagleton's work (esp. 1990, 1991).

5. For an excellent overview of this see Kevin Passmore (2003). For effective applications of Foucauldian approaches in management theory, historical sociology and political theory, see Burchell *et al.* (1991), Dean (1994, 1999), Barry *et al.* (1996), Lemke (1997, 2003), Bröckling *et al.* (2000), Anderson (2003), Bratich *et al.* (2003), and McKinlay and Starkey (2004).

2 Foucault's Critical Historicism

1. See also, Jones and Porter (1994) and Scull (1990 and 2007). For a discussion of the reception of Foucault by academic historians see Megill (1987), Brieler (2003) and Gutting (2005b, 49–73), for an assessment of Foucault as a historian and the heuristic implications of his work for historical research, see Goldstein (1994) and Maset (2002).
2. For an overview of the debate between Habermas and Foucault, see Kelly (1994), Ashenden and Owen (1999), Biebricher (2005) and Ingram (2005). For an concise account of Foucault's 'mapping of history', see Flynn (2005b).
3. For the checkered career of 'historicism', see Popper (1957), Meinecke (1972), Reil (1975), Scholtz (1989), Rüsen (1993), Copjec (1994), Veeser (1994), Gallagher and Greenblatt (2000), Berger (2003), Hamilton (2003) and Iggers (2005).
4. Though he resisted the widespread impression that he had *founded* his theory of history on the notion of discontinuity (see e.g. Foucault, 2002c, 113f.). For the link between discourse analysis, archaeology and history, see also Foucault (1994a, 467ff).
5. Instead, he displaces the primacy of the conscious subject of traditional historiography by taking the past on its unconscious terms, as it were, in which it was unbeknown to itself.
6. For an interesting complementary reading of Foucault and Žižek for the purpose of ideology analysis, see Danaher (2002).
7. To be sure, historical perspectivism was not absent from his earlier writings. In *The Order of Things*, for example, it was embodied in his notion of different *epistemes*. But in *The Order of Things* and *The Archaeology of Knowledge* it was not coupled with the political passion that typified his works in the 1970s.
8. Ian Hacking's historical ontology (2002) and Lorraine Daston's historical epistemology (e.g. 2000) are two prominent examples for an effective utilisation of Foucauldian historicist frameworks today. For a critical discussion of Hacking's notion of 'local historicism' (Hacking, 2002, 53), see Davies (2006, 149–52).

3 The *Positive Unconscious*: in Search of the Matrix

1. The type of existence to which Copjec refers here 'is subject *only* to a judgement of existence' – i.e., 'we can say that it does or does not exist, without being able to say what it is, or to describe it in any way' –, as

opposed to an existence which 'is subject to a predicative judgement as well as to a judgement of existence', i.e. 'an existence whose character or quality can be described'. Thus the truth of the former will 'always be located outside knowledge'. Copjec's prime example for the 'Lacanian inflection' in Foucault is the latter's discussion of 'plebness' (Copjec, 1994, 3f.).

2. The term 'historical *a priori*' is not a Foucauldian invention. For the relationship between Foucault's and Husserl's concepts of the historical *a priori* (Husserl, 1970, 369–78), see Han, 2002, 4 and 65f.

3. Gary Gutting aptly calls the discursive level to which it refers 'the "intellectual subconscious" of scientific disciplines' (Gutting, 2005b, 9).

4. Žižek remarks in this context that it often goes unnoticed 'that Foucault's rejection of the psychoanalytic account of sexuality also involves a thorough rejection of the Freudian Unconscious' (Žižek, 2000a, 366). What holds for volume one of Foucault's *History of Sexuality* is equally true of his account of the human sciences in *The Order of Things*. Foucault's rejection of Freud's conceptualisation of the unconscious can be traced back to his 1954 introduction to Ludwig Binswanger's *Traum und Existenz*, where he criticises Freud for construing the unconscious as determined by a metaphysics of desire and comes to the conclusion that 'Freud caused the world of the imaginary to be inhabited by *Desire* as classical metaphysics caused the world of physics to be inhabited by Divine Will and Understanding: a theology of meanings, in which truth anticipates its own formulations and completely constitutes them' (Foucault, 1986b, 35).

5. Hubert Dreyfus and Paul Rabinow have exposed the ambiguous nature of these rules in detail: Are they '*descriptive*, so that we should say merely that people act *according to* them' or are they 'meant to be efficacious, so that we can say that people actually *follow* them?' Can they be 'discursive regularities and prescriptive working principles' at the same time (Dreyfus and Rabinow, 1982, 81–4, quotes: 81 and 84)? For Foucault's 'empirico-transcendental confusion that assimilated empirical contents to their own conditions of possibility', see also Han (2006, 66–9, quote: 66). Žižek observes in this context that what Lacan elevates into the position of an *a priori* 'is not a particular constellation – performativity, social practices or whatever – it's rather a negative form of a priori. What is a priori is just a certain negativity or impossibility' (in Žižek and Daly, 2004, 76).

6. Foucault endorses here Deleuze's position. In one of his last interviews, he clarified the scope of his 'kinship with Deleuze' as 'definitely not' extending to the Deleuzian notion of desire (Foucault, 2000a, 446).

7. In this essay, Foucault had famously predicted that 'perhaps one day, this century will be known a Deleuzian' (Foucault, 2002c, 343). For Žižek's take on 'the strange complementarity of the relationship between Deleuze and Foucault', see Žižek (2004c, 71–2), and for Baudrillard's take on this (Baudrillard, 1987, 17ff.); for a wide-ranging assessment of Deleuze's work, see Buchanan (1999).

8. For Foucault's understanding of and suspicion towards dialectics, see also Foucault, 1994a, 471; and 1981, *passim*.

4   Suspending Ontological Questions

1. David Howarth is right to say that Foucault's 'archaeological and genealogical writings develop an original approach to the analysis of ideologies and political discourses' (Howarth, 2001, 2). His assessment is based on Michael Freeden's definition of ideologies 'as systems of political thinking, loose or rigid, deliberate or unintended, through which individuals and groups construct an understanding of the political world they, or those who preoccupy their thoughts, inhabit, and then act on that understanding' (Freeden, 1996, 3). Howarth's own analyses have proved convincingly how productive such an approach can be. Whether it is, however, correct to say that Freeden's definition of ideology would represent a 'neutral position' which allows us to bypass the 'thorny issue as to whether the concept [of ideology] is either negative/critical or positive/descriptive' (Howarth, 2001, 9) is debatable. Freeden employs a concept of ideology which is descriptive-interpretative and affirmative, as the following quote illustrates: 'What, one may ask, does the study of ideology do for those who insist, as do the normative political philosophers, that political thought is about creating a better society? The posing of such a question is itself telling. Would we ask such a question of anthropology, concerned as it is with observing the behaviour of human beings in cultural contexts?' (Freeden, 2003, 125f.) Freeden's approach replaces the critique of ideology with the analysis of ideologies. In other words, rather than in the critical-interventionist tradition of Marx, Freeden's conceptualisation of ideology stands in the scholarly tradition of Max Weber, according to which the task of the social scientist is to strive for an 'analytical ordering of empirical reality' (Weber, 1949, 52).

2. See e.g. Foucault (1970, xix–xxiv; 1990, 11f.; 2002a, 142–4; 2003e, xxi–xxii; and 2000g, 261f.). Béatrice Han points out that 'Foucault never questions *the nature of the understanding of truth belonging to each epoch*. ... the truth through which recognition is held to work only appears in his analysis as a set of theses whose ontological presuppositions are never challenged. ... Foucault does not wonder about the "essence of truth", and never considers the possibility of a first opening from which different historical understandings of truth could be defined' (Han, 2002, 193). With regard to Foucault's 'invalidation of any normative perspective', Han stresses the fact that although Foucault takes the question of truth seriously, 'he is not concerned with the truth-value of individual statements. On the contrary, one of the functions of archaeology is to bracket the legitimacy of normative judgments by referring each formation of knowledge to the *épistémè* from which it arises, and from which alone it can be judged' (ibid., 43). Is not Foucault's notorious reluctance to be located intellectually and to account for the very possibility of the place from which he was speaking the flip side of this (see e.g. Foucault, 2002a, 19, and 1994d, 553)?

3. Foucault aligns himself in this essay with the Annales school.

5 Matrix Reloaded: Žižek's Ideology Critique

1. For a discussion of Žižek's *descriptive* account of ideology as developed particularly in *The Sublime Object of Ideology* and *On Belief*, which is not central to our analysis here, see Myers (2004) and Kay (2003).
2. As is well known, Althusser turned to Pascal in order to substantiate his argument that ideological belief is generated by the very acts performed by the subject, which are in turn regulated by the material rituals and practices imposed by the state (see Althusser, 1970). Žižek refines Althusser's insight by quoting a passage from Pascal's *Pensées* where the ritualistic basis of belief is directly linked to an unconscious, 'automaton-like' mode of enjoyment (see Žižek, 1989, 36–40). The implication is that belief is always sustained by a paradoxical 'belief before belief', an unconscious disposition to follow the law not because of its positive content, but rather because of its 'irrational', fundamentally traumatic and incomprehensible character: 'Althusser speaks only of the process of ideological interpellation through which the symbolic machine of ideology is "internalised" into the ideological experience of Meaning and Truth: but we can learn from Pascal that this "internalization", by structural necessity, never fully succeeds, that there is always a residue, a leftover, a stain of traumatic irrationality and senselessness sticking to it, and that *this leftover, far from hindering the full submission of the subject to the ideological command, is the very condition of it*' (Žižek, 1989, 43).
3. It could be surmised that the ultimate difference between Derrida and Žižek is the way in which they conceptualise difference: while in Derrida difference signals the impossibility of 'full identity', in Žižek it stands for that radical externality which, precisely as *impossible*, incarnates identity itself (see Žižek, 2002b, 37).

6 Locating Antagonism: the Return of Class Struggle

1. The idea that resistance to capitalism must come from a multitude of heterogeneous sites – an idea expressed most notably by Michael Hardt and Toni Negri in widely-read writings such as *Empire* and *Multitude* – is criticised by Žižek as intimately idealistic.

7 Beyond Anti-capitalism and Liberal Democracy

1. From a more general theoretical viewpoint, Žižek's reproach stems from what he regards as the secret Kantianism of these philosophers, i.e. their insistence on the notion of a regulative and unattainable Idea, the concept of empty universality which can never be filled by a particular content. What Žižek refuses, therefore, is 'the Kantian opposition between the constituted order of objective reality and the Idea of Freedom that can function only as a regulative point of reference, since it is never ontologically fully actualized. ... the moment a political movement pretends

fully to realize Justice, to translate it into an actual state of things, to pass from the spectral *démocratie à venir* to "actual democracy", we are in total-itarian catastrophe – in Kantian terms, the Sublime changes into the Monstrous'. The problem with this logic, which we may call of 'self-inhibited agency', is that it 'includes its own failure in advance' as it 'sticks to its marginal character as the ultimate sign of its authenticity'. In other words, it misunderstands the role and consistency of power: 'it *needs* it as the big enemy ("Power") which must be there in order for us to engage in our marginal/subversive activity – the very idea of accomplish-ing a total subversion of this Order ("global revolution") is dismissed as proto-totalitarian' (Žižek, 2000a, 232–4).

2. For Žižek's critique of Cultural Studies and their focus on struggles for recognition see, for example, the section 'Theoretical state apparatuses' (Žižek, 2001b, 225–9).

3. 'Lacan's wager is that even and also in politics, it *is* possible to accom-plish a more radical gesture of "traversing" the very fundamental fantasy – only such gestures which disturb this phantasmic core are authentic *acts*' (Žižek, 2000a, 266).

4. Significantly, in 'Enjoyment within the Limits of Reason Alone', the Foreword to the second edition (2002) of his *For They Know Not What They Do: Enjoyment as a Political Factor*, Žižek explicitly proposes to get rid of the 'remnants of the liberal-democratic stance' which characterised his earlier work (Žižek, 2002b, xviii).

5. Žižek argues that in today's postmodern 'post-politics' democracy is totally 'fetishised': 'In post-politics, the conflict of global ideological visions embodied in different parties which compete for power is replaced by the collaboration of enlightened technocrats (economists, public opinion specialists...) and liberal multiculturalists. ... Post-politics thus emphasizes the need to leave old ideological divisions behind and confront new issues, armed with the necessary expert knowledge and free deliberation that takes people's concrete needs and demands into account'. The aim of today's post-politics is thus to find 'ideas that work', when of course this means that 'one accepts in advance the (global capitalist) constellation that determines what works'. The necessary correlative to such a mode of democratic consensus is the radical suspension (or foreclosure) of authentic political interventions, which in turn produces 'returns in the Real', i.e., new forms of what Žižek also calls *Id*-Evil, 'a cruelty whose manifestations range from "fundamen-talist" racist and/or religious slaughter to the "senseless" outbursts of violence by adolescents and the homeless in our megalopolises, ... a violence grounded in no utilitarian or ideological reason' (Žižek, 2000a, 198–201).

6. His main examples here are the academia and parental education: in the first instance, 'the more professors renounce "authoritarian" active teach-ing, imposing knowledge and values, the more they are experienced as figures of power' (since they decide on the students' grades anyway); in the second case, 'a father who exerts true transferential authority will

never be experienced as "oppressive" – on the contrary, it is, a father who tries to be permissive, who does not want to impose his views and values on his children, but allows them to find their own way, who is denounced as exerting power, as being "oppressive"...' (Žižek, 2004a, 118).

7. In his Introduction to *The Parallax View*, Žižek refers more generally, and with obvious disapproval, to 'the usual gang of democracy-to-come-deconstructionist-postsecular-Levinasian-respect for Otherness suspects' (Žižek, 2006a, 11).

Part II
On Power and How To Enjoy It

Among the key Foucauldian ideas Žižek has subjected to criticism, few have been more thoroughly queried than Foucault's notions of power and resistance. The following six chapters trace Žižek's notion of the political act against the background of Foucault's theory of power and resistance as it emerged from *Discipline and Punish* and volume one of the *The History of Sexuality*. In a nutshell, our argument is this: in order to effect social change, it is not enough to be aware of the existing state of subjection as the latter is itself part of a power mechanism that is inescapably eroticised and ultimately sustained by the disavowed pleasure we derive from being caught in it. By taking into serious account the Foucauldian insight that knowledge is always-already implicated in the workings of power, critical theory needs to conceptualise the correlation and crucial difference between the circular movement of permanent resistance and the political act. Predicated upon the Lacanian psychoanalytic notion of the act as a radical intervention in social reality that simultaneously shifts the symbolic coordinates of the subject who accomplishes it, Žižek's theorizations of social transformation go a long way towards achieving this. Whether they amount to a model for social change based on collective political practice is, however, questionable.

We will develop the argument as follows: chapter 8 takes a closer look at Foucault's account of power and resistance before we turn to Žižek's critique of Foucault (Chapter 9) and consider its validity with regard to Foucault's much-acclaimed late work (Chapter 10). Chapters 11, 12 and 13 explore in detail how exactly Žižek conceives of the relationship between socio-symbolic power and agency.

8
'Where There Is power...'

If Foucault's historicist brand of discourse analysis was one of his best-received contributions to the humanities and social sciences, his theory of power was its linchpin. The lasting impact of his discourse analyses cannot be accounted for without due attention to the distinctive concept of power which he developed in the 1970s, i.e. the period customarily referred to as his 'genealogical' phase. Foucault himself underlined repeatedly the importance of the link between discourse and power analysis, stressing that 'it is in discourse that power and knowledge are joined together' (Foucault, 1990, 100; see also 1994a, 464ff.). In his inaugural lecture at the *Collège de France* from 1970, which can be seen as a bridge between his writings on knowledge systems and those explicitly committed to the analysis of power technologies, Foucault outlined how 'in every society the production of discourse is at once controlled, selected, organised and redistributed by a certain number of procedures whose role is to ward off its powers and dangers, to gain mastery over its chance events, to evade its ponderous, formidable materiality' (Foucault, 1981, 52). The procedures of control over and mastery of discourse were at once manifestations of the positive unconscious of discourse, which we discussed in Chapter 3, and techniques of power.

In keeping with the ethos underlying his discourse theory, Foucault's theory of power was not peddling a purely academic agenda. His reconceptualization of the question of power was in large measure driven by political considerations, among which the endeavour to draw some lessons from the developments of the

1960s and the concomitant discourses of liberation and revolution was of particular importance.

> What often embarrasses me today ... is that all this work done in the past fifteen years or so ... functions for some only as a sign of belonging: to be on the 'good side', on the side of madness, children, delinquency, sex. ... One must pass to the other side – the good side – but by trying to turn off these mechanisms which cause the appearance of two separate sides. ... This is where the real work begins (Foucault, 1988, 120f.).

While there were historical moments when in principle it was useful and necessary to resort to dualistic simplifications, he argued, this would not be a viable strategy in the contemporary struggles of the 1970s. It was therefore time to move beyond 'the idea that under power with its acts of violence and its artifice, we should be able to rediscover the things themselves in their primitive vivacity: behind the asylum walls, the spontaneity of madness; through the penal system, the generous fever of delinquency; under the sexual interdict, the freshness of desire' (Foucault, 1988, 120). What was required was nothing less than a radically new attitude to the problematic of power which would leave behind 'a certain aesthetic and moral choice' according to which 'power is bad, ugly, poor, sterile, monotonous, and dead', and at the same time question the common lore that 'what power is exercised upon is right, good, and rich' (ibid.). From the beginning of the 1970s until his untimely death, Foucault's (now explicit) intellectual ambition was to ground the possibility of effective resistance in a theoretical edifice whose intelligibility and political efficacy did not, in any way, rely on some convenient ideological self-deception. During the 1970s, he considered the formulation of an adequate notion of power to be the keystone of this edifice.

The concept of power which Foucault developed in *Discipline and Punish* (1975) and volume one of *The History of Sexuality* (1976) was first and foremost directed against what he termed the 'juridico-discursive' models of power represented most prominently by Marxism and psychoanalysis (Foucault, 1990, 82ff.). In these models, Foucault argued, power was primarily conceptualised as centred and operating by prohibition and repression. Construed as a negative and limiting relationship – it 'can "do" nothing but say no' (ibid., 83) – power was guaranteed by institutions that upheld a central law. The liberationist appeal of these models derived from their inherent promise that, in principle, it was possible to step outside of and overcome the grip of power. Against such juridico-discursive conceptions of power, Foucault demanded that '[w]e must cease once and for all to describe the effects of power in negative terms: it "excludes", it "represses", it "censors", it "abstracts", it "masks", it "conceals"' (Foucault, 1991, 194). What was needed instead was an appreciation of modern technologies of power as a positing rather than negating force, as generative rather than destructive, as giving rise to new realities, 'domains of objects and rituals of truth' (ibid.) rather than impeding them.

In consequence of his critique, Foucault proposed a theoretical model which decentred power and rejected the thought that it could be held by one person or group while others lacked it. Power was a relationship between social forces and as such it was fragile, unstable and thus alterable and reversible. In other words, Foucault no longer conceived of power as an external force exerting itself on society, but as immanent in the system of social relations; not as a detached institution imposing itself on social processes, repressing or distorting them, but as an effective network of relationships pervading the social body.

> The analysis, made in terms of power, must not assume that sovereignty of the state, the form of the law, or the overall unity of a domination are given at the outset, rather, these are only the terminal forms power takes. It seems to me that power must be understood in the first instance as the multiplicity of force relations immanent in the sphere in which they operate and which constitute their own organization as the process which, through ceaseless struggles and confrontations, transforms, strengthens, or even reverse them; as the support which these force relations find in one another; and lastly, as the strategies in which they take effect, whose general design or institutional crystallization is embodied in the state apparatus, in the formulation of the law, in the various social hegemonies (Foucault, 1990, 92–3).

In volume one of *The History of Sexuality*, Foucault was turning his attention to 'sexuality' as a privileged marker of power in its modern, normalizing form. The juridico-discursive model of power was now criticised as the conceptual backbone of the 'repressive hypothesis' which Foucault mocked delightfully in the opening part 'We "Other Victorians"'. The book, however, is not about sex, nor should it be read primarily as a 'day of reckoning' with psychoanalysis.

To be sure, Foucault intended to redefine the problematic of sexuality by detaching it from the paradigm of repression. He did reject the repressive hypothesis as a flawed model of the relation between power and sex, but not on the grounds that there had been no repression of sexuality since the Victorian age. What he rejected was the attempt to *centre* the history of sexuality on mechanisms of repression (see ibid., 115ff.). The very notion of repression smacked of a negative obstacle to a positive, quasi-natural drive. It seemed to presuppose an anthropological norm or *status naturalis* from which we had been alienated for centuries. Ahistorical constants of this kind, however, were untenable presuppositions to Foucault as we have seen in Chapter 2, and it was only being consistent that he did not entertain the notion of natural drives, whether in relation to sex or otherwise.[1]

And yet, Foucault's critique of the hypothesis that since the 17th century, as part and parcel of the evolution of capitalism, sexuality had been systematically repressed – i.e. repressed in the sense of 'oppressed' and 'suppressed' as well as in the Freudian sense of *verdrängt* –, was embedded in a more comprehensive enterprise outlined in the final part of his book entitled 'Right of Death and Power over Life'. This final part was the staple of Foucault's 1976 project of a history of sexuality, which lent it its distinctive character as a 'conjectural history' of the deployment of power in the modern age. The function of the critique of the repressive hypothesis within the framework of this venture was to expose the predominant form which power had assumed since the dawn of the modern age, a form of power which was all-pervasive and yet impalpable enough that it had been largely overlooked. This new paradigm, which would mark the *differentia specifica* of Western modernity, was 'bio-power'. But what precisely did this term mean?

Foucault's account of bio-power encapsulated a theory of modernity – advanced as an alternative to Marx and Weber (see ibid., 140–3) – within which power was identified as 'power over life'. In the course of the past four centuries, Foucault argued, it had developed in two interrelated forms: first, as *'anatomo-politics of the human body'* based on the 'procedures of power that characterised the *disciplines*', and second, as *'bio-politics of the population'* effected by procedures of power that were 'situated and exercised at the level of life, the species, the race, and the large-scale phenomena of population' (ibid., 139). While the former was centred on the 'body as a machine' which it aimed to discipline, to optimize, to utilize, to drill and to subject to systems of socio-economic control, the latter focussed on the 'species body' whose biological functioning (from propagation and mortality to life-expectancy and health issues) it sought to supervise and regulate. The 'disciplines of the body' on the one hand, and the 'regulation of the population' on the other, combined to form the 'two poles around which the organization of power over life was deployed' (ibid.). This bipolar conception of bio-power – 'anatomic and biological, individualizing and specifying, directed towards the performances of the body, with attention to the processes of life' (ibid.) – thus integrated the microphysics of disciplinary power, which Foucault had elaborated in *Discipline and Punish*, into a complex model of power which now extended to the level of macro-sociology.

Modern technologies of power 'that take life as their objective' differed, according to Foucault, from traditional technologies insofar as 'the ancient right to *take* life or *let* live was replaced by a power to *foster* life or *disallow* it to the point of death' (ibid., 138, 152). While traditional 'sovereign power' as symbolised by the figure of the King was ultimately evidenced only 'through the death he was capable of requiring', bio-power was quintessentially 'a life-administering power' set on generating forces rather than destroying them (ibid., 136). A society would reach the 'threshold of modernity' when the sovereign power of death was superseded by the 'administration of bodies and the calculated management of life', that is, when man – no longer an Aristotelian 'living animal with the additional capacity for political existence' – would wager 'the life of the species ... on its own political strategies' (ibid., 139f., 143). The entire evolution of capitalism, Foucault maintained, would be unthinkable 'without the controlled insertion of bodies into the machinery of production and the adjustment of the phenomena of population to economic processes' (ibid., 141), i.e.

without the process of social disciplining through the combined deployment of anatomo- and bio-politics, ranging from populations statistics and eugenics to statist racism.

The most important and far-reaching consequence of the development of bio-power was, however, the rise in the West of a 'normalising society'. As a technology of power centred on life, Foucault argued, bio-power did not have to rely any longer on a 'line that separates the enemies of the sovereign from his obedient subjects': bio-power 'effects distributions around the norm' instead (ibid., 144). When, in the course of the 18th and 19th centuries, individuals were measured and described according to developmental norms and administrative classification systems were produced which construed variations as deviations and rendered deviating individuals subject to disciplinary action, the control of individuals as objects of power-knowledge systems was paralleled and underpinned by effective self-scrutinisation on the part of the subjects who as a rule internalised what was deemed normal. Even the workings of those institutions most clearly connected with the law, like the judiciary, the police and the prison system, could not be accounted for without reference to the process of normalisation, as Foucault pointed out: 'I do not mean to say that the law fades into the background or that the institutions of justice tend to disappear, but rather that the law operated more and more as a norm, and that the judicial institution is increasingly incorporated into a continuum of apparatuses (medical, administrative, and so on) whose functions are for the most part regulatory' (ibid.). As the historical outcome of the development of bio-power, normalisation had thus become, in Foucault's view, the most fundamental and ubiquitous form which power assumed in the modern world.[2]

It was precisely here, in the historical context of bio-power and normalisation, that sex acquired its significance as a political issue for Foucault. When in the course of the 19th century disciplinary power and population controls came together in institutional formations of power and knowledge (*dispositifs*), the 'regime of power-knowledge-pleasure that sustained the discourse on human sexuality' (the sexuality *dispositif*) emerged as one of them, and, as Foucault pointed out, 'one of the most important' (ibid., 11, 140). 'Sex', Foucault argued, was 'at the pivot of the two axes along which developed the entire political technology of life. On the one hand it was tied to the disciplines of the body. ... On the other hand, it was applied to the regulations of populations'. In short, 'sex was a means of access both to the life of the body and the life of the species' (ibid., 145, 146). What, though, was he trying to uncover?

> I am looking for the reasons for which sexuality, far from being repressed in the society of that period, on the contrary was con-stantly aroused. The new procedures of power that were devised during the classical age and employed in the nineteenth century were what caused our societies to go from *a symbolics of blood* to *an analytics of sexuality*. Clearly, nothing was more on the side of the law ... the symbolic, and sovereignty than blood; just as sexuality was on the side of the norm, knowledge, life, meaning, the disciplines, and regulations (ibid., 148).

Here psychoanalysis comes back into the equation. Although volume one of *The History of Sexuality* should not be read primarily as a kind of Foucauldian 'judgement day' for psychoanalysis, as pointed out earlier, it surely was an outright attack. While in *The Order of Things* – in spite of some acerbic criticism (see Chapter 3) – psychoanalysis had occupied a privileged position as one of the three 'counter-sciences' paving the way for a new regime of thought which would supplant the crumbling episteme of 'man' someday (see Foucault, 1970, 373–86), this was no longer the case in 1976. Psychoanalysis now became the privileged target for Foucault's cri-tique to the extent that he located it at the very heart of the *disposi-tif* of sexuality.[3] Psychoanalysis did not seem to recognise that the *dispositif* of sexuality was inextricably linked with the normalising technologies of bio-power. On the contrary, to Foucault it repre-sented historically 'the theoretical effort to reinscribe the thematic of sexuality in the system of law, the symbolic order, and sover-eignty'. Such conceptualisation of the sexual in terms of the law, however, was in Foucault's view rooted in the pre-modern era and thus ultimately 'a historical retro-version'. Foucault put his counter-argument in a succinct formula: 'We must conceptualize the deploy-ment of sexuality on the basis of the techniques of power that are contemporary with it' (ibid., 149f.). Historicism and critique of power were joining forces in a compelling counter-argument which unfolded as follows:

People are going to say that I am dealing in a historicism which is more careless than radical; that I am evading the biologically established existence of sexual functions for the benefit of phenomena that are variable, perhaps, but fragile, secondary, and ultimately superficial; and that I speak of sexuality as if sex did not exist (ibid., 150f.).

Did he not in fact leave out of consideration the very thing 'on the basis of which sexualization was able to develop'? While on the one hand, prior to Freud, 'one sought to localize sexuality as closely as possible' and, in the process, 'fell back upon a biological minimum: organ, instinct, and finality', did *he* not, on the other hand, adopt 'a symmetrical and inverse position' from which 'there remain only groundless effects, ramifications without roots, a sexuality without a sex'? In the final analysis, was this not 'castration once again?' (ibid., 151). Far from it, Foucault retorted:

the purpose of the present study is in fact to show how deployments of power are directly connected to the body – to bodies, functions, physiological processes, sensation, and pleasure; far from the body having to be effaced, what is needed is to make it visible through an analysis in which the biological and the historical are not consecutive to one another ... but are bound together in an increasingly complex fashion in accordance with the development of the modern technologies of power that take life as their objective (ibid., 151f.).

The history of sexuality he envisaged would not deal with the question of the sexual body on the level of perceptions, meanings and values. Rather than a mere history of mentalities, it would be 'a "history of bodies" and the manner in which what is most material and most vital in them has been invested' (ibid., 152). Stressing that the analysis of sexuality must neither biologise the notion of sex nor simply circumvent the level of the corporeal reality of the body, he proposed an account of the body and sexuality which was at once anti-essentialist and attentive to the materiality of the body. What is more, if it could be shown that the *corporeal reality* of the body was shaped historically by cultural forces and power inscribed itself *directly* into the body, the opposition between the (natural) body and its cultural (de)formation, and between sex as such and historically conditioned sexuality, had to be called into question.

Still, while his critics might perhaps agree with him that 'sexuality is not, in relation to power, an exterior domain to which power is applied, that on the contrary it is the result and an instrument of power's designs', they would still insist that sex is 'the "other" with respect to power', that it is 'the center around which sexuality distributes its effects'. Yet it was 'precisely this idea of sex *in itself*' which Foucault did not accept (ibid., 152). The idea of 'sex in itself' is the crux of Foucault's critique of psychoanalysis and, by extension, of the repressive hypothesis and the juridical notion of power. To Foucault, sex was not the transhistorical anchorage point of sexuality. Rather, the *dispositif* of sexuality was what established the 'fictitious point of sex' which was 'the most speculative, most ideal, most internal element in a deployment of sexuality organized by power in its grip on bodies' and their polymorphous pleasures (155f.). Far from being the ultimate reference point and 'universal secret' of human activity, sex was not some origin but the most insidious effect of the modern regime of power-knowledge-pleasure sustaining the discourse on human sexuality. In short, sex was a discourse-*'effect with a meaning-value'* (ibid., 148). For Foucault, there could be no such thing as 'sex' outside the range of discourses which constituted sexuality historically.

What is interesting in this context is the fact that Foucault's critique of sex as some pre-discursive domain to be liberated or an origin to be restored, failed to engage with Lacanian psychoanalysis. Lacan did not entertain the idea of 'sex' as a pre-discursive entity. At the same time, however, he questioned the notion that sexual difference (*sexuation*) – which Foucault failed to consider altogether – could be grasped on the level of discourse. In Lacan, sexual difference was strictly correlative with the notion of the Real and thus did not refer to some pre-symbolic reality but to the process of symbolic representation itself: it emerged, as Žižek put it, 'at the very point where symbolisation fails' (Žižek, 1994a, 160). Yet as a residue of the process of symbolisation the Real of sexual difference was foreclosed from the symbolic order and, in this sense, did not exist but 'ex-isted': it remained outside of it in the sense of being excluded from within, as its 'ex-timate' core, constitutive exception or 'limit-obstacle' (see esp. Lacan, 1998b).[4] By the same token,

Foucault's historicist objection to the essentialist rhetoric of alienation according to which we would be alienated from some original,
authentic being, did not consider Lacanian psychoanalysis either. In
Lacan, 'alienation' denoted a constitutive feature of the subject and
referred to the alterity that inhabits the innermost core of the
subject as a condition from which there is no escape. Put crudely, as
Lacanian subjects we are not alienated *from* our authentic being –
we do not exist as subjects to start with – but we are alienated *in* the
symbolic order as the condition of possibility for our existence as
subjects (see Lacan, 1998a, ch. 16).[5]

The fact that Foucault's critique of the repressive hypothesis left
Lacanian psychoanalysis out of consideration in important respects
was arguably no coincidence, and nor was the fact that Lacan's name
was absent from volume one of *The History of Sexuality*.[6] Foucault's
non-engagement with Lacan is indicative of the nature and direction
of his criticism which was first and foremost a historicist critique of
essentialist interpretations of sexuality and liberation.[7] This is further
confirmed by Foucault's choice of opponent. His attack was mainly
aimed at the discourse of Freudo-Marxism à la Wilhelm Reich. In a
lecture from the same year 1976, he even referred to the repressive
hypothesis as 'Reich's hypothesis' (Foucault, 2003d, 16). Reich's 'historico-political critique of sexual repression' (Foucault, 1990, 131) had
instigated a trend during the middle decades of the last century which
allocated sexuality a central place in critical theory. In the 1930s, Reich
was one of the first to forge a link between psychoanalysis and
Marxism and their respective resistances to sexual and economic
repression, a theme which found widespread popular expression in the
discourse of sexual liberation and revolution during the 1960s. If, historically as well as politically, sexual freedom was incompatible with
the capitalist work imperative and system of exploitation, and thus
doomed to prohibition and taboo, was not the struggle against sexual
repression a political struggle against capital and for future liberation?
Foucault was suspicious of the rhetoric of sexual liberation which he
considered to be the expression of a 'tactical shift and reversal in the
great deployment of sexuality', yet not 'a basis for a movement to dis-
mantle it' (ibid., 6f. and 131).[8]

> We must not think that by saying yes to sex, one says no to
> power; on the contrary, one tracks along the course laid out by

the general deployment of sexuality. It is the agency of sex that we must break from, if we aim – through a tactical reversal of the various mechanisms of sexuality – to counter the grips of power with the claims of bodies, pleasures, and knowledges, in their multiplicity and their possibility of resistance. The rallying point for the counterattack against the deployment of sexuality ought not to be sex-desire, but bodies and pleasures (ibid., 157).[9]

For Foucault this was as much a general political strategy as it was a personal one.

9
'... There Is Resistance'

Perhaps at this stage we can hazard a summary of key aspects of Foucault's 'strategic model' of power as developed in *Discipline and Punish* and the introductory volume of *The History of Sexuality*.

1. Power is not an object that can be 'acquired, seized, or shared, something that one holds on to or allows to slip away' – power is a relationship, to be understood nominalistically 'as the name one attributes to a complex strategical situation in a society' (Foucault 1990, 92 and 94).
2. Rather than radiating downwards from a superstructural position, power circulates, 'comes from below' and a multiplicity of different sources – we must conceive of power 'without the king' (ibid., 94 and 91).
3. Power relations do not reside in a 'position of exteriority with respect to other types of relationships ... but are immanent in the latter' (ibid., 94) – like a 'network which runs through the whole social body' (Foucault, 2002c, 119).
4. Since power is ubiquitous and operates in a capillary fashion throughout the social body, it has to be explored at the micro-level, in its concrete local effects. It is from here, primarily, that power relations can be challenged.
5. The micro-practices of power do 'not merely reproduce, at the level of individuals, bodies, gestures and behaviour, the general form of the law or government; ... there is neither analogy nor homology, but a specificity of mechanism and modality' (Foucault, 1991, 27).

6. On the other hand, the 'micro-physics of power' could not function if, 'through a series of sequences, it did not eventually enter into an over-all strategy' (Foucault 1990, 99) embodied in state apparatuses and other institutions.
7. 'Power relations are both intentional and non-subjective'; the fact that 'there is no power that is exercised without a series of aims and objectives ... does not mean, that it results from the choice or decision of an individual subject'; there is no 'headquarters that presides over its rationality' (ibid., 94f.).
8. The procedures of power through which human beings are made subjects are manifold and complex. They range from the structuring of possible fields of action and the governing of conduct, to continuous surveillance and ensuing self-surveillance, and the shaping of individuals' very "fabric" (bodily attributes, capacities and functions) through the repeated performance of discursive norms. *Normalisation* is the most pervasive form which power assumes in the modern world.
9. Modern technologies of power are quintessentially 'life-administering' forces (*bio-power*) set on 'the administration of bodies and the calculated management of life'. – '[D]irectly connected to the [human] body' as their privileged objective, they 'can materially penetrate the body in depth without depending on the mediation of the subject's own representations' (Foucault 1990, 136, 139, 151, and 2002c, 186).
10. Far from being merely negative, repressing what they want to control, power relations 'have a directly productive role, wherever they come into play'. Power 'traverses and produces things ... induces pleasures, forms of knowledge, produces discourse' (Foucault 1990, 94, and 2002c, 119).
11. The notion 'that knowledge can exist only where the power relations are suspended' should therefore be relinquished. Power does not distort knowledge – knowledge is a form of power. 'There is no power relation without the correlative constitution of a field of knowledge, nor any knowledge that does not presuppose at the same time power relations' (Foucault 1991, 27).
12. Last but not least: 'Where there is power, there is resistance' – '[w]e can never be ensnared by power: we can always modify its grip in determinate conditions and according to a precise

strategy'. However, 'resistance is never in a position of exteriority in relation to power'; rather, it is 'inscribed in the latter as an
irreducible opposite'. Resistance, then, does not predate power
but relies on and grows out of the situation against which it
rebels (Foucault 1990, 95f., and 1988, 123).[1]

The final point, which is of crucial importance here, has been elaborated by Chris Weedon, who has extensively utilized Foucauldian
frameworks for feminist theory:

> In Foucault's work, discourses produce subjects within relations
> of power that potentially or actually involve resistance. The
> subject positions and modes of embodied subjectivity constituted
> for the individual within particular discourses allow for different
> degrees and types of agency both compliant and resistant. ...
> While there is no place beyond discourses and the power rela-
> tions that govern them, resistance and change are possible from
> within (Weedon, 1999, 119f).

While Weedon is representative of an affirmative–critical interpretation of the capacity of Foucauldian theory to ground the possibility of
resistance, other critics have been more dismissive. For Joan Copjec,
one of Foucault's fiercest critics, it is precisely in his notion of total
immanence – '[h]is disallowance of any reference to a principle ...
that "transcends" the regime of power he analyses' – where the
problem resides, as we have seen in Chapter 3. If society coincides
with a regime of power relations, as it tends to in Foucault, and if,
consequently, there is no form of negation which could not be
absorbed by the power regime it contests, how can effective resistance
be accounted for (Copjec, 1994, 6, 7, 10)? As early as 1982, Hubert
Dreyfus and Paul Rabinow had concluded their seminal analysis of
Foucault with a similar question whose urgency is undiminished
today: 'Is there any way to resist the disciplinary society other than to
understand how it works and to thwart it whenever possible? Is there
a way to make resistance positive, that is, to move toward a "new
economy of bodies and pleasure"?' (Dreyfus and Rabinow, 1982, 207).

From the infinite list of charges levelled against Foucault's theorisation of power and resistance, we want to highlight the following
five clusters.[2] The first complex of criticisms is aimed at the very way

in which Foucault conceptualised power, which makes it impossible to conceive of effective resistance in the first place. 'Just as "life" was once elevated by Bergson, Dilthey, and Simmel to the basic transcendental concept of philosophy', his critics argue, 'so Foucault now raises "power" to a basic transcendental–historicist concept' (Habermas, 1985, 298). If power was elevated to the basic ontological concept, all talk about resistant agency could be no more than a rhetorical manoeuvre. It was thus no coincidence that, while his historical analyses 'seem[ed] to bring *evils* to light', Foucault distanced himself from any suggestion 'that the negation or overcoming of these evils promote[d] a good' (Taylor, 1986, 69). While rhetorically gesturing towards an emancipatory politics in often passionate terms, Foucault's theorisations would in effect undermine any possibility of adopting such a position. Worse still, 'he seems to raise the question whether there is such a thing as a way out' (ibid.). The burning question fuelling this cluster of criticisms is whether the problem of resistance can be conceptualised at all without a proper theory of the subject as the centre and source of possible resistance (see also Honneth, 1991 and Walzer 1986).

The second objection is closely linked to the first one. Paul Allen Miller points out that Foucault conceptualises resistance as a 'reactive force "co-constituted" with power', which one would associate with the image of a 'static blocking action rather than a dynamic counter-force' (P.A. Miller, 1997, 196), and Baudrillard, relating Foucault's version of power with Deleuze's notion of desire, brands Foucault's genealogical inquiries as completely lacking in transformative potential: '*it's simply that in Foucault power takes the place of desire*'; like desire in Deleuze, Foucault's power is 'always already there, purged of all negativity, a network, a rhizome, a contiguity diffracted ad infinitum' (Baudrillard, 1987, 17f.). What would ultimately disable Foucauldian theory is its substitution of the Bataillean notion of transgression for the Hegelian notion of dialectical negation: While '[n]egation implies an intervention in the reigning positive order that possesses the potential to transform that order', transgression 'leaves that which it transgresses untouched' and is therefore 'incapable of accounting for historical change' (P.A. Miller, 1997, 197f.).[3]

In this context in which, in Frederic Jameson's words, we are left with 'a wholly positivist landscape from which the negative has evaporated' (Jameson, 1991, 323), we can situate a significant strand of Marxist critique of Foucault insofar as it has been directed at the amorphous and anti-dialectical nature of his theory of power on the one hand, and its contemplative–descriptive character on the other. Foucault's 'happy positivism' (Foucault, 1981, 59) failed to recognise the historical role of social antagonism without which neither resistance nor radical political change could be grasped, let alone be effected.[4]

The third objection regards the failure of Foucault's historicist account of power to offer any criteria designed to justify and motivate resistance. Striving to rise to 'a more rigorous objectivity' than displayed by what he dismissed as the human pseudo-sciences, Foucault could 'give no account of the normative foundations of [his] own rhetoric' (Habermas, 1985, 344). As Nancy Fraser put it, Foucault's theorisations of power did not only construe modern society as being without redeeming features, it also and perhaps more importantly denied him the possibility of condemning any of modern society's objectionable aspects. Her penetrating criticism summarises perfectly the normativist Foucault-critique:

> Why is struggle preferable to submission? Why ought domination to be resisted? Only with the introduction of normative notions of some kind could Foucault begin to answer this question. Only with the introduction of normative notions could he begin to tell us what is wrong with the modern power/knowledge regime and why we ought to resist it. ... Clearly, what Foucault needs, and needs desperately, are normative criteria for distinguishing acceptable from unacceptable forms of power (Fraser, 1989, 29, 33).

Fraser's take on Foucault leads us, fourthly, to the feminist Foucault-critique which has targeted a great number of distinctive issues, ranging from Foucault's neglect of the question of sexual difference in general, to his failure to consider the gendered nature of disciplinary technologies in particular. With regard to power and resistance, we want to highlight two positions. The first one argues along the lines of essentialist Marxism and grounds women's resistance to the patriarchal order in the notion of an authentic experience, emphasising that without the assumption of a subject-individual that exists prior to her being formatted by disciplinary power mechanisms, it is not possible to account for resistance at all.

If individuals are reduced to the effects of power relations, who then are the agents with the capacity to resist (see e.g. Hartsock, 1990)? The second position is represented by Wendy Brown and advocates a political practice which goes beyond the scope of a Foucauldian politics of resistance. The latter by itself, Brown argues, 'goes nowhere in particular, has no inherent attachments and hails no particular vision': it does not 'contain a critique, a vision, or grounds for organized collective efforts to enact either', and thus has to be supplemented by political practices enabling us to articulate a political vision which transcends the horizon of mere resistance to the status quo (Brown, 1995, quote: 49).[5]

Finally, charge number five has been levelled at Foucault's notion of power/knowledge and, more concretely, at what has been perceived as his Nietzschean reduction of truth to power. The criticisms contained in this cluster were voiced from various angles, ranging from the insistence that truth-claims were either adequate or inadequate, a problematic which must not be confused with the question of what impact power might have on knowledge, to the critique of the ambiguity of Foucault's own, if implicit, truth-claims: Was Foucault not trying to tell us the truth about the impossibility of telling the truth, thus criticising the project of the Enlightenment while at the same time secretly relying on it? As a result, not only the adequacy but the very credibility of Foucault's account of power and resistance are being called into question (see e.g. Habermas, 1985, Taylor, 1986 and McCarthy, 1991).

Where, then, does Žižek's critique of Foucault fit in? Let us take a closer look at his major work *The Ticklish Subject* which contains Žižek's most detailed and coherent discussion of Foucault's notion of power as developed in *Discipline and Punish* and volume one of *The History of Sexuality* (Žižek, 2000a, 247–57). It is fuelled by Žižek's customary blend of Lacanian, Hegelian and Marxist motifs and can be situated against the background of the criticisms outlined above as cluster one and two. To begin with, Žižek resumes the established Foucault-critique by stressing that for Foucault the relationship between power and resistance is 'circular, and one of absolute immanence: power and resistance (counter-power) presuppose and generate each other'. From this follows that, if *effective* resistance means resistance which does not merely conform to the rules of the game but allows 'the subject to assume a position that exempts him' from the controlling and regulating grip of power, it cannot be accounted for with reference to Foucault (ibid., 251).

Foucault's notion of 'absolute continuity of resistance to power', Žižek proceeds, can be seen as symptomatic of perversion as an intellectual practice. The transgressive practices of perversion would not only preclude the political potential of the Freudian unconscious – which is inaccessible through the phantasmic scenarios the pervert is acting out – they would also and most importantly obscure it. It is thus no surprise, Žižek argues, that Foucault ('a perverse philosopher if ever there was one' – ibid., 251), like all critics who champion the subversive potential of perversions, winds up denying the Freudian negative unconscious and its theoretical-political worth:

> the pervert, with his certainty about what brings enjoyment, obfuscates the gap, the 'burning question', the stumbling block, that 'is' the core of the Unconscious. The pervert is thus the 'inherent transgressor' *par excellence*: he brings to light, stages, practices the secret fantasies that sustain the predominant public discourse (ibid., 248).

The subject of today's 'post-politics', Žižek maintains, is caught in a perverse loop of consummate transgression without 'burning question', impelled incessantly by the super-ego injunction 'Enjoy!'. The political task is, therefore, to break free from the loop of 'the pervert's false transgression' and to try and 'hystericise the subject' caught in this loop by instilling 'the dimension of lack and questioning in him' (ibid., 247–9). This is the specific angle and starting point of Žižek's critique of Foucault's conception of power in *The Ticklish Subject*.

However, Žižek insinuates that when, with obvious enjoyment, Foucault relentlessly varies the motif of power and resistance as presupposing and generating one another, what he brings to light is not without its merits. On the contrary, the weakest point of his theoretical edifice is simultaneously its fundamental achievement. As Žižek's account implies, there are at least two lessons which should be heeded from *Discipline and Punish* and volume one of *The History of Sexuality*: first, that the object which modern technologies of power aim to control and regulate 'is already their effect', and second, that 'the very subject who resists these disciplinary measures and tries to elude their grasp is, in his heart of hearts, branded by them' (ibid., 252). Žižek's illustrates this with a veritably Foucauldian example, that is the 19th century movement for the liberation of labour. The worker bent on liberating himself from the fetters of capital, was he not 'in his heart of hearts' already branded by the disciplinary work ethics of contemporary capitalism, to the extent that all he was striving for was to 'establish himself as the disciplined worker who works for himself, who is fully his own master (and thus looses the right to resist, since he cannot resist himself ...)' (ibid.)?

Žižek's appraisal of Foucault carries the distinct message that one must not walk into the traps of essentialism and try to return to a state before Foucault. Power and resistance *are* caught in a deadly mutual embrace. Where there is power, there *is* resistance, since the former 'needs an X which eludes its grasp'. By the same token, Žižek's critique suggests that it is worth considering the anti-essentialist implications of the Foucauldian notion that there is no resistance without power inasmuch as the latter 'is already formative of that very kernel on behalf of which the oppressed subject resists the hold of Power' (ibid., 252–4).

And yet, the crucial question looming large in Žižek's argument is whether power and resistance are *simply* or *entirely* caught in a deadly mutual embrace. If we want to account for social discipline and subordination, can we entirely skirt the question of 'how individuals ideologically subjectivize their predicament, how they relate to their conditions of existence'? Can the disciplinary tec niques of bio-power really 'constitute individuals *directly*, by penetrating individual bodies and *bypassing* the level of "subjectivisation"' (ibid., 253)? In the final analysis, Žižek's critique boils down to one basic question: is the deadlock of power and resistance our inescapable fate? His answer is of course No! We have to recast the Foucauldian account of power and resistance by moving *beyond* Foucault.

To start with, Žižek argues, there is no reason to accept the conclusions which Foucault drew from his enquiries as inevitable. The Foucauldian premise

according to which resistance to power is inherent and immanent to the power edifice (in the sense that it is generated by the inherent dynamic of the power edifice) in no way obliges us to draw the conclusion that every resistance is co-opted in advance, included in the eternal game Power plays with itself (ibid., 256).

In a second step, Žižek complements this observation by highlighting the critical aspect which is missing from Foucault's account:

> the key point is that through the effect of proliferation, of producing an excess of resistance, the very inherent antagonism of a system may well set in motion a process which leads to its own ultimate downfall (ibid.).

Yet, this is precisely the notion of antagonism which Foucault, 'the anti-dialectician par excellence' (ibid., 253), would not entertain:

> from the fact that every resistance is generated ('posited') by the Power edifice itself, from this absolute inherence of resistance to Power, he seems to draw the conclusion that resistance is co-opted in advance, that it cannot seriously undermine the system – that is, he precludes the possibility that the system itself, on account of its inherent inconsistency, may give birth to a force whose excess it is no longer able to master and which thus detonates its unity, its capacity to reproduce itself. In short: Foucault does not consider the possibility of an effect escaping, outgrowing its cause, so that although it emerges as a form of resistance to power and is as such absolutely inherent to it, it can outgrow and explode it (ibid., 256).

Although Foucault's account, ironically, confirms 'the Hegelian thesis on how reflexive probing into a transcendent In-itself produces the very inaccessible X that seems forever to elude its final grasp', it lacks the dialectical notion of an effect that can 'outgrow' its cause, for one thing, and the 'properly Hegelian self-referential turn' in the relationship between power and resistance, for another, which is – Žižek contends – why Foucault neglects the very process through which power technologies become 'contaminated' by what they endeavour to control (ibid., 252–4).

One is thus tempted to reverse the Foucauldian notion of an all-encompassing power edifice which always-already contains its transgression, that which allegedly eludes it: what if the price to be paid is that the power mechanism cannot even control *itself*, but has to rely on an obscene protuberance at its very heart? In other words: what effectively eludes the controlling grasp of Power is not so much the external In-itself it tries to dominate but, rather, the obscene supplement which sustains its own operation (ibid., 256f.).

Žižek's verdict on Foucault is unequivocal: within the scope of Foucault's theorisation of power, where resistance is always-already co-opted in advance, the prospects 'for individuals to rearticulate and displace the power mechanisms they are caught in' are practically zero (ibid., 253). Foucauldian theory does not allow for a subversive act which would bring about a 'thorough restructuring of the hegemonic symbolic order in its totality' (ibid., 262). On the contrary, the circular movement of resistance to power amounts exactly to what Žižek calls 'the ultimate ideological operation', namely the 'elevation of something into impossibility as a means of postponing or avoiding encountering it' (in Žižek and Daly, 2004, 70).

If it is true that (a) regimes of power generate their own surplus with potentially destabilising consequences, yet that (b) capitalism has the 'profound capacity to ingest its own excesses and negativity: to redirect (or misdirect) social antagonisms and to absorb them within a culture of differential affirmation' (Daly, 2004, 16); and that (c) in order to effect political change it is not enough to be in the know about the existing state of subjection as the latter is itself part of a power mechanism that is inescapably eroticised and ultimately sustained by the disavowed pleasure we derive from being caught in it; then the key question to be raised is how we can conceive of a political intervention which breaks free from the vicious circle whereby regimes of power reproduce themselves by continuously creating and obliterating their own excess.

In order to answer this question, however, one has to part company with Foucault and turn to Lacan, Žižek concludes, because it is Lacan, and not Foucault, who would enable us 'to conceptualize the distinction between imaginary resistance (false transgression that reasserts the symbolic status quo and even serves as positive condition of its functioning) and actual symbolic rearticulation via the intervention of the Real of an *act'*, that is 'a passage through "symbolic death"' (Žižek, 2000a, 262).

Even though Žižek has confined his critique of Foucault's account of power and resistance explicitly to *Discipline and Punish* and the first volume of *The History of Sexuality* (see ibid., 306, note 3), it also holds on the whole for Foucault's much-acclaimed late writings in which he addresses one of the cardinal problems of his entire work, that is the question of the subject. Before we move on to Žižek's account of the political Act in Chapters 11, 12 and 13, we want to take a brief look at this.

10
The Missing Subject

To begin with, let us recapitulate the argument so far. Foucault was not concerned with language as a matter of linguistics. From the start, his problem was rather how social reality, as we know it, was constituted in discourse. 'My problem is essentially the definition of the implicit system in which we find ourselves prisoners; what I would like to grasp is the system of limits and exclusion which we practice without knowing it; I would like to make the cultural unconscious apparent' (Foucault, 1989, 71). What bedevilled Foucault's archaeology of knowledge in the late 1960s was, however, that he conceptualised discourse formations as autonomous, self-sufficient systems, the functioning of which could be explained without reference to some system-external outside. In this context, the subject was conceived as an effect of discourse and would amount to little more than a mirror image of the subject-positions produced within a given discursive regime. While in the 1970s Foucault's agenda shifted from the analysis of knowledge systems to the analysis of power-knowledge apparatuses, this lack of agency which typified his earlier works was not remedied. With disciplinary power 'cut[ting] individuals to its measure' (Gros, 2006, 511), the subject was now the product of regimes of normalisation inside which it (dis)appeared as 'the alienated correlate of apparatuses of power-knowledge from which the individual drew and exhausted an imposed, external identity beyond which the only salvation was madness, crime, or literature' (ibid., 513). It is not without irony that towards the end of his journey Foucault should rediscover the problematic which had served as his foil at its beginning, namely the problem of the subject. Indefatigably as he had worked towards the fulfilment of his own prophecy according to which the subject 'would be erased, like a face drawn in sand at the edge of the sea' (Foucault, 1970, 387), the late Foucault, in his endeavour to anchor the possibility of effective resistance to technologies of power in an ethics of existence based on technologies of the self, was haunted once again by the spectre of the transcendental 'in the form of the idea of a free and autonomous self-constitution of the subject' (Han, 2002, 196). The irony of this did not escape Foucault. In the introduction to volume two of *The History of Sexuality* from 1984, where he gave an account of the theoretical shift towards the analysis of the subject, he mused:

> There is irony in those efforts one makes to alter one's way of looking at things, to change the boundaries of what one knows and to venture out a ways from there. Did mine actually result in a different way of thinking? Perhaps at most they made it possible to go back through what I was already thinking, to think it differently, and to see what I had done from a new vantage point and in a clearer light (Foucault, 1985, 11).

When two years before, in 1982, Foucault had declared that 'it is not power, but the subject, that is the general theme of my research' and went so far as to contend that this had been 'the goal of my work during the last twenty years', it came as a surprise to many friends and critics alike (Foucault, 2002b, 326f.). With the benefit of hindsight, he could now portray his itinerary as centred on the exploration of different modes of subjectivation:

> My work has dealt with three modes of objectivization that transform human beings into subjects. The first is the modes of inquiry that try to give themselves the status of sciences. ... In the second part of my work, I have studied the objectivizing of the subject in what I shall call 'dividing practices'. ... Finally, I have sought to study – it is my current work – the way a human being turns him- or herself into a subject. For example, I have chosen the domain of sexuality – how men have learned to recognize themselves as subjects of 'sexuality' (Foucault, 2002b, 326f.; see also 2000a, 452).

His lectures from 1980–81 on *Subjectivity and Truth* and, even more so, those from 1981 to 1982 on the *Hermeneutics of the Subject* bear witness to the fact that the late Foucault believed increasingly in the possibility of a subject in the sense of subjectivation rather than subjection (Gros, 2006, 512). The step from subjection (the constitution of the subject through domains of knowledge and tactics of power) to subjectivation (the emergence of the subject in practices of the self, i.e. 'self-subjectivation' [Foucault, 2006, 214]) was the project Foucault was feverishly working on during the late 1970s until his death in 1984. His entire late work was devoted to seeking an anchoring point for his new-found notion of the subject. After all, there was an eight-year silence between the appearance of the first volume of *The History of Sexuality* in 1976 and its second and third volumes in 1984, during which the intended six-volume series of explorations into the history of sexuality had turned into a different project (Gros, 2006, 508).

In his lecture course on the history of modern governmentality, which he began in January 1978, Foucault had thoroughly reworked his notion of power. He was now concerned with 'techniques for "governing" individuals – that is, for "guiding their conduct" – in domains as different as the school, the army, and the workshop' (Foucault, 1984, 337f.). In the form of liberal government as it came into being in the course of the 18th century, effective power was now conceived by Foucault as predicated on the freedom of the individual which would mark its inherent limit (Foucault, 2004, 79 and 1994c, 272f.). Four years later, in 1982, he differentiated rigorously between power and domination and between relationships of power and relationships of violence:

[W]hat defines a relationship of power is that it is a mode of action that does not act directly and immediately on others. Instead, it acts upon their actions: an action upon an action, on possible or actual future or present actions. A relationship of violence acts upon a body or upon things; it forces, it bends, it breaks, it destroys, or it closes off all possibilities. Its opposite pole can only be passivity, and if it comes up against any resistance it has no other option but to try to break it down (Foucault, 2002b, 340).

Although violence could be an instrument or the result of the exercise of power, it would not constitute the nature of a power relationship as such:

> A power relationship ... can only be articulated on the basis of two elements ...: that 'the other' (the one over whom power is exercised) is recognized and maintained to the very end as a subject who acts; and that, faced with a relationship of power, a whole field of responses, reactions, results, and possible inventions may open up. ... [Power] operates on the field of possibilities in which the behavior of active subjects is able to inscribe itself. ... [I]t is always a way of acting upon one or more acting subjects by virtue of their acting or being capable of action (ibid., 340f.).

A reappraisal of the notion of the subject followed logically from this. However, it is not volume two and three of *The History of Sexuality* from 1984 but the lectures on the *Hermeneutics of the Subject* from 1981 to 1982 which represent the final twist in this story of the return of the subject. The lectures develop the material for a project devoted to the practices of the self (see Gros, 2006: 507–17). It was meant to carry the enterprise of a history of the subject beyond the scope of the history of sexuality by isolating *techniques of the self* understood as

> the procedures, which no doubt exist in every civilization, suggested or prescribed to individuals in order to determine their identity, maintain it, or transform it in terms of a certain number of ends, through relations of self-mastery or self-knowledge. In short, it is a matter of ... 'govern[ing] oneself' by performing actions in which one is oneself the objective of those actions, the domain in which they are brought to bear, the instrument they employ, and the subject that acts (Foucault, 2000b, 87).

Had this project not been interrupted by his early death, Frederic Gros presumes, Foucault would have found this 'the crowning achievement of his work' (Gros, 2006, 515).[1]

What, then, might be criticised about Foucault's late attempt to work out how a subject could emerge that was no longer simply constituted but constituting itself through techniques of the self, a subject that would ultimately give body to the 'insubordination and ... essential obstinacy on the part of the principles of freedom' which Foucault had located at 'the heart of power relations' all along (Foucault, 2002b, 346)?[2]

Historian Philipp Sarasin, who has worked extensively with Foucauldian frameworks (see Sarasin 2001, 2003 and 2004), offers an interesting assessment of Foucault's final turn. In his analysis of Foucault's reading of the Oedipus myth,[3] he argues that the notion of the subject sketched out in Foucault's late work presupposes a *modus operandi* of self-subjectivation that dispenses with any reference to the symbolic. Foucault's premise would be historically incorrect and philosophically untenable – there never was a society where self-technologies were practiced without reference to some symbolic order, nor would any such society be conceivable. Recurring to Lacan, Sarasin stresses that, on the contrary, communities of speaking animals cannot but subject themselves to a symbolic law. The alternative would be psychosis. While Foucault's genealogical deconstruction of ostensibly eternally-valid laws, norms and values had proved extremely fruitful historiographically, his disregard for the symbolic would be fundamentally flawed. In his endeavour to reveal the possibility of immanent forms of subjectivation beyond the law, Foucault rejected not only what he took to be the psychoanalytic notion of the law but eventually cut any reference to the symbolic order (Sarasin, 2005, 197–207).

Sarasin's critique confirms Žižek's assessment of Foucault's late work in the *The Ticklish Subject*. How could one conceive of a more active model of subjectivity in which the subject was capable of adopting a position which would exempt it from the *dispositifs* of power described in *Discipline and Punish* and volume one of *The History of Sexuality*? Was this not, Žižek insinuates, Foucault's implicit question? Foucault believed he had found such an exception in Antiquity, Žižek argues, insofar as 'the Antique notions of the "use of pleasure" and "care of the Self"' would 'not yet involve reference to a universal Law'. And yet:

the image of Antiquity deployed in Foucault's last two books is *stricto sensu* phantasmic, the fantasy of a discipline which, even in its most ascetic version, needs no reference to the symbolic Law/Prohibition of pleasures without sexuality. In his attempt to break out of the vicious cycle of power and resistance, Foucault resorts to the myth of a state 'before the Fall' in which discipline was self-fashioned, not a procedure imposed by the culpabilizing universal moral order (Žižek, 2000a, 251f.).

The Use of Pleasure and *The Care of the Self*, Žižek concludes, are tacit acknowledgements of the failure of his earlier work to ground effective resistance sufficiently, but they do not develop a viable alternative to this deadlock. On the contrary, 'Foucault's description of the Self in pre-Christian Antiquity is the necessary Romantic-naive supplement to his cynical description of power relations after the Fall, where power and resistance overlap' (ibid., 252).

In fact, the notion of the subject Foucault championed in his late work was 'rather a classical one', as Žižek explains in *The Sublime Object of Ideology*: 'subject as the power of self-mediation and harmonizing the antagonistic forces, as a way of mastering the "use of pleasures" through a restoration of the image of self'. If until the mid-1970s Foucault had remained within the anti-humanist death-of-the-subject paradigm which construed the subject as an effect of pre- or non-subjective processes, the late Foucauldian notion of subject re-entered 'the humanist–elitist tradition: its closest realization would be the Renaissance ideal of the "all-round personality" mastering the passions within himself and making out of his own life a work of art' (Žižek 1989, 2). Either way Foucault was failing to account for the subject before subjectivation.

The Lacanian notion of the split subject which Žižek mobilises against the poststructuralist subjectlessness offers a third way between what Ernesto Laclau (in Žižek, 1989, xiv) called the 'essentialism of the substance' and the 'essentialism of the subject'. In Žižek's Lacanian reading the '*subject* is ... to be strictly opposed to the effect of *subjectivation*', for prior to subjectivation through acts of identification with the forms of identity offered by various discursive arrangements – i.e. prior to becoming somebody – the subject is the subject of a lack: 'what the subjectivation masks is not a pre- or transsubjective process ... but a lack in the [symbolic] structure', a constitutive void which is the subject itself – 'the subject as absolute negativity' (Žižek 1989, 174f.). If the latter is 'decentred', this is not because objective unconscious mechanisms govern our subjective experience. Rather, the subject is decentred because 'I am deprived of even my most intimate subjective experience, ... the fundamental fantasy that constitutes and guarantees the core of my being, since I can never consciously experience it and assume it' (Žižek 2006c, 53). What the wealth of forms of subjectivation masks ultimately is the split ('decentred') subject as its own generative matrix.

Jean Hyppolite, Foucault's famous teacher and predecessor at the Collège de France, once described *The Order Of Things* sympathetically as a tragic book. One should extend this assessment to all of Foucault's major works up to the first volume of *The History of Sexuality* in 1976. They are intriguing histories which demonstrate compellingly how from the 16th century a system of prison walls has encroached insidiously on every nook and cranny of modern society, formatting individuals to size in the process. Yet the stories they tell are too compelling for their own good: the prison system is impenetrable, the construction has no loopholes, walls seem to be all there is. They are the stories of 'a power without an exterior' (Ewald, 1992, 169). If these works are therefore tragic, Foucault's late works – to use a well-worn bon mot – bear the hallmarks of a farce. While the former throw the baby out with the bathwater, the latter place the baby right next to the bathtub. Foucault's attempt to isolate the practices of the self from the symbolic order in which they 'make sense' and to theorize the emergence of the subject as self-subjectivation, without reference to some symbolic order and beyond the law, could only fail.

The intellectual event 'Foucault' would probably not exist had he started his itinerary with his final insights on the subject. The Foucauldian project has been particularly elucidating when it was at its most controversial. This is especially true of *The Order of Things*, *Discipline and Punish*, and volume one of *The History of Sexuality*. Thus his work should not be read as an intellectual trajectory which culminated in the account of the subject advanced in his late work.

The ethical and political consequences of Foucault's account of power, the subject and resistance in his late work are reflected in the philosophical ethos of the 'historical ontology of ourselves' outlined in his 1984 essay *What Is Enlightenment*:

[C]riticism is no longer going to be practised in the search for formal structures with universal value but, rather, as a historical investigation into the events that have led us to constitute ourselves, and to recognize ourselves as subjects of what we are doing, thinking, saying. ... this criticism is not transcendental, ... it is genealogical in its design and archaeological in its method. ... [It] will be genealogical in the sense that ... it will separate out, from the contingency that has made us what we are, the possibility of no longer being, doing, or thinking what we are, do, or think (Foucault, 2003a, 53f.).

Foucault then goes on to spell out the practical–political implications of this:

Yet if we are not to settle for the affirmation or the empty dream of freedom. ... the historical ontology of ourselves must turn away from all projects that claim to be global or radical. In fact, we know from experience that the claim to escape from the system of contemporary reality so as to produce the overall programs of another society. ... another culture, another vision of the world, has led only to the return of the most dangerous traditions (ibid., 54).

To be sure, this is not a new position for Foucault to adopt. It rather confirms his attitude *vis-à-vis* political change as expressed, for example, in his famous interview with Bernard-Henri Lévi from 1977. When asked 'Do you want the revolution? Do you want anything more than the simple ethical duty to struggle here and now, at the side of one or another oppressed and miserable group, such as fools or prisoners?', Foucault – evoking the spectre of really-existing Stalinism – called into question 'the very desirability of the revolution' as a liberating struggle (Foucault, 1988, 122f.). He advocated the ideal of an intellectual who, in the here and now, 'locates and marks the weak points, the openings, the lines of force', who is constantly on the move without ever being certain as to his ultimate destination as he is too focussed on the present, who 'contributes to posing the question of knowing whether the revolution is worth the trouble, and what kind ... it being understood that the question can be answered only by those who are willing to risk their lives to bring it about' (ibid., 124).[4] Now, in 1984, while essentially confirming his earlier convictions, he is far more direct:

I prefer the very specific transformations that have proved to be possible in the last twenty years in a certain number of areas which

concern our ways of being and thinking, relations to authority, relations between the sexes, the way in which we perceive insanity or
illness; I prefer even these partial transformations, which have been
made in the correlation of historical analysis and the practical attitude, to the programs for a new man that the worst political
systems have repeated throughout the twentieth century. I shall
characterize the philosophical ethos appropriate to the critical
ontology of ourselves as a historico-practical test of the limits we
may go beyond, and thus as work carried out by ourselves upon
ourselves as free beings (Foucault 2003a, 53f.).

The implications of this have been interpreted in profoundly different ways. While to James Bernauer and Michael Mahon '[h]is
thought moved toward an ever-expanding embrace of otherness, the
condition of any community of moral action', testifying to 'an impa-
tience for ... a freedom that does not surrender to the pursuit of
some messianic future but is an engagement with the numberless
potential transgressions of those forces that war against our self-cre-
ation' (Bernauer and Mahon, 2005, 164), Tilman Reitz is concerned
about the neoliberalist implications of Foucault's ethics. Questioning
Nancy Fraser's contention that Foucault's oeuvre belongs to the
Fordist era and has thus become a matter for historians (see Fraser,
2003), Reitz argues that, on the contrary, Foucault is an eminently
topical thinker, in that he has contributed to the expansion of a neo-
liberal constellation from a leftist position. Foucault's opposition to
the disciplinary apparatuses of normalisation would combine with
his penchant for fragmentation to develop a brand of critique which,
ultimately, exhausts itself in a mere affirmation of individual difference, diversity and particularistic identity, without due attention to
hierarchical relations of power and domination (Reitz, 2003). Reitz is
right: although it can hardly be maintained that Foucault had
intended to forge a coalition with the neo-liberal political milieu, his
late writings prove intellectually attractive in many quarters of
academia where neo-liberal aspirations have come to the fore.[5]

* * *

In his disputation with Ernesto Laclau and Judith Butler, Žižek remarks
that 'the problem for me is *how to historicise historicism itself*. The

passage from "essentialist" Marxism to postmodern contingent politics (in Laclau), or the passage from sexual essentialism to contingent gender-formation (in Butler) ... is not a simple epistemological progress but part of the global change in the very nature of capitalist society. It is not that before, people were "stupid essentialists" and believed in naturalized sexuality, while now they know that genders are performatively enacted'. In order to account for this passage from essentialism to the awareness of contingency, Žižek calls upon 'a kind of meta-narrative' such as 'the Foucauldian notion of the shift in the predominant *épistème*' (in Butler *et al.*, 2000, 106). In other words, while Foucault has not gone far enough with regard to the historicisation of historicism (see Chapters 1–4), a Foucauldian analysis of the intellectual shift in which he himself has played a prominent part, would go a long way towards achieving this.

Žižek's acknowledgement coincides in many respects with our assessment. Foucauldian analyses are at their most telling when they force us to confront those 'implicit system(s) in which we find ourselves prisoners' (Foucault, 1989, 71). His archaeology is at its most compelling when, by uncovering the historical *a priori* of knowledge formations, it brings to light the interplay of absence and presence, revealing from either side of an epistemic break how a movement is eclipsed (see J.-A. Miller, 1992, 60). Foucault the genealogist is at his most irresistible, when as a political historian of truth he shows us 'to what extent the effort to think one's own history can free thought from what it silently thinks, and so enable it to think differently' (Foucault, 1988, 116).

Yet, at the same time, the Foucauldian work has come to stand for a type of knowledge which renders social reality as a hermetic world of powers and counter-powers, mutually inciting, reinforcing and obliterating one another, a type of knowledge akin to the tradition of determinist materialism. In such a world, where there is no rupture in the 'great chain of being', freedom is 'news from elsewhere' (Deary, 2004, 25) and paradigm change either mirage or miracle. How, then, can we conceive of an intervention that breaks free from the vicious circle by which regimes of power reproduce themselves by constantly generating and obliterating their own excess?

11
Liberation Hurts: Žižek on Superego, Masochism and Enacted Utopia

What emerges from our analysis so far is that the difference between an act proper (radical agency) and performative activity within a certain hegemonic structure, hinges on the way in which we position ourselves towards the excess produced by the discursive field. Radical agency is first of all conceived by Žižek in classic Hegelo-Marxist dialectical terms (also articulated by the Frankfurt School), as a way of 'reading the troubling excess that occurs in the realization of some global [universal] project as the symptomal point at which the truth of the entire project emerges' (Žižek, 2000a, 347); then, crucially, as a kind of endorsement (which the Frankfurt School did *not* subscribe) of this very 'troubling excess', implying that the subject suspends its immersion in the socio-symbolic order (its alienation) by way of assuming the very abyssal negativity that structures such order (separation). Thus the subject truly 'identifies with the exception': the best way to undermine power, for Žižek, lies in overidentifying with the negativity (the structural exception/excess) which (su)stains its space. What remains to be seen is what this act of endorsement actually (concretely) entails.

Let us return to Žižek's argument on the fundamental difference between Foucault's and Lacan's notions of resistance/transgression in order to clarify the question. What qualifies a free act, according to Žižek, is an intervention whereby 'I do not merely choose between two or more options WITHIN a pre-given set of coordinates, but I choose to change this set of coordinates itself' (Žižek, 2001c, 121).

For Lacan, there is no ethical act proper without taking the risk of
... a momentary 'suspension of the big Other', of the socio-symbolic network that guarantees the subject's identity: an authentic
act occurs only when the subject risks a gesture that is no longer
'covered up' by the big Other (Žižek, 1993, 262–4).

One of the most urgent questions that Žižek's radical formulation of
the act poses is how to conceive of the relationship between the
symbolic "big Other" (the discursive field) and the Real mobilised by
the act, insofar as this relationship is mediated by the subject. This
is evidently crucial for Lacan himself, who claims that the authentic
act is a way to 'treat the real by the symbolic' (Lacan, 1998a, 15). As
Žižek reminds us time and time again, Lacan's point is that the
Symbolic alone guarantees our access to the Real (and, conversely,
that only the Real allows us to truly resignify the Symbolic). The
centrality of the Symbolic–Real relationship suggests that the act
cannot be quickly dismissed as a violent, psychotic suspension of
the subject's immersion in the socio-symbolic order, or else we miss
the originality of Lacan's point and, consequently, of Žižek's argument. Rather, the intrinsically violent character of the act implies,
strictly speaking, nothing but the *repetition* of a creative intervention
that disturbs what was always-already there, at the heart of the symbolic network. Repetition is a recurrent term in Žižek's opus, regularly deployed in connection with the notion of agency (see Žižek,
2001a, 69–110). Essentially, it connotes the mental (and implicitly
political) effort to repeat a given historical situation by rendering
visible its fundamental deadlock, the 'scandal' of its abyssal openness. The main reference here is, naturally, Walter Benjamin's
Theses on the Philosophy of History, where revolution itself is conceived as the repetition of a certain interference that suspends the
ostensible linearity of historical progress: 'What repetition repeats is
not the way the past "effectively was" but the virtuality inherent to
the past and betrayed by its past actualization' (Žižek, 2004c, 12). In
Benjamin, revolution implies the paradox of a 'static intervention',
i.e. the interruption of historical progression aimed at bringing
about the a-historical kernel of history itself. Precisely because it is
linked to revolution, then, repetition appears to Žižek also as an
eminently theological concept, which he relates not only to
Benjamin's proverbial mysticism but also to Kierkegaard's appraisal

of the scandal of Christianity against its institutionalisation: repeating Christ, for Kierkegaard, entails the 'religious suspension of the ethical', the scandal of a revolutionary act that inscribes a break in the normal state of things. The act thus represents a paradigmatic case of the Hegelian coincidence of opposites: it is at once the highest embodiment of agency/change, *and* another name for stasis – for the exceptional emergence of an explosive impasse within a regime of continuous activity. As such, it sanctions the existence of the foundational gap around which the whole socio-symbolic network is structured. This is also why the act is, in stark contrast to what today's multiculturalist ethical attitude suggests, the only way for the subject to truly 'reach out for the other', in the precise sense of fully endorsing the radical otherness on which the functioning of the symbolic field hinges.

Perhaps the best way to approach the intricate theme of agency as developed along the lines of 'subjectivity, violence and otherness', is by looking at one of the many examples on popular culture offered by Žižek's writing. In *Revolution at the Gates*, he focuses on David Fincher's film *Fight Club* (1999) precisely to clarify the meaning of the act as the endorsement of the disavowed excess which sustains symbolisation. This reading also allows us to focus on Žižek's main political concern, the critique of late capitalist ideology. The basic question posed by the film's hero (Norton) is extremely simple and yet absolutely pressing: how is the modern subject to break out of 'the futility of a life filled with failure and empty consumer culture' (Žižek, 2002a, 250)? The suggested answer is equally simple, although apparently absurd: through self-beating. This strategy is epitomised in what is perhaps the most significant scene of the film, when the hero, whilst arguing with his boss over his salary, decides to enact his boss's repressed anger and suddenly starts beating himself up violently in his office. According to Žižek, this apparently masochistic act represents the only way 'to suspend the fundamental abstraction and coldness of capitalist subjectivity', insofar as

> we cannot go directly from capitalist to revolutionary subjectivity: the abstraction, the foreclosure of others, the blindness to the other's suffering and pain, has first to be broken in a gesture of taking the risk and reaching directly out to the suffering

other – a gesture which, since it shatters the very kernel of our identity, cannot fail to appear extremely violent (Žižek, 2002a, 252).

Radical agency is here formulated in connection with an apparently masochistic intervention 'which is equivalent to adopting the position of the proletarian who has nothing to lose'. In Žižek's Lacanian terms, the emergence of pure subjectivity coincides with an 'experience of radical self-degradation' whereby I, the subject, am emptied 'of all substantial content, of all symbolic support which could confer a modicum of dignity on me'. The reason why such a (humiliating and potentially perverse) position of self-degradation is to be assumed, Žižek argues, is that within a disciplinary relationship (between 'master and servant'), self-beating is, in its deepest configuration, nothing but the staging of the other's secret fantasy; as such, this staging allows for the suspension of the disciplinary efficacy of the relationship by bringing to light the obscene supplement which secretly cements it. Žižek's central point is that the obscene supplement ultimately cements the position of the servant: what self-beating uncovers is 'the servant's masochistic libidinal attachment to his master', so as 'the true goal of this beating is to beat out that in me which attaches me to the master' (Žižek, 2002a, 252).

Žižek's analysis highlights a fundamental political question: it is not enough to be aware of our state of subjection to change things, as that very subjection – insofar as it is part of a power mechanism – is inevitably 'eroticised', sustained by the disavowed pleasure we find in being caught in it:

When we are subjected to a power mechanism, this subjection is always and by definition sustained by some libidinal investment: the subjection itself generates a surplus-enjoyment of its own. This subjection is embodied in a network of 'material' bodily practices, and for this reason we cannot get rid of our subjection through a merely intellectual reflection – our liberation has to be *staged* in some kind of bodily performance; furthermore, this performance *has* to be of an apparently 'masochistic' nature, it *has* to stage the painful process of hitting back at oneself (Žižek, 2002a, 253).

Ultimately, the passage from 'oppressed victim' to 'active agent of the revolution' requires a move whereby the subject endorses that disavowed excess/symptom which 'anchors' his identity in the socio-symbolic order *qua* power mechanism: *'the only true awareness of our subjection is the awareness of the obscene excessive pleasure (surplus-enjoyment) we derive from it*; this is why the first gesture of liberation is not to get rid of this excessive pleasure, but actively to assume it' (Žižek, 2002a, 254).

Žižek's reflections on masochism thematise one of his most recurrent theoretical argumentations: the question of the Lacanian superego as the bearer of a formidable command to enjoy. The obscene call of the superego is to be understood as complementary to the letter of the law; for instance, the injunction 'Thou shalt not kill' from the Ten Commandments is inevitably accompanied by 'the obscene intrusive reverberation of "Kill! Kill!"' (Žižek, 2003b, 104). More precisely, superego pressure is detectable in the presence of the 'pure' prohibition devoid of substantial content ('You shall not!'), which is always integral to the specific character of the prohibition itself ('You shall not kill!'). The abstract injunction nestled in the particular text of the prohibition embodies the obscene superego call ('you shall!'), since it functions as an unfathomable ban generating an unbearable feeling of guilt borne out of our intimate desire to transgress, to disobey the prohibition itself. The proper paradox here is that the more we obey the law, the more we feel guilty, since our obedience to the law is a sign that, deep down, we want to transgress it. Guilt, in other words, refers to the fact that we have compromised our desire to transgress the law, and the superego feeds precisely on this guilt.

It is this understanding of superego pressure that brings Žižek to state that 'psychoanalysis does not deal with the severe authoritarian father who forbids you to enjoy, but with the obscene father who enjoins you to enjoy, and thus renders you impotent or frigid much more effectively' (Žižek, 2000a, p. 245) – the point being that the permissive father (and by extension our permissive society) *directly actualises the superego call to enjoyment*, thus accomplishing the most effective neutralisation of the subject's potential for transgression. Along these lines, Žižek argues that the post-modern regime of hedonistic injunctions, supplemented by the cynical distance towards ideological identification, is strictly correlative to the re-emergence of the nationalistic obsession with the ethnic Thing, or with New Right political populism (see Žižek, 2001b, 229–56; 1993, 202–3; 1994a, 57): direct investment in pleasure-seeking has its truth in violent explosions of unmediated/psychotic forms of obscene 'ideological enjoyment' such as racism, neo-Nazi brutality, etc. The late capitalist universe, therefore, can be said to fully vindicate the merciless character of the superegoic injunction to enjoy, as opposed to our standard conception of the law:

> Lacan's fundamental thesis is that superego in its most fundamental dimension is an injunction to enjoyment: the various forms of superego commands are nothing but variations on the same motif: 'Enjoy!' Therein consists the opposition between Law and superego: Law is the agency of prohibition which regulates the distribution of enjoyment on the basis of a common, shared renunciation (the 'symbolic castration'), whereas superego marks a point at which permitted enjoyment, freedom-to-enjoy, is reversed into obligation to enjoy – which, one must add, is the most effective way to block access to enjoyment (Žižek, 2002b, 237).

Most of Žižek's early writings are aimed at unmasking the nexus between superego transgressions and ideological formations as a key to understanding regressive phenomena such as nationalism and racism in our liberal democracies. All in all, superego transgressions in the form of unbearable injunctions "to enjoy" (to release libidinal pressure) are to be considered as functional to the strengthening of the ideological apparatus from which they emanate.

"Enjoy!" is therefore rightly regarded as one of the key terms in Žižek's dialectics. As such, it is the purely formal, unwritten, internalised, and thus all the more irresistible injunction to enjoy (i.e. to transgress) that secretly sustains the very space of the law. It is important to emphasise how, thus conceived, the law never presents itself simply as a neutral, rational set of prohibitions; rather, it comes into being as an irrational, impenetrable, libidinally invested superego command grounded in the assumption that we are always-already guilty, since the law presents itself, first and foremost, as an abstract prohibition devoid of content.[1] The law is the law on the ground of its formal dimension; if brought down to its essentials, the law is form without content, an empty, implicitly eroticised injunction that, as reflected in Kafka's work, 'insists without properly existing' (Žižek, 2006a, 115).[2] More precisely, the enjoyment under scrutiny here corresponds to the non-symbolizable, trans-historical excess that determines the condition of (im)possibility of a given hegemonic field.[3]

However, rather than just decry and/or attempt to repress the explosions of superego excess so as to revert to the precarious balance of the system from which they emerge, Žižek claims that what is needed is the recognition of their symptomatic revolutionary potential. Drawing on the central theme of Walter Benjamin's previously mentioned *Theses on the Philosophy of History*, he suggests that 'symptomatic' events such as 'the very rage of the anti-Semitic pogroms' down to today's 'post-Communist outbursts of neo-Nazi violence' are to be regarded as 'a negative proof of the presence of these emancipatory chances' (Žižek, 2002a, 256). Ultimately, according to Žižek the strategy of endorsing 'obscene' superego excesses as a means to break out of a given ideological predicament must coincide with the politicisation of these excesses insofar as they are none other than missed revolutionary opportunities.[4]

Žižek, of course, knows very well that these acts of politicisation are risky, precisely because there is no guarantee that the superego obscenity which sustains power is actually turned into authentic revolutionary force. However, he holds on to his defence of redemptive violence in the form of the 'enacted utopia' (Žižek, 2002a, 261) of the revolutionary act:

> As Deleuze saw very clearly, we cannot provide in advance an unambiguous criterion which will allow us to distinguish 'false' violent outburst from the 'miracle' of the authentic revolutionary breakthrough. The ambiguity is irreducible here, since the 'miracle' can occur only through the repetition of previous failures. And this is also why violence is a necessary ingredient of a revolutionary political act (Žižek, 2002a, 259).

Again, we should underline the strategic role played by masochism. Our contention is that Žižek's apology of masochism effectively targets the structural imbalance of the law as a set of empirical prescriptive measures supplemented by superegoic stimuli. This side of the argument can be developed further by calling into question the well known philosophical question concerning sado-masochism. Let us go back to Žižek's central question: why is masochism the first necessary step towards liberation? Firstly, as we have seen, because the staging of a masochistic gesture is the only way for the subject to cut the Gordian knot of his or her libidinally-invested subjection to the law itself. Secondly, and simultaneously, because the economy of masochism brings into contention the insidious figure of the Sadean executioner of the law, the embodiment of the law's dark underside (the superego). How, exactly?

Here we should go back to the previously mentioned thesis on the consubstantiality of law and superego pressure, perhaps reminding ourselves of Lacan's crucial postulation that the law, fundamentally, 'enjoys'.[5] Already in 1962, with his essay 'Kant avec Sade' (see Lacan, 1989), Lacan objects to the fact that Kant, in his positing the autonomous and self-determining character of the law, conveniently forgets to include in the picture the law's obscene addendum, that is, the underworld of enjoyment (*qua* practices of domination) introduced by Sade.[6] From Žižek's viewpoint, the problem we are faced with is, therefore, how to expose this obscene superegoic addendum of the law – since, if the law enjoys, this means that the law is fundamentally imbalanced, sustained by a scandalous, irrational and strictly speaking unlawful (criminal) will to enjoy. Paraphrasing Žižek's comment on a passage from P. D. James' *A Taste for Death* (see 1994a, 93), we could say that what compels the executioner of the law to show his dirty underside of enjoyment is 'the experience of having his desire to kill the victim coincide with the victim's death-drive'.

The point not to be missed is that, as Gilles Deleuze has noted in *Coldness and Cruelty*, what supremely frustrates the sadistic executioner is the masochistic fervour of his victim: a genuine sadist could never tolerate a masochist victim (which also means: he would be compelled to destroy him, to engage in a violent *passage á l'acte*). The immediate reason for this frustration is that masochism forces the sadist to acknowledge that the object of his desire – the body of the other – is *already the object of the other's desire*, and as such it can only function as a kind of ersatz enjoyment. Consequently, the sadist realises that he has been thoroughly objectified, cynically used by the masochist as an instrument to generate his own (the masochist's) pleasure in pain.

And what is the awareness of this 'missed encounter with the Thing' if not the very distinctive feature of *jouissance*? Put differently, the masochist makes visible the very extent to which the (executioner of the) law is enslaved to the lack that pertains to desire;[7] the *jouissance* of the masochist affirms its speculative identity with the *jouissance* of the law, hence revealing the strict correlation between the self-affirming character of the law itself and the groundlessness of the law's desire. To sum up: masochism brings out the dark underside of the law, demonstrating how the latter is always supplemented by a sadistic, obscene injunction to enjoy, which ultimately reveals the self-destructive character of the law as well as its fundamental inconsistency and changeability. In view of this, Žižek suggests that one of the ways to challenge the perverse functioning of the law/power is by assuming, in a supreme act of masochistic expenditure, the Real of its obscene *jouissance*, the vertiginous dimension of superego enjoyment. It is within this context that Žižek insists on the (paradoxically) revolutionary character of the superego's injunction 'Enjoy!' If taken literally, the superego leads us directly to the Real. Just as, according to Freud, dreams, jokes and slips of the tongue constitute 'the royal way to the unconscious', we could surmise that to Žižek the superego represents 'the royal way to the Real'.

We can also see, now, how Žižek turns around Kant's claim that the moral law is the measure of the subject's freedom: it is not that the unbearable pressure of the moral law coincides with disinterestedness and freedom (Kant), but that freedom can only be posited as an unbearable (implicitly traumatic) pressure to face the empty kernel of the law. The daring equation between freedom and masochism thus targets the tautological foundations of the law: the real scandal is that, as Deleuze put it apropos of Kant's *Critique of Practical Reason*, 'the law ... is self-grounded and valid solely by virtue of its own form. ... the object of the law is by definition unknowable and elusive'. Such a perspective implies the psychoanalytic awareness that 'the object of the law and the object of desire are one and the same, and remain equally concealed' (Deleuze, 1991, 82–5); or, as Lacan claims at the end of *Seminar XI*, that 'the moral law ... is simply desire in its pure state, the very desire that culminates in the sacrifice, strictly speaking, of everything that is the object of love in one's human tenderness – I would say, not only in the rejection of the pathological object, but also in its sacrifice and murder. That is why I wrote *Kant avec Sade'* (Lacan, 1998, 275–76).

Kant and Sade provide two opposite examples of how to disturb the Real. Kant's moral law designates the intervention of subjective freedom within the order of Being: the ethical act is essentially self-grounded, authorised only in itself, regardless of utilitarian considerations or natural propensities ('the starry heavens above me and the moral law within me', from the *Critique of Practical Reason*). With Sade, freedom is also conceptualised as a rupture with causality, with natural order, as an unconditional injunction to enjoy regardless of natural propensity or utilitarian considerations. The paradox noted by Lacan, however, is that in both cases, regardless of the radically different points of enunciation, we effectively have a break with the Freudian pleasure principle, i.e. an intervention of drive leading to *jouissance*.

By coupling Sade with Kant, Lacan underlines the non-pathological thrust of the categorical imperative: Sade's 'unconditional injunction to enjoy' is correlative to Kant's 'unconditional injunction to do one's duty', as both are ultimately 'pure desire' – they are delivered from any utilitarian concern with the actual attainment of the object (in other words, they are 'desire turned drive'). The truth of Sade's injunction to enjoy the body of the other beyond any possible limit is to be found in Kant's moral law, since the latter presupposes a fracture between the positive content of the law and its (empty, frustratingly unattainable) form: the encounter with the object of desire, whether it is body or law, is necessarily a missed encounter, to the extent that this missed encounter inevitably becomes eroticised, i.e. it turns into the very source of enjoyment (which is the exact definition of drive). What 'Kant avec Sade' reveals, therefore, is that, if developed through to its 'bitter end', Kant's revolutionary insight into morality conflates with Sade's notion of absolute excess.[8] Lacan claims that the moral law cannot serve as a stabilising device which prevents us from encroaching upon the abyss of the noumena; quite on the contrary, it represents the Real 'in disguise', an irresistibly transgressive injunction sustained by a traumatic excess. And, again, the distinctive feature of Žižek's position here seems to be that the scandal of the law's inconsistency can only be fully articulated from the point of view of the masochist *vis-à-vis* the Sadean executioner.

This position can also be elaborated in terms of guilt. If the gap that separates the law from its positive content makes the subject a priori guilty (for, as in Kafka's novels, the subject never knows where he stands with respect to the 'irrational' law), it is the subject's full assumption of this indelible guilt that can break the vicious circle of the law and its superego supplement. What counts here is, again, Žižek's *topos* of the (Christian) masochist, who signals the intervention of a mode of enjoyment outside the law. The emancipatory potential of this intervention resides in the fact that it suspends the law's unbearable pressure, for it reveals (i.e. it makes visible by way of repro-duction) how this pressure is always-already the effect of an obscene injunction to enjoy. When a subject stages a masochistic scenario and says 'I am a priori guilty, and therefore I *want* to be punished!', it is the law that, in effect, reveals its impotence and frustration, since its uni-versalistic foundations are exposed as merely functional to the super-ego command ('Enjoy!'). If a subject does not need the law to punish him, for he can do it himself outside the remit of the law, the latter inevitably loses its coercive character and exhibits its fundamental lack of purpose, its being anchored in *jouissance*. The masochist, therefore, teases out and identifies with the libidinal (fundamentally irrational and self-destructive) kernel of the law itself.

The following passage from Deleuze focuses with unequalled accuracy on the subversive potential of masochism:

We all know ways of twisting the law by excess of zeal. By scrupulously applying the law we are able to demonstrate its absurdity and provoke the very disorder that it is intended to prevent or to conjure. ... we then behave as if the supreme sover-eignty of the law conferred upon it the enjoyment of all those pleasures that it denies us; hence, by the closest adherence to it, and by zealously embracing it, we may hope to partake of its pleasures. ... A close examination of masochistic fantasies or rites reveals that while they bring into play the very strictest applica-tion of the law, the result in every case is the opposite of what might be expected (thus whipping, far from punishing or pre-venting an erection, provokes and ensures it). It is a demonstra-tion of the law's absurdity (Deleuze, 1991, 88).

We need to add that the law's absurdity is nothing but the excessive force with which it destabilises the domain of the pleasure principle. The scandalous excess of the law is, ultimately, the absolute transgression that shatters the notion of life as idiotic homeostatic balance (i.e., it is drive at its purest).

To conclude, we could note that Žižek's insight into masochism seems all the more pertinent today, with the so called 'decline of Oedipus'. The more symbolic authority is being fragmented, diluted and neutralised through a multitude of formal practices of liberalisation and democratisation – whose underlying aim is to de-politicise the social field so as to optimise capitalist profitability – the more it would appear that the only way to antagonise power is by assuming its clandestine surplus-enjoyment.

12
The Leninist Act

What we encounter at this stage of our critical enquiry is once again the very 'bone in the throat' of Žižek's theory of agency, that notion of the act which makes his strategy so uncomfortable to many. Apropos of the empirical dimension of this notion, the first point to make concerns the relationship between the conscious symbolic activity of the subversive subject (say, the knowledge that the economy needs to be repoliticised) and the explosive, excessive, irreducible dimension attached to the act *qua* actual practical intervention. How are we to understand such relationship? Or, to put it in hysterical terms, what do we have to do when we know what we have to do? Significantly, Žižek keeps conscious activity separated from the act, insofar as the act 'occurs *ex nihilo*, without any phantasmic support' (Žižek, 2000a, 374), whereas activity is always secretly sustained by an underlying fantasy. Consequently, the act radically divides the subject, who is unable to 'assume it as "his own", posit himself as its author–agent – the authentic act that I accomplish is always by definition a foreign body, an intruder which simultaneously attracts/fascinates and repels me, so that if and when I come too close to it, this leads to my *aphanisis*, self-erasure'. The paradox of the Žižekian act as the privileged form of agency becomes, at this stage, rather obvious: when we act, we are in fact acted, we enter a kind of 'uncharted territory' where our gestures are performed blindly, as if we were guided by an invisible hand: 'The paradox is thus that, in an authentic act, the highest freedom coincides with the utmost passivity, with a reduction to a lifeless automaton who blindly performs its gestures' (Žižek, 2000a,

375). The act, in other words, is not on the level of the subject, but of the object, insofar as the object in question is none other than the internalised excess, or surplus-enjoyment, which always-already attaches itself to any process of subjectivization: 'If there is a subject to the act, it is not the subject of subjectivization, of integrating the act into the universe of symbolic integration and recognition, ... but, rather, an uncanny acephalous subject through which the act takes place as that which is "in him more than himself"' (Žižek, 2000a, 374–5).

Put differently, the act is correlative to what Žižek often calls 'substanceless subjectivity': to act we need first to empty our subjective frame from its wealth of subject positions and emerge as 'pure subjects'. Far from relying upon an idealistic (or idealised) perspective, this emphasis on substanceless subjectivity takes us straight into the heart of a militant materialism: 'Materialism is not the assertion of inert material density in its humid heaviness – such a "materialism" can always serve as a support for Gnostic spiritualist obscurantism. In contrast to it, a true materialism joyously assumes the "disappearance of matter", the fact that there is only void' (Žižek, 2004c, 25). Or, more comprehensively put, materialism means that

> we should assert that 'objective' knowledge of reality is impossible precisely because we (consciousness) are always-already part of it, in the midst of it – the thing that separates us from objective knowledge of reality is our very inclusion in it ... the correct materialist position (which draws the radical Hegelian ontological consequence from Kant's antinomies) is that *there is no universe as a Whole*: as a Whole, the universe (the world) is Nothing – everything that exists is *within* this Nothing (Žižek, 2002a, 180–1).

Žižek's basic materialistic thesis is that 'society doesn't exist', that there is no positive order of being, in the sense that no hidden ground appears through it: through it there is only the void of Nothingness. The properly political point is to reappropriate this void through a universal cause such as, first and foremost, the subject. Therein lies the reason of Žižek's fascination with biogenetics. What we get with biogenetic planning is precisely the potential disappearance of 'the illusion of the autonomy of personhood' (Žižek, 2004c, 18). Thinking the human body as a technologically modifiable unit and the self as an insubstantial genetic formula already means reconnecting the subject (together with the idea of external reality it harbours) with its empty/virtual core. It is easy to see, then, how the new existential scenario opened up by biogenetics takes us back to the old scenario described by Lacanian psychoanalysis, with its emphasis on the fundamental non-existence (or virtuality) of the subject.[1] However destined to generate anxiety, the potential inscribed in technological self-manipulation is, in Žižek's view, thoroughly revolutionary, since it opens up a universe of unpredictable possibilities: 'Who knows what this "posthuman" universe will reveal itself to be "in itself"? What if there is no singular and simple answer ...? What if it is only and precisely this technological prospect that fully confronts us with the most radical aspect of our finitude?' (Žižek, 2003b, 196). Anxiety itself, in a properly Lacanian reading of the term (i.e., anxiety as the result of our over-proximity to the object-cause of desire), becomes symptomatic of a potential encounter with the abyss of freedom intended as the possibility to reconfigure drastically the meaning and function of our consciousness.

It is this crucial equation of self and void that allows us to grasp the theoretical value of the act as formulated by Žižek. The act can only be conceived against the background of a notion of lack intended as 'generative absence' (Žižek, 2004c, 35), as a missing link through which the chain of being has a chance to suddenly and radically reconstitute itself. From this angle, transcendence is nothing but an illusion created by the very constitutive gap/rupture within immanence (herein, according to Žižek, lies Hegel's lesson). The truth of transcendence is the gap between immanent perceptions/appearances, and it is precisely the explosive potential inscribed into this gap that is mobilised by the act.

The emptying operation that accompanies and qualifies radical agency can be fully grasped by looking at what is perhaps the key psychoanalytic notion deployed by Žižek, i.e. the Freudian death-drive: 'Death-drive means precisely that the most radical tendency of a living organism is to maintain a state of tension, to avoid final "relaxation" in obtaining a state of full homeostasis. "Death drive" as "beyond the pleasure principle" is this very insistence of an organism on endlessly repeating the state of tension' (Žižek, 2004c, 24). Far from relating to death or a suicidal tendency, in fact, death-drive according to Žižek designates *the opposite of dying*, the insistence of the excess of life itself beyond any conceivable limit, beyond life itself in its finitude. Death-drive is

> the very opposite of dying – a name for the 'undead' eternal life itself, for the horrible fate of being caught in the endless repetitive cycle of wondering around in guilt and pain. The paradox of the Freudian 'death-drive' is therefore that it is Freud's name for its very opposite, for the way immortality appears within psychoanalysis, for an uncanny *excess* of life, for an 'undead' urge which persists beyond the (biological) cycle of life and death, of generation and corruption. The ultimate lesson of psychoanalysis is that human life is never "just life": humans are not simply alive, they are possessed by the strange drive to enjoy life in excess, passionately attached to a surplus which sticks out and derails the ordinary run of things (Žižek, 2003b, 62).

How does drive relate to the fundamental inconsistency of the big Other? Contrary to desire, which is essentially an intentional stance towards the missing object, drive is characterised by its blind repetitiveness: the subject is literally caught in the compulsion to endlessly circulate around a particular object, to the extent that, eventually, this movement generates an explosive *jouissance* of its own. In the incessant, libidinally-invested repetition of the missed encounter with the object, the subject, as it were, *becomes the object*, i.e. encounters itself in all its traumatic emptiness and meaninglessness.

The second point to make, strictly linked to the first, concerns the already mentioned question of terror. In his (to many infamous) defence of 'the Good Terror', Žižek reiterates that there is 'something inherently "terroristic" in every authentic act, in its gesture of thoroughly redefining the "rules of the game", inclusive of the very basic self-identity of its perpetrator'. Nevertheless, Žižek maintains a firm distance from terrorism. Despite acknowledging that the act is always 'catastrophic (for the existing discursive universe)', he specifies that one should resist the temptation of willingly provoking a catastrophe (i.e. engage in terroristic activity), while at the same time resisting 'the opposite temptation of the different modalities of dissociating the act from its "catastrophic" consequences'. In short, he claims that despite the fact that 'the act always and by definition appears as a change "from Bad to Worse"' (Žižek, 2000a, 377), we should not associate it to terrorism, for the latter is either a pseudo-radical activity sustained by a symbolic fiction or a 'perverse' over-identification with the act, equivalent to 'a kind of hysterical acting-out bearing witness to their [the terrorists'] inability to disturb the very fundamentals of economic order (private property, etc.)' (Žižek, 2000a, 270; see also 380).

To these mystifying forms of radical intervention, Žižek opposes 'the Leninist act', which he locates in the space between the two Russian revolutions of 1917: the anti-tsarist revolt of February 1917, aimed at democratising society, and the second, decisive October revolution, which replaced liberal democracy with socialism. Succinctly put, Lenin's great achievement was that of discerning the unique chance for a radicalisation of the revolutionary process: 'In February, Lenin immediately perceived the revolutionary chance, the result of unique contingent circumstances – if the moment was not seized, the chance for the revolution would be forfeited, perhaps for decades'. Despite widespread scepticism and open resistance within his own Bolshevik Party (to the extent that his own wife, Nadezhda Krupskaya, concluded that he had gone mad) Lenin was able to sustain 'the abyss of the act', aware as he was that the revolution only legitimises itself by itself, irrespective of opportunistic calculations, and that 'those who wait for the objective conditions of the revolution to arrive will wait forever (Žižek, 2002a, 6–9).[2] As anticipated, Žižek is adamant that any revolutionary intervention is founded upon the suspension of the principle of sufficient reason:

> A revolutionary process is not a well-planned strategic activity with no place in it for a full immersion into the Now without regard to long-term consequences. Quite the contrary: the suspension of all strategic considerations based on hope for a better future, the stance of *on attaque, et puis, on le verra* (Lenin often referred to this slogan of Napoleon), is a key part of any revolutionary process (Žižek, 2004c, 203).

Even more pointedly: 'the true revolution is "revolution with revolution", a revolution that, in its course, revolutionises its own starting presuppositions' (Žižek, 2004c, 211). As regards Lenin, the key issue is that, in his 1917 writings 'between the two revolutions', 'what he [Lenin] insists on is that the exception (the extraordinary set of circumstances, like those in Russia in 1917) offers a way to under-mine the norm itself' (Žižek, 2002a, 10). The force of Žižek's plea to 'identify with the exception' of a given socio-symbolic order, i.e. to assume its excess, is thus perfectly embodied by Lenin's act, which combines the ability to read the 'symptomatic' revolutionary potential of a certain historical situation, and the readiness to take the risk of a radical intervention without guarantees of a positive outcome. The violence implicit in radical agency is not that of a terroristic violation which simply breaks the legal norm, but rather that of an intervention which implicitly 'redefines what *is* a legal norm':

> The act is therefore not 'abyssal' in the sense of an irrational gesture that eludes all rational criteria; it can and should be judged by uni-versal rational criteria, the point is only that it changes (re-creates) the very criteria by which it should be judged – there are no antecedent universal rational criteria that one 'applies' when one accomplishes an act (Žižek, 2001b, 170).

This radical redefinition of the symbolic coordinates of a given his-torical configuration is exactly what qualifies the Žižekian act. That is to say: a truly radical intervention does not aim at recklessly anni-hilating a given order; rather, it performs the much more sophisti-cated transformation of the general principle that sustains that order. For example, when we deal with today's opposition between 'wild' capitalism and welfare state capitalism, a true act would cir-cumvent both extremes and implement 'a new structural principle of social life that would render the very field of the opposition between market and state obsolete' (Žižek, 2004c, 73).

What is the significance of Lenin's act today? Or, more to the point, what does the invitation to 'repeat Lenin' imply for our era of global capitalism? Žižek clearly warns us from a simple return to Lenin, to the 'good old times of the revolution', since he knows full well that such a nostalgic ideological reappropriation would be utterly anachronistic and illusory. Nonetheless, he insists that today's state of affairs is, once again, exceptional, and as such it demands intervention. After the fall of the Berlin Wall and the end of Communism, and after the 'ten-year honeymoon of triumphant capitalism' (Žižek, 2002a, 296), what has emerged is the fundamental inability of the liberal-democratic state to tackle successfully crucial world issues such as the spreading of poverty, ecological and healthcare crises, the role and power of multi-national corporations, etc. According to Žižek, 'the only logical conclusion is that we urgently need a new form of politicization which will directly "socialize" these critical issues'. Lenin, therefore, 'stands for the compelling freedom to suspend the stale existing (post-)ideological co-ordinates, the debilitating *Denkverbot* (prohibition on thinking) in which we live – it simply means that we are allowed to think again' (Žižek, 2002a, 11).

If the first seeds of this 'thinking new forms of politicization' could be discerned in the series of movements emerged from Seattle 1999, he claims that these social movements are symptoms of a profound malaise which needs to be given the form of a 'universal political demand' (Žižek, 2002a, 296), without which they remain caught 'in the vicious circle of "resistance", one of the big catchwords of "post-modern" politics ... the last thing we want is the domestication of anti-globalization into just another "site of resistance" against capitalism'. Ultimately, the political radicality of Žižek's theorisation of agency is encapsulated in his defence of the dimension of universality on behalf of the symptom, the excluded part, and 'the limit of these movements is that they ... lack the dimension of universality – that is to say, they do not relate to the social totality' (Žižek, 2002a, 297). Žižek's paradox is that universality becomes 'actual' only through the politicisation of the concrete exclusion(s) upon which it hinges.

Repeating Lenin, then, implies something much more complex and sophisticated than mere repetition. It implies, first of all, accepting that Lenin's time is gone forever, that what he proposed resulted in grim failure, that the opportunity was missed; however, it is precisely in its ultimate failure that – making the most of the Benjaminian lesson – we should be able to discern the flicker of the utopian light that shone through Lenin's project. The return to Lenin, particularly if contemplated from today's postmodern and post-political horizon, is the return to the field of possibilities opened up by his act. To put it in Žižek's psychoanalytic language, it entails the intervention of drive, the libidinally-sustained compulsion to circulate again and again around the missed encounter with the Thing.

13
Commodity Fetishism: From Desire to Drive

Žižek's ruminations on capitalism often begin with a reference to what in Marxian terms is normally referred to as commodity fetishism. Typically, he notes how in Volume I of *Capital* Marx suggests that the most intimate core of the commodity is to be found in its *form* rather than in its empirical content. Consequently, he claims that the logic of late capitalism is sustained by the 'virtual soul' of the commodity, the empty core of a sublime object responsible for the endless circulation of desire:

> the real problem is not to penetrate to the 'hidden kernel' of the commodity – the determination of its value by the quantity of the work consumed in its production – but to explain why work assumed the form of the value of a commodity, why it can affirm its social character only in the commodity-form of its product (Žižek, 1989, 11).

And again:

> In other words, classical political economy is interested only in contents concealed behind the commodity-form, which is why it cannot explain the true secret, not the secret *behind* the form but *the secret of this form itself*. In spite of its quite correct explanation of the "secret of the magnitude of value", the commodity remains for classical political economy a mysterious enigmatic thing – it is the same as with dreams: even after we have explained its hidden meaning, its latent thought, the dream remains an enigmatic phe-

nomenon; what is not yet explained is simply its form, the process by means of which the hidden meaning disguised itself in such a form (Žižek, 1989, 15).

Žižek's wager is that the enigma of the commodity-form can only be approached by bringing Lacan's Real into the equation, that most fundamental and sublime of abstractions whose role is to allow us to perceive ourselves as subjects capable of articulating a certain relationship with knowledge. More specifically, he focuses on the deepest and most displaced dimension at work in Marx's notion of commodity fetishism, the mechanism necessary for the notion itself to emerge as a contested philosophical domain. The originality of this analytical method – and simultaneously its most misperceived quality – coincides with the determination to confront the pivotal presuppositions around which a given cognitive field (in our case late capitalism) is structured. The crucial contribution of Lacanian psychoanalysis and Hegelian dialectics to Žižek's thought is the pervasive awareness that any knowledge, or discursive field, hinges upon a mechanism of foreclosure, which is therefore its fundamental kernel, its disavowed 'truth'. This means that the reality into which we intervene is always-already *the product* of our intervention. Every particular and conscious act is necessarily preceded by a formal (unconscious) decision to convert the inert objective reality into something 'posited' by the subject. The crucial significance of Hegel's concept of 'positing the presuppositions' lies in this formal gesture of retroactively setting up the framework for our intervention:

> in his particular-empirical activity, the subject of course presupposes the 'world', the objectivity on which he performs his activity, as something given in advance, as a positive condition of his activity; but his positive-empirical activity is possible only if he structures his perception of the world in advance in a way that opens the space for his intervention – in other words, only if he retroactively posits the presuppositions of his activity, of his 'positing'. This 'act before the act' ... is a purely formal 'conversion' transforming reality into something perceived, assumed as a result of our activity (Žižek, 1989, 218).

A similar mechanism of foreclosure is in place in commodity fetishism, with such force that, according to Žižek, it sustains the entire logic of capitalism. For instance, the significance of Žižek's contested assertion that 'capital is Real' depends on the understanding of capital as the foreclosed hard kernel embodied by the Marxian commodity, i.e. that 'mysterious entity full of theological caprices' (Žižek, 2003b, 145) already acknowledged by Marx himself. Žižek banks on the evidence that Marx, against what most Marxists would be prepared to admit, was briefly but all the more crucially stricken by the religious/auratic character of the object of exchange: for a few lines he put aside his ponderous and undoubtedly momentous empirical dissection of capital to focus on the sublime, elusive and fundamentally repressed dimension that pertains to the commodity.

It is the emergence of this dimension that brings Žižek to claim that capital is the Real of our times:

> In socioeconomic terms, one is tempted to claim that Capital itself is the Real of our age. ... it is 'real' is the precise sense of determining the structure of the material social processes themselves: the fate of whole strata of the population, and sometimes of whole countries, can be decided by the 'solipsistic' speculative dance of Capital, which pursues its goal of profitability in a benign indifference. ... Here we encounter the Lacanian difference between reality and the Real: 'reality' is the social reality of the actual people involved in interaction and in the productive processes, while the Real is the inexorable 'abstract' spectral logic of Capital which determines what goes on in social reality (Žižek, 2000a, 276).

Žižek knows full well that capital is not invisible, in the sense that its presence reveals itself through various modes of exploitation. However, he claims that the secret of its global success and resilience (our acceptance of capitalism as our ultimate existential horizon) is fully detectable only by addressing the thorny issue of our attachment to the strictly speaking *missing* kernel of the commodity. In Lacanian terms, what is established here is the direct connection between the big Other and the small other (*a*): *objet a* does not merely correspond to the traditional notion of fetish, i.e. an ordinary object surreptitiously endowed with disproportionate value, but rather it is posited as strictly correlative to the emptiness of the big Other. The partial object, as Žižek puts it in *The Parallax View*, is linked to the big Other by a kind of umbilical cord (see Žižek, 2006a, 108), which implies that our symbolic existence ultimately emerges and materialises itself in a contingent and excessive element without a proper place in the order of being (this is the psychoanalytic equivalent of the Hegelian thesis that 'Spirit is a bone'). The commodity is thus the metonymical element directly embodying the inconsistency of the symbolic order, and therein lies its 'secret'.

We can look at this from a different angle. In traditional Marxian terms, Žižek maintains that capitalism, far from seeking to satisfy people's needs, is actually a self-propelling 'mad dance' whose sole aim is the endless generation of ever-increasing amounts of money. If this is capitalism, he adds, one should look for the secret cause of its irresistible self-generating movement, the crucial factor that sustains its symbolic efficiency. Here we can again draw on psychoanalysis to argue that, in order to perpetuate itself indefinitely, capitalism exploits the logic of desire, since it addresses individuals by soliciting in them an ever changing array of desires for which it proposes an ever changing array of commodities. With capitalism, as it were, desire is exposed for what it truly is: the desire to constantly delay the satisfaction of desire (i.e. the desire to desire). Nonetheless, Žižek is convinced that despite its obvious parasitic manipulation of desire, capitalism should rather be understood in relation to drive:

> Drive inheres to capitalism at a more fundamental, *systemic*, level: drive is that which propels the whole capitalist machinery, it is the impersonal compulsion to engage in the endless circular movement of expanded self-reproduction. ... (Here we should bear in mind Lacan's well-known distinction between the aim and the goal of drive: while the goal is the object around which drive circulates, its (true) aim is the endless continuation of this circulation as such). Thus the capitalist drive belongs to no definite individual – rather, it is that those individuals who act as direct 'agents' of capital (capitalists themselves, top managers) have to display it (Žižek, 2006a, 61).

Capitalism exploits the excess of life best epitomised by the previously outlined notion of drive (*'Pure life is a category of capitalism'*,

Žižek, 2006a, 118), the uncanny libidinal urge to circulate incessantly around a missing object incarnated by the commodity. Even
more accurately: the drive of capitalism is the fixation on a certain
motion whose aim is to introduce a radical imbalance which, in
turn, functions as the condition for the eternalisation of that very
movement. This capitalistic drive is such that it turns the failure to
reach its object into its success, which is precisely the satisfaction
that comes from the infinite circulation around the object.

Here we should go back to the key role of the commodity *qua*
form, since the significance of Žižek's insight rests on the idea that
the perpetually self-revolutionising movement of capital hinges on
its inherent obstacle, the whimsical heart of the commodity. Far
from being misplaced, such a reference brings to light the partly
repressed nub of Marx's notion of commodity fetishism: however
materially and historically accountable, the commodity *qua* fetish
(ultimately, money itself, the mother of all commodities) is
nothing but the stand-in for the very trace of void which bestows a
sublime aura upon the commodity itself. This explains Žižek's fond-
ness of the section from volume 1 of *Capital* entitled 'The Fetishism
of the Commodity and its Secret' where Marx writes: 'A commodity
appears at first sight an extremely obvious, trivial thing. But its
analysis brings out that it is a very strange thing, abounding in
metaphysical subtleties and theological niceties' (Marx, vol. 1,
1990, 163).[1] The way Žižek reads this passage bears witness to his
axiomatic belief in 'locating the Real in what appears symbolic
fiction': the commodity is not merely the embodiment of social
relations, but it actually represents an uncanny object endowed
with magical/religious powers – and the more people deny this
dimension, the more they are caught in the spell of the commodity.

With regard to this uncanny attribute of the commodity that
defines the nature of our libidinal attachment to capitalism, Žižek's
endeavour to identify a breaking point is more crucial than ever.
The question is to avoid the Foucauldian 'perverse' stance of claiming that there is no revolutionary position we can occupy since capitalism erases all references to externality and forces us to 'enjoy
even what we hate'. To steer clear of this kind of resignation, Žižek
would seem to propose an ethics of over-identification, encouraging
us to adopt a position of full immersion into the symbolic order sus-

tained by capitalism, *inclusive of its crucial relationship to enjoyment.*
In fact, this is how, for Žižek, enjoyment becomes a political factor.

Before carrying out a full evaluation of Žižek's brand of anti-
capitalism, let us briefly summarise the key Žižekian question of
enjoyment in its connection with the Real. In his first books he had
insisted on the centrality of the concept of 'political enjoyment',
especially by way of establishing a connection between enjoyment,
nationalism, and racism. Thus conceived, enjoyment coincides with
the way a particular ethnic community organises their way of life
(ceremonies, rituals, etc.): 'A nation *exists* only as long as its specific
enjoyment continues to be materialised in a set of social practices and
transmitted through national myths that structure these practices'
(Žižek, 1993, 202). What is relevant here is the relationship between
the non-discursive Real of enjoyment and the symbolic domain: the
community is held together by a secret reliance on forms of enjoyment which are essentially 'other', that is to say, externalised and
non-conceptual, available only through secret fantasy scenarios.
Again, one can read in this assertion a strong reliance on universalism: strictly speaking, the historically changeable idea of nation is
anchored in the Real of enjoyment, which is always-already compromised with the Symbolic and yet it functions as 'a formal universal', since every symbolic configuration owes its positive existence
to its inherently non-discursive obstacle.

The main argument hereby articulated is that the Real of enjoyment confers upon us a certain particular identity and yet does not
belong to us, we never possess it, since it is, in actual fact, an empty
framework filled by fantasy, the deadlock that shapes our being
from within. In a similar way, *joussance* is what is at stake in racism:
'what really bothers us about the "other" is the peculiar way he
organises his enjoyment, precisely the surplus, the "excess" that pertains to this way: the smell of "their" food, "their" noisy songs and
dances, "their" strange manners, "their" attitude to work' (Žižek,
1993, 202–3). Fundamentally, Žižek understands racism as a psychological ploy we make use of in order to blind ourselves to our own
inconsistency as subjects. By hating the other we effectively demonstrate our profound frustration at being unable to bring our own
kernel of enjoyment under control. What we hate is the fact that
'we are in us more than ourselves': *'The hatred of the Other is the
hatred of our own excess of enjoyment'* (Žižek, 1993, 206). This leads to

an important conclusion apropos of desire, which turns around the standard wisdom about the subversive quality implicit in the very act of desiring (from Wilhelm Reich to Deleuze and Guattari). Desire, according to Žižek, 'can never be grounded in (or translated back into) our "true interests": the ultimate assertion of our desire ... is to act *against* our Good' (Žižek, 1993, 215). As anticipated, Žižek's Lacanian insight into desire is that, if taken to its extreme, it cannot but turn into drive. As a result, traversing the fantasy – the ethical act par excellence in Žižek's Lacanian terms – is in effect the same as keeping up (not giving up on) one's desire: it implies a scandalous over-identification with *jouissance*. The Lacanian motto 'don't give up on your desire' means 'traverse the fantasy and confront the explosive Real of enjoyment'. This explains why, according to Žižek, the fear of excessive identification that characterises our postmodern politically correct attitude is the 'fundamental feature of the late-capitalist ideology: the Enemy is the "fanatic" who "overidentifies" instead of maintaining a proper distance towards the dispersed plurality of subject-positions' (Žižek, 1993, 216).

Apropos of over-identification, Žižek is fully aware that to sustain the (inherently masochistic) Lacanian injunction regarding desire today, in our capitalist society, is increasingly arduous, as the presence of others is more and more perceived as violent and dangerous: the other is the smoker, the stalker, the sexual harasser, the paedophile, etc. The postmodern subject who sees the other as a threat is effectively a cynic who forecloses any possibility of identification, withdrawing more and more into a 'monadic' state of masturbatory solipsism. The key point is that the cynical distance of the modern subject inevitably frees up considerable space for the circulation of capital, since capitalist ideology functions precisely by demanding that we keep a distance from its all-pervasive nucleus of explosive enjoyment – i.e. that we believe in the guise of not believing. Modern hedonism fits perfectly the coordinates of capitalism for two main reasons: as a rule 1) it strives towards the balance of the pleasure principle (obsession with fitness, healthy lifestyle, 'having a good time', etc.) and 2) when it does (inevitably) explode as excessive enjoyment, it remains stuck at the level of asocial/masturbatory *jouissance* (from extreme forms of sexual enjoyment to various modalities of drug addictions). As modern advertising tells us, capitalism operates on the basis of a constant displacement of the collective enjoyment it demands from us; by forcing us to enjoy, it makes sure its core of self-propelling enjoyment (the constant self-revolution of capital) remains secretly operative.

We can approach this question from a different angle. As is well known, Marx located the main antagonism of capital in the disparity between use-value and exchange-value: the latter acquires full autonomy over the former, which is seen as its dispensable temporal embodiment. According to Marx, economic crises emerge precisely because of this gap, i.e. when reality catches up with the illusion that money is self-propelling. And, today, the gap between the virtual universe and the real universe seems indeed to be enlarging, as epitomised by the procedure of offering commodities deprived of their substance, such as decaffeinated coffee and beer without alcohol. Žižek, however, turns around the coordinates of the entire question:

> What if the problem of capitalism is not this solipsistic mad dance, but precisely the opposite: that it continues to disavow its distance from 'reality', that it presents itself as serving the real needs of real people? The originality of Marx is that he played both cards simultaneously: the origin of capitalist crises is the gap between use- and exchange-value, *and* capitalism constrains the free development of productivity (Žižek, 2002a, 279).

Along these lines, he claims that the true horror of what we refer to as today's 'frictionless capitalism' lies in the fact that frictions (i.e. class struggle) continue to exist but are constantly disavowed, reallocated outside our post-industrial universe, away from our delicate sight. If on the one hand (in classic Marxian terms) our material reality is ruled by the invisible circulation of capital in its self-propelling movement around the sublime nucleus of the commodity, on the other hand it is our material reality itself, the way we experience it, that becomes increasingly 'spectralised' – as confirmed above all by the progressive virtualisation of the status of real money (from paper money to electronic money).

It is in this 'metastatic spectralisation' of everyday reality that Žižek identifies the key problem concerning the status of the modern individual faced by the onslaught of capital. Our predicament is that the farther away we position ourselves from the volatile

'Real enjoyment' of capitalism, the more smoothly capitalism reproduces itself. If the strength of capital is that 'it enjoys' by making sure that we keep a distance from its Real enjoyment, then the potential of full identification would be to bring about what is 'in capital more than capital itself', i.e. the disavowed core of enjoyment embodied by the commodity (insofar as the commodity represents this unbearable/impossible libidinal attachment). This is why, incidentally, Žižek maintains that to truly identify with the other means to identify with something that the other *is not aware of possessing* – that is to say, precisely the excessive (Real) core of *jouissance*. This also holds for ideological identification, or what in Althusserian terms we would call interpellation: since the ultimate support of ideology is a nonsensical kernel of enjoyment, the best way to expose the failure of ideology to coincide with itself (to impose itself as a self-transparent, neutral and consistent set of ideas) is *to identify with it completely, inclusive of its concealed underside of obscene enjoyment.* Since obscene enjoyment is nothing but a gentrification (the positive side) of the abyssal inconsistency of ideology, bringing this obscene enjoyment to the surface is tantamount to revealing the inconsistency of the ideological edifice.

We are of course tapping again into the central paradox of Žižek's theoretical system: liberation from a given socio-symbolic order or ideological predicament implies full over-identification with it, insofar as only through the replication of the *entire* logic that sustains symbolic attachment are we able to bring to light the repressed/excessive/symptomatic element that both closes off the Symbolic and, at a deeper level, reveals its inconsistency. In over-identification, therefore, the Real excess is exposed as consubstantial with the Symbolic. Žižek insists on the constitutive ambiguity of over-identification: liberation can only arise from the risky staging of the submissive position that seems to confirm the fundamental logic of ideological interpellation. Similarly, fully embracing the law (inclusive of its 'dirty superego underbelly') becomes the most effective strategy to break its spell.

At this stage, however, we should add a crucial observation. Žižek knows full well that the strength and originality of capitalism as an ideological apparatus is that, in contrast to previous modes of domination, it elevates its own excess into the very principle of social identification: the norm of capitalism is that it constantly revolutionises the norm, relentlessly exceeding its own limits. This implies that the mere politicisation of excess *qua* external surplus might not work with capitalism, since with capitalism excess is, in fact, the norm. This observation effectively shifts the context of the struggle within the enemy's camp, since it tells us that the main weapon against capitalism actually coincides with capitalism's main strength. According to Žižek, however, such implication does not decree the failure of the critical method; rather, it calls for the radicalisation of its application:

> This is why we should remain faithful to Marx's fundamental insight: unbridled capitalist expansion encounters its limit not in an external factor – the available ecological resources, for example – but in itself: the limit of capitalism is absolutely intrinsic to it – or, as Marx himself put it, the limit of capitalism is capital itself (Žižek, 2002a, 277).

It is in connection with this insight that Žižek asks the crucial question: for how long will capitalism be able to contain its own excess through the spectralisation of our lives? And, conversely, should we not, rather than trying to contain the spectrality of capital and its impact on our lives (its solipsistic 'mad dance'), fully identify with it as its symptom, the place where its truth emerges? Should we not, making the most of Marx's insight into commodity fetishism, confront the enemy on its own ground, taking its 'metaphysical subtleties and theological niceties' (its radical inconsistency) absolutely seriously? And, ultimately, does this not imply that today's predominant anti-capitalist belief in/reliance upon purely political forms of democratisation (from a composite field of contemporary leftist philosophers including, amongst others, Laclau, Badiou, Balibar, Rancière, Hardt and Negri) misses the point, since it tends to ignore the importance of the economy as the crucial battlefront?

What emerges from all of Žižek's writings is that there is no universal formula or practice which would instantly allow us to accede to the explosive Real of capital. If the question of enjoyment and its politicisation is indeed to be regarded as the driving topic of his work, it is a topic defined by a degree of seemingly indelible ambiguity, which could be summed up through a final reference to the psychoanalytic notion of symptom. Already in *The Sublime Object of Ideology*, he had made it explicit that the subject 'loves his symptom more than himself' (Žižek, 1989, 74), the implication being that, even after we have realised how our consistency is fully externalised in a symptom (*qua* sinthome, an inert stain of non-symbolisable enjoyment), we are still not prepared to renounce it: 'symptom is an element clinging on like a kind of parasite and "spoiling the game", but if we annihilate it things get even worse: we lose all we had' (Žižek, 1989, 78). This is why Žižek never tires of repeating that today's crucial (and extremely problematic) ethical choice is between Bad and Worse: we either stay with our symptom (bad) or we try to annihilate it (worse). His ultimate ethico-political injunction is that we need to find a way to bring about *the worse outcome*, the only one from which the symbolic/ideological field can be radically resignified.

* * *

Žižek's merciless drilling for a dialectical understanding of the social, the subject and human agency results in the exposure of what he takes to be 'the ultimate ideological operation' of deconstructionist criticism, namely, 'the very elevation of something into impossibility as a means of postponing or avoiding encountering it' (Žižek and Daly, 2004, 70). Rather than constructing social reality as 'realtight', Žižek conceptualises it as fissured and self-external, his wager being 'that reality itself is already based on some exclusion or inconsistency – reality is not-all' (Žižek and Daly, 2004, 102). The Lacanian Subject he invokes is the name for this gap in the social substance. It is at once the driving force and limit of all forms of subjectivation and thus correlative to the Real. It is therefore only consequent that, to Žižek, the proper space for critical theory 'consists of these very gaps and interstices opened up by the "pathological" displacements in the social edifice' (Žižek and Daly, 2004, 53). The true intellectual challenge and task on hand 'is not to recognize fiction behind reality ... but to recognize the Real in what appears to be mere symbolic fiction (Žižek and Daly, 2004, 102).

The Real, however, is not some kind of immutable Thing-in-itself 'about which you can do nothing except symbolize it in different terms'. It is rather 'freedom as a radical cut in the texture of reality', the point being 'that you *can* intervene in the Real' (Žižek and Daly, 2004, 150, 166). The act is *Real* insofar as it is not determined by the existing symbolic order and cannot rely on its normative support; it is *free*, for as a 'mad' gesture it can only be made sense of retroactively; it is *ethical* inasmuch as 'you assume that there is no big Other' (Žižek and Daly, 2004, 163), and *revolutionary* because it is the condition of possibility for any radical break with the generative matrix of global capitalism. The ethico-political act, then, is the third manifestation (beside the subject and the Real) of Žižek's key Hegelian motif of *absolute self-relating negativity*. As an emancipatory 'answer of the Real' (Žižek, 2001a, 31), it is the keystone of Žižekian theory.

What bedevils Žižek's politics, as Ian Parker points out, is the fact that the psychoanalytic act is insufficient as a model for social transformation – if the latter is meant to be a *collective* emancipatory enterprise. His concept of the act is indispensable, we would argue, for it uncovers the crucial inconsistencies of poststructuralist resistance theories; if taken for a self-sufficient model of social transformation, however, it is wanting. In fact, within the terms of Žižek's theory the question of how collective political practice could lead to a new type of society that 'realizes the full potential of open collective self-management' cannot be framed. One of the reasons for this is his tendency to conceptualise social processes of identification/subjectivation as rearticulations of primary processes of identity formation. This results in an overly spontaneist conception of human agency and in some respects a reductive take on political practices (see Parker, 2004, esp. 74–104, quote: 88).

It is, however, surprising that, in his account of Alain Badiou, Peter Hallward comes to the conclusion that Žižek peddles 'an effectively static or structural conception of the real' as opposed to Badiou's 'essentially interventionist or activist approach' (Hallward, 2003, 150). Žižek addresses this criticism in *The Parallax View* where he confronts Bruno Boostel's Badiouian objection to the notion of death-drive as the embodiment of an intervention that devalues in advance 'every project of imposing a new Order, fidelity to any positive political Cause' (Žižek, 2006a, 64). As we shall see in the following chapter, Žižek's Real is not symmetrically opposed to symbolisation but integral to it, absolutely inherent to the process of 'naming reality'.

Notes

8 'Where There Is Power ...'

1. For Foucault's historicist take on the connection between sex and death drive, see Foucault (1990, 156).
2. We draw here heavily on McWhorter (2001, 251). For an illuminating account of the workings of norms in the process of subjectivation, see Macherey (1992), and on the politics of sexual normalisation, McWhorter (1999).
3. In his view, a modern history of sexuality could 'serve as an archaeology of psychoanalysis' (Foucault, 1990, 130).
4. Žižek's account of sexual difference and its implications will be explored in detail in Chapters 15–18.
5. In the same vein, Foucault's critique of the juridico-discursive conception of power as being negative-repressive 'missed' Lacan's point as well, that is his notion of the relationship between law and desire. While Foucault admitted freely that 'the assertion that sex is not "repressed" is not altogether new' – some psychoanalysts had said for some time that 'one should not think that desire is repressed, for the simple reason that the law is what constitutes both desire and the lack on which it is predicated' – he insisted that the juridico-discursive conception of power 'governs both the thematics of repression and the theory of the law as constitutive of desire'. For Foucault it marks the deadlock of psychoanlytic discourse as such. Whether 'the analysis [is] made in terms of the repression of instincts' or 'in terms of the law of desire', they 'both rely on a common representation of power which, depending on the use made of it and the position it is accorded with respect to desire, leads to two contrary results: either to the promise of a "liberation", if power is seen as having only an external hold on desire, or, if it is constitutive of desire itself, to the affirmation: you are always-already trapped' (Foucault, 1990, 81–91; quotes: 81–3). Žižek, by comparison, emphasises how the late (i.e. post 1960) Lacan has subverted 'the opposition that provides the axis of the entire history of psychoanalysis: either the resigned-conservative acceptance of Law/Prohibition, of renunciation, of "repression", as the *sine qua non* of civilisation; or the endeavour to "liberate" drives from the constraints of the Law. There is a Law which, far from being opposed to desire, is the Law of desire itself, the imperative that sustains desire, that tells the subject not to give up his or her desire – the only guilt this law acknowledges is the betrayal of desire' – i.e. a law that enjoins the subject to *Enjoy* 'beyond the pleasure principle' and irrespective of his or her well-being (Žižek, 1994a, 173f.; see also 198f.). For a Lacanian critique of Foucault's account of the law-desire relation, see Copjec (1994, 24ff.).

John Forrester insinuates that Foucault's critique has missed the point of late-Freudian theory as well, since in *Inhibitions, Symptoms and Anxiety* (1926) Freud would have replaced the concept of repression with that of defence, and that 'the defences invoked by psychoanalysis are much more varied than the simple negative absence connoted by repression; indeed, they correspond quite closely to the broader, more positive forms of power that Foucault wishes to accentuate' (Forrester, 1990, 304–5). We owe this hint to Joel Black (1997, 45f). On the relationship between Foucault and psychoanalysis more generally, see Chapter 1, p. 67, note 2.

6. On a biographical level, it is interesting to note how Foucault professed to be illiterate in 'Lacanese'. *Vis-à-vis* Jacques Alain Miller he declared that 'One of these days you'll have to explain Lacan to me' (J.-A. Miller, 1992, 62). And when in an interview on the occasion of the publication of volume one of *The History of Sexuality* Miller quoted Lacan's axiom that there was no such thing as a sexual relationship, and explained that this 'implies that sexuality isn't historical in the sense that everything else is, through from the start', Foucault replied that he 'didn't know there was this axiom' (Foucault, 1980, 213). Foucault was of course anything but illiterate in Lacanian theory, and more often than not his observations on Lacan where highly appreciative (see e.g. Foucault, 2006, 30, 187–9, and idem 1994b; see also Macey, 1995, *passim*). Yet the demonstrative absence of Lacan's name from Foucault's major works is striking. While it is clearly Lacanian psychoanalysis which Foucault had in mind when, in *The Order of Things*, he elevated psychoanalysis to the status of a counter-science, he did not quote Lacan here either (Foucault, 1970, 273–85; see also 1990, 81ff). Miller believes that 'one has not fully grasped *L'Histoire de la sexualité* unless one recognises in Foucault ... an explication which runs alongside Lacan' (J.-A. Miller, 1992, 62).

7. Joel Whitebook stresses that in volume one of *The History of Sexuality* Foucault had reversed his position *vis-à-vis* psychoanalysis. While the version of psychoanalysis which Foucault had praised in *The Order of Things* for sounding the death-knell for humanism and the humanities 'was the structuralist psychoanalysis of Lacan', the kind of psychoanalysis which he criticised now was 'the very embodiment of humanism, which itself had to be uprooted with archaeological critique ... and ... the supposed "refutation" of the repressive hypothesis' (Whitebook, 2005, 338f.).

8. For a critique of Foucault as being more utopian than the Freudian left he criticised, see Whitebook (2005, 337f.) and his article 'Michel Foucault: A Marcusean in Structuralist Clothing', in *Thesis Eleven* I (November 2002), pp. 52–70.

9. One of Foucault's most striking examples illustrating the reasons for his rejection of 'sex' as a marker for liberation was the drama of childhood: 'Some say that the child's life is sexual. From the milk-bottle to puberty, that is all it is. Behind the desire to learn to read or the taste for comic strips, from first to last, everything is sexuality'. And yet it is apparent, Foucault continues, 'that the child has an assortment of pleasures for which the "sex" grid is a veritable prison' (Foucault, 1988, 117).

9   '... There Is Resistance'

1. For a detailed discussion of various aspects of Foucault's account of power, see Burchell *et al.* (1991), Barry *et al.* (1996), Hindess (1996), Lemke (1997), Gordon (2002), Rouse (2005) and Paras (2006, 75–97).
2. The following draws on Lemke (1997, 10–27) and Kögler (2004, 99–115, 176–83).
3. Foucault himself was quite candid about the scope of his analyses: 'I am not a prophet, at most a diagnostician' (Foucault, 1988, 116).
4. On the relationship between Foucault and Marxism, see Chapter 1, p. 67, note 2; for Nancy Hartsock's critique of Foucault's amorphous concept of power – 'Power is everywhere, and so ultimately nowhere' – and its denial of the possibility of liberation, see Hartsock (1990, quote: 169), and for Terry Eagleton's take on Foucault, see for instance (Eagleton, 1990, 384f.).
5. See esp. Larmour *et al.* (1997, 17–22), Weedon (1997, 104–31), Sawicki (1998, 2005) and Armstrong (2006). On the relationship between Foucault and Feminism see Allen (1999), Diamond and Quinby (1988), McNay (1992), Ramazanoglu (1993) and Hekman (1996). Judith Butler's work is arguably the most influential appropriation of Foucault's conceptualisation of power and resistance for feminist theory today (see esp. J. Butler, 1990, 1993, 2003).

10   The Missing Subject

1. On the adequacy of Foucault's conceptualisation of sexuality in *The Use of Pleasure* and *The Care of the Self* for Greco-Roman Antiquity, see esp. P. A. Miller (1997) and Cohen and Saller (1994), on the question of what prompted Foucault to return to the issue of the subject and to recast his project of a history of sexuality, see Foucault (1985, 3–13), Dews (1989), Eagleton (1990, 384–95), Macey (1993, 457–71), Black (1997), Reitz (2003), Davidson (2005) and Gros (2006, 507–21).
2. For a critical assessments of Foucault's late work, see Larmour et al. (1997); for his political thought, see Moss (1998); for a spirited defence of Foucault, see Amy Allen's critique of the 'anti-subjective hypothesis' (Allen, 2000).
3. In his lectures on the *Hermeneutics of the Subject* from 1981 to 1982, Foucault construes the Oedipus story as a (divine) test in order to demonstrate how an autonomous subject – in the sense of self-subjectivation rather than subjection – could emerge in practices of the self (see Foucault, 2006, 444f.).
4. For his notion of the 'specific intellectual', see Foucault (1977).
5. See also Cathren Müller's excellent essay 'Neoliberalismus als Selbstführung', which demonstrates how governmentality studies, by building on Foucault's work on technologies of the self, tend to 'reduce social theory to a descriptive reproduction of neo-liberal ideologies', thus rendering

invisible the elements of coercion and domination within neo-liberalist regimes (Müller, 2003). For the former, more affirmative view, see also Bernauer (1990).

11 Liberation Hurts: Žižek on Superego, Masochism and Enacted Utopia

1. Žižek (1994, 20) argues that 'the superego is a Law in so far as it functions as an incomprehensible, nonsensical, traumatic injunction, incommensurable with the psychological wealth of the subject's affective attitudes'.
2. The classic Žižekian reference here regards the status of bureaucracy in Kafka: 'Kafka's genius was to eroticize bureaucracy, *the* nonerotic entity if ever there was one. ... What can be more "divine" than the traumatic encounter with the bureaucracy at its craziest – when, say, a bureaucrat tells me that, legally, I don't exist? It is in such encounters that we get a glimpse of another order beyond mere earthly everyday reality. Like God, bureaucracy is simultaneously all-powerful and impenetrable, capricious, omnipresent and invisible. ... it is only in this sense that Kafka's works stage a search for the divine in our secular world – more precisely, they not only search for the divine, they find it in state bureaucracy' (Žižek, 2006a, 115–16). This, according to Žižek, is therefore the proper 'mystery of the institution', in as much as its 'truth-content' is fully externalised in its mere (reified) presence – which, like the commodity (see chapter 13) exerts a libidinal hold on us. The crucial paradox is that there is more truth in the external form of the institution than in its supposed inner/profound significance.
3. For the development of the notion of the 'traumatic "ahistorical" kernel' as the non-symbolizable excess which determines the difference between historicism and historicity (see Butler *et al.*, 2000, 111–12).
4. Similarly, the law *qua* unbearable superego pressure (for example, the injunction to do one's duty that characterises Kant's moral law) takes us beyond the pleasure principle, connecting us with the unconscious domain characterised by the Real of *jouissance*: 'the basic lesson of psychoanalysis is that the Unconscious is, at its most radical, not the wealth of illicit "repressed" desires but *the fundamental Law itself*' (Žižek, 2000a, 366).
5. 'I will remind the jurist that law basically talks about what I am going to talk to you about – jouissance. Law does not ignore the bed' (Lacan, 1998b, 2).
6. This disturbing appendix to Kant's moral construct had already been identified by Freud, who in his 'The economic problem of masochism' explicitly links Kant's categorical imperative to the cruelty of the superego: '... this super-ego is as much a representative of the id as of the external world. It came into being through the introjection into the ego of the first objects of the id's libidinal impulses – namely, the two parents. In

this process the relation to those objects was desexualized; it was diverted from its direct sexual aims. Only in this way was it possible for the Oedipus complex to be surmounted. The super-ego retained essential features of the introjected persons – their strength, their severity, their tendency to supervise and to punish. ... The super-ego – the conscience at work in the ego – may then become harsh, cruel and inexorable against the ego which is in its charge. Kant's Categorical Imperative is thus the direct heir of the Oedipus complex' (Freud, 1961, 167).

7. The relationship between the executioner and the masochist offers itself as an interesting variation on the classic Hegelian couple lord-bondsman (master-slave). In the *Phenomenology of Spirit*, Hegel claims that it is through his complete submission to the lord that the bondsman actually gains self-consciousness, insofar as he externalises himself in the objects of his labour: 'the bondsman realizes that it is precisely in his work wherein he seemed to have only an alienated existence that he acquires a mind of his own' (Hegel, 1977, 119). As the standard Marxist interpretation has it, it is therefore the bondsman, and not the lord, who can claim to occupy an autonomous subject-position. However, does not the figure of the masochist challenge the lord/executioner precisely by undermining the belief in such autonomy? What the masochist makes manifest is the fact that his 'being-for-itself' is grounded in the unfathomable abyss of his own enjoyment, which is homologous to the Hegelian notion of absolute negativity. Hegel emphasises this crucial point by insisting on the tie between the bondsman's self-consciousness-through-labour and 'absolute fear': 'If consciousness fashions the thing without the initial absolute fear, it is only an empty self-centred attitude; for its form or negativity is not negativity per se, and therefore its formative activity cannot give it a consciousness of itself as essential being' (Hegel, 1977, 119).

8. The couple Kant-Sade can also be read through the notion of symptom. As Žižek puts it in *The Parallax View*, 'Sade is the symptom of Kant ... of how Kant betrayed the truth of his own discovery' (Žižek, 2006a, 94).

12   The Leninist Act

1. 'The crucial thing one has to bear in mind here is that this uncanny experience of the human mind directly integrated into a machine is not the vision of a future or of something new but the insight into something that is always-already going on, which was here from the very beginning since it was co-substantial with the symbolic order' (Žižek, 2004c, 18).

2. Žižek argues that 'Lenin's counterargument against the formal-democratic critics of the second step is that this "pure democratic" option is itself utopian: in the concrete Russian circumstances, the bourgeois-democratic state has no chance of survival – the only "realistic" way to protect the true gains of the February Revolution (freedom of organization and the press, etc.) is to move on to the Socialist revolution, otherwise the tsarist reactionaries will win' (Žižek, 2002a, 9).

13 Commodity Fetishism: From Desire to Drive

1. The religious dimension is crucial, as it brings us back to the notion of belief as obscene/displaced libidinal attachment: 'If, as Benjamin asserted, capitalism is actually, at its core, a religion, then it is an obscene religion of the "undead" spectral life celebrated in the black masses of stock exchanges' (Žižek, 2006a, 118).

Excursus: Žižek In and Out of Europe

In June 2005, in the wake of the French and Dutch 'No' to the European Constitution, a number of leading broadsheets from across the globe published a short article written by Žižek – often with different titles and slightly changed contents – where the Slovenian philosopher confirms his Eurocentric stance through a stern defence of the result of the two referenda. The article to which we will refer is 'The constitution is dead. Long live politics proper', published in *Guardian* on June 4 (Žižek, 2005c). Here Žižek argues that reading the referenda results as a worrying blow to the hopes of a United Europe against the overwhelming geopolitical power of the United States, as most liberal commentators did, is symptomatic of a widespread patronising attitude: 'in their reaction to the no results, they [the political and media elite] treated the people as retarded pupils who did not understand the lessons of the experts' (Žižek, 2005c). Just as the vigorous lobbying for the Yes vote (as a matter of knowledge and expertise versus ignorance and ideology) exposed the political failure to give the people 'a clear symmetrical choice', the No results confirm the short-sightedness of a political class which can now consider itself properly detached from the true hopes and aspirations of the French, Dutch and Europeans as a whole.

The pragmatic counterargument to Žižek's is that the No actually expresses either the people's calculated and opportunistic rejection of what was perceived, in practical terms, as an unfavourable deal; or simply the mystified reaction to an over-elaborated and obscure body of bureaucratic norms and cavils. What should not be forgotten, however, is that despite the lack of a consistent alternative political vision sustaining the No campaign, the latter nevertheless reflected two distinctly different but equally passionate forms of ideological attachment, that of the radical left and the neo-populist right. In other words, it would be too easy to dismiss the No as a post-political answer to a post-political offer. Far from forcing an impossible argument on to a phenomenon that can be explained by reference to 'objective reasoning' and clear-cut empirical coordinates, Žižek's analysis offers a reading of the recent referenda that unravels the deep-seated, one would be tempted to say *unconscious* cause of an ambiguous political choice. To put it bluntly, Žižek believes that the No results hold the same intrinsic political potential of the Lacanian act, in as much as they effectively open up the space for a radically alternative vision of Europe's future – one which demands a thorough and ruthless probing into the foundations and limits of the European legacy. Before we substantiate our view of Žižek's stance with an exploration of its scope, rationale and implications, we are now going to take a cursory glance at the history of Marxist thought on Europe. More specifically, we shall focus our attention on Lenin's position as expressed in his 1915 article 'On the Slogan for a United States of Europe'. A contextualised reading of this article will allow us to introduce and start evaluating what Žižek regards as the fundamental formal dimension of the political act.

Lenin's *no!* to the United States of Europe

Marxist thought on the question of Europe can be traced back to its earliest documents. In fact, the very first sentence of *The Communist Manifesto* situates a political message in a historical–geographical space: 'A spectre is haunting Europe – the spectre of Communism'. Along with its closing appeal ('Proletarians of all countries, unite!'), which articulates the universalist claim of Marxist politics, it captures in a nutshell one of the tenets of Marxist discourse over the past one and a half centuries, i.e. the belief that the key to emancipating the disenfranchised and exploited of all countries is to be found inside Europe. Marx's belief in (especially Western) Europe's unique position with regard to economic progress, human civilisation, and proletarian emancipation is expressed most comprehensively in *Capital: Volume One,* where he refers to 'Western Europe' as 'the home of Political Economy', whilst also presuming that 'this ready-made world of capital' holds the key to understanding the future of the rest of the world which, rather sooner than later, would be forced into the same developmental mould (Marx, 1975–2005, vol. 35, 9, 751ff.; see also Marx, 1970ff, vol. II.6, 634 and vol. II.7, 12f.). Although in antagonistic form, Western Europe possesses the politico-economic resources necessary to toll the 'knell of capitalist private property' and ensure that eventually the 'expro-priators are expropriated' (Marx, 1975–2005, vol. 35, 749).

A strikingly different idea, however, is the notion of a United States of Europe (European Confederation), which was entertained by the organised labour movement since the second half of the 19th century as an alternative to the aggressive foreign policy of 'the powers of old Europe' (Marx, 1975–2005, vol. 6, 481). As early as 1875 (only four years after the end of the Franco-Prussian war and the bloody suppression of the Paris Commune) Friedrich Engels warned about the nationalist and pacifist implications of a European Confederation, insisting on 'the principle that the workers' move-ment is an international one'. In a scathing criticism of the (in)famous 1875 draft programme of the future united Social-Democratic Workers' Party of Germany, he queried the political rationale behind the idea of a United States of Europe:

> And what is left of the internationalism of the workers' move-ment? The dim prospect – not even of subsequent co-operation among European workers with a view to their liberation – nay, but of a future 'international brotherhood of peoples' – of your Peace League bourgeois 'United States of Europe' (Marx, 1975–2005, vol. 45, 61).

Forty years later, in the midst of the First World War, Rosa Luxem-burg was still firmly advocating both the European and the interna-tionalist agenda. Like Marx and Engels, she was convinced that the signal for the revolution that would end the 'regression into bar-barism' of 'our lofty European civilization' (Luxemburg, 2000, 55) and finally emancipate the human race, could only originate from a united European proletariat. In her prison pamphlet *The Crisis of Social Democracy (The Junius Pamphlet),* written in early 1915, she makes a point of stressing that the workers of Europe's leading capitalist countries

> are exactly the ones who have the historical mission of carrying out the socialist transformation. Only from out of Europe … will the signal be given when the hour is ripe for the liberating social revolution. Only the English, French, Belgian, German, Russian, Italian workers together can lead the army of the exploited and

enslaved of the five continents. When the time comes, only they can settle accounts with capitalism's work of global destruction (Luxemburg, 2000, 162).

European bourgeois society – 'wading in blood, dripping filth' – had revealed itself 'in its true, its naked form' (Luxemburg, 2000, 66). Now workers needed to 'awake from their stupor, extend to each other a brotherly hand' and drown out the chorus of capitalist hyenas 'with labor's old and mighty battle cry: Proletarians of all lands, unite!' (Luxemburg, 2000, 164).

For Trotzky too 'Europe' initially designated both the site of imperialist powers and revolutionary hope. In the course of the 1920s, however, with the increasing dominance of the USA in Europe in the wake of the Dawes Plan, he came to the conclusion that 'America is today the basic force of the capitalist world', thus supplanting European capitalism as a world-historical power. In *Europe and America* Trotsky argued that the United States had become the new main enemy also in as much as it was shoring up the (social-democratic) reformism in Europe in order to prevent the European revolution, for 'a revolution in Europe and Asia would inevitably inaugurate a revolutionary epoch in the United States'. At the same time, he contended that America 'is now the greatest lever of the European revolution', in that it will not allow capitalist Europe to rise again, which in turn will 'impel the [European] proletariat onto the revolutionary road'. Anticipating the ensuing confrontation between America and Europe, Trotsky considered that:

It is quite possible that all that books and our own experience have taught us about the fight of the privileged classes for their domination will pale before the violence that American capital will try to inflict upon revolutionary Europe.

The task of uniting Europe for this momentous battle with America was, however, 'beyond the strength of the European bourgeoisie'; only the victorious proletariat, which would bring about the 'Socialist United States of Europe', could unify Europe. Towards the end of his piece Trotsky formulated the project of a 'Soviet United States of Europe' which, along with Asia, would form a 'mighty bloc of peoples' that will prove 'infinitely more powerful that the United

States'. Ultimately, the 'European-Asiatic Federation of peoples' would 'wrest from American capital the control of world economy and will lay the foundations for the Federation of Socialist Peoples of the whole earth' (Trotsky, 1926).

Antonio Gramsci, who shared Trotsky's diagnosis that Europe had lost its historical importance (see Gramsci, 1975, vol. 2, §24), discussed the question of Europe explicitly in his analyses of *Americanism*. On the one hand, he argued, Americanism was itself an extension and intensification of European civilisation (see Gramsci, 1975, vol. 3, §11); on the other hand, it represented in civilisatory terms a step forward compared to a Europe characterised by the continued existence of parasitic classes without any economic function (see Gramsci, 1975, vol. 1, §61).

It was left to Lenin, however, to express most explicitly the historical ambiguity of the notion of Europe's (emancipatory and civilisatory) 'historical mission', which large parts of the European labour movement shared with the liberal elites. On the one hand, Lenin was convinced that (Western) Europe was still the epitome of progress, if in antagonistic form; on the other hand, he concluded from his politico-economic analyses that the European imperialist state system had become the central reference point and hotbed of the international counter-revolution, and thus the counterpole of the emerging communist movement. For Lenin, abstract 'Europeanism' was therefore an untenable position. He never tired of stressing the importance of distinguishing imperialist-chauvinist and romanticised petit bourgeois visions of Europe from the true Europeanism of 'the real Europe, the Europe of revolutionary traditions and tense class struggle of the broad masses' (Lenin, 1960ff, vol. 11, 364, note 1).

In 1915, Lenin wrote a number of articles and pamphlets in which he developed his position with regard to the bankruptcy of the Second International and the practicability of revolutionary upheaval under the conditions of war.[1] From our angle, however, his most telling piece on the subject is the article 'On the Slogan for a United States of Europe' (Lenin, 1960ff, vol. 21, 339–43). Without delving into the thick ramifications of the debate that developed within the European Left,[2] we are now going to take a closer look at Lenin's argument, as it allows us to catch a glimpse of the political logic of his stance on Europe.

In August 1915, at the height of World War One, Lenin took issue with his party over the 'purely political character' of the ongoing debate on the question of the United States of Europe. Against the shared view that favoured a United Europe, he argued that

> while the slogan of a republican United States of Europe – if accompanied by the revolutionary overthrow of the three most reactionary monarchies in Europe, headed by the Russian – is quite invulnerable as a political slogan, there still remains the highly important question of its economic content and signifi-cance. From the standpoint of the economic conditions of impe-rialism – i.e., the export of capital and the division of the world by the 'advanced' and 'civilised' colonial powers – a United States of Europe, under capitalism, is either impossible or reactionary (Lenin, 1960ff, vol. 21, 340).

However, let us recall that only one year before, in August 1914, Lenin had drafted a set of theses, immediately approved by the Bolshevik leadership, which included as one of the targets of the revolutionary social democracy during the war precisely the forma-tion of the United States of Europe (see Lenin, 1960ff, vol. 21, 18). Furthermore, the slogan for a republican United States of Europe had long been part of the consensus within the pre-WWI Second International, finding particularly strong support in the Second International's leading theorist, Karl Kautsky, who took the view that the creation of a federative European community would be instrumental in bringing about the international revolution. So why did Lenin, in 1915, suddenly change his mind?

Two observations clarify his stance. As the above excerpt indi-cates, Lenin's reservations with regard to the idea of a United Europe were rooted in a coherent politico-economic argument. He highlighted the reactionary nature of any international agree-ment amongst a handful of capitalist states (Britain, France, Russia and Germany) whose very power was strictly correlative to their plundering large parts of the rest of the world's population (their colonies). He put this view in unambiguous terms when he stated that '[a] United States of Europe under capitalism is tanta-mount to an agreement on the partition of colonies' (Lenin, 1960ff, vol. 21, 341).[3] In contrast to Kautsky, Lenin was convinced that in

1915 a United States of Europe could only represent the interests of the European capitalists, a belief that he elaborated further in his 1916 pamphlet *Imperialism: The Highest Stage of Capitalism* (see Lenin, 1960ff, vol. 22, 185–304). And yet, it would be erroneous to assert that Lenin discovered the colonialist spirit of early 20th century capitalism in 1915 – which implies logically that the reasons for his change of mind over Europe must be sought elsewhere.

Towards the end of his article on Europe, Lenin reminded his readers of the basics of Marxist internationalism by pointing out that a 'United States of the World (not of Europe alone) is the state form of the unification and freedom of nations which we associate with socialism'. However (and this is the whole point of Lenin's piece):

> As a separate slogan ... the slogan of a United States of the World would hardly be a correct one. ... because it may be wrongly interpreted to mean that the victory of socialism in a single country is impossible (Lenin, 1960ff, vol. 21, 342).

This captures in a nutshell what made Lenin write his piece, namely the prospect of making revolution in one's own country as the starting point of a process to be completed globally (see Conrad, 2002). Consequently, in the final part of his article Lenin formulated for the first time the idea of the possibility of a victorious revolution 'in several or even one capitalist country alone' (Lenin, 1960ff, vol. 21, 343). The whole political logic of Lenin's thought is here thrown into sharp relief.

Lenin did not study the question of a United States of Europe from the 'aperspectival' viewpoint of an enlightened but fundamentally disinterested observer. Rather, he approached his subject in search of a political breaking point. While Rosa Luxemburg, for example, could not shake the knowledge that, whatever the outcome of the war, the European working class would pay the greatest price in blood and suffering, Lenin believed in and searched feverishly for the revolutionary opportunities presented by the war. The voting for war credits in August 1914 undoubtedly proved to be a traumatic moment for the European Left. Those who had worked for and wholly believed in the ability of the organised labour movement to stand against war now saw the major social democratic parties of Germany, France, and Britain rush to the defence of their fatherlands. Under those circumstances, the internationalist idea of a simultaneous European revolution turned into the nightmare vision of what Žižek calls 'interpassivity: of doing things not in order to achieve something, but to prevent something from really happening, really changing' (Žižek, 2002a, 170). Turning the tables on the war-mongers by staging a proletarian revolution in Tsarist Russia, of all countries, Lenin attempted to achieve what in that specific situation appeared impossible. His vision can be said to denote 'the singular emergence of the truth of the entire situation' (Žižek, 2002a, 177), since it essentially contends that the idea of a pan-European proletarian revolution can only survive in the struggle of Europe's most disavowed exception. As Žižek has often remarked, true universality coincides with the point of exclusion of a given paradigm.

In practical terms, the point to be emphasised is that Lenin's No! to a United States of Europe was the result of a political strategy which culminated in the Russian October Revolution. Lenin's No! was undoubtedly a risky one, not least because the indication that socialism may for a long time be victorious only in single countries remained open to many a nationalist (reactionary) interpretation.[4] However, the opposite is equally true, as the idea of a United States of Europe was openly supported in many reactionary camps. The German elites, for example, had already predicted a leading role for their country within fortress Europe.

More important still for our argument is the fact that the primary target of Lenin's choice was the social democratic Left and its phoney internationalism. The growing strength of the German social-democratic party, for instance, only convinced Lenin of the opportunistic and imperialistic tendencies within European social democracy (see Lenin, 1960ff, vol. 39, 113). Ultimately, his decision to oppose the slogan for a United Europe should be read as an attempt to regain the political capacity to act by drawing a clear line of demarcation *vis-à-vis* those leftists whom by then he referred to, with a fair degree of contempt, as Kautskyites, scolding them for performing what Žižek dubs 'the ultimate ideological operation', that is 'the very elevation of something into impossibility as a means of postponing or avoiding encountering it' (Žižek and Daly,

2004, 70). What should be retrieved from Lenin, therefore, is the *formal* dimension of his gesture. His No! to Europe should be read as part of a strategy to defend the authentic revolutionary potential within Europe itself.

Unravelling Žižek's Eurocentrism

Žižek has never made a secret of his political lineage. Quite on the contrary, he has not only frequently and openly admitted his intellectual and political sympathy for Lenin, but has also claimed for himself an 'almost Maoist' allegiance (see Žižek, 2002d; see also Žižek, 2004c, 203–13). Furthermore, in the attempt to reopen a serious political debate on the origins and nature of Stalinism, he has urged us 'to confront the radical ambiguity of Stalinist ideology which, even at its most "totalitarian", still exudes an emancipatory potential' (Žižek, 2001b, 131); elsewhere, he has extensively referred to 'the inner greatness of Stalinism' (Žižek, 2002a, 191–7), while simultaneously firmly rejecting its socio-political outcome (see also Žižek, 2006a, 288–95). And yet, although his views are infused with an unmistakable desire to resignify and thus reenergize the socialist project, the theoretical scope of his approach to the question of contemporary Europe exceeds the confines of the Marxist tradition. Despite its apparent simplicity, Žižek's argument is anchored in a complex theoretical edifice which, as we hope this book clarifies, combines Marx's political economy, Hegelian philosophy and Lacanian psychoanalysis. As with most of his political thought, the main aim of Žižek's 'plea for a leftist Eurocentrism' (see Žižek, 1999a) is that of providing us with a challenging model of ideology critique whose essential message could be summed up in the following excerpt:

> The perspective of the critique of ideology compels us to invert Wittgenstein's 'What one cannot speak about, thereof one should be silent' into 'What one should not speak about, thereof one cannot remain silent'. If you want to speak about a social system, you cannot remain silent about its repressed excess. The point is not to tell the whole Truth but, precisely, to append to the (official) Whole the uneasy supplement which denounces its falsity (Žižek, 2002a, 168).

Our exploration of Žižek's Eurocentrism unravels its key theoretical premises, explaining why it provides an original contribution to one of today's nodal geopolitical debates.

In his *Iraq: The Borrowed Kettle*, he develops a series of tightly related points concerning the relationship between Europe and the United States. Provided that his fundamental presupposition is a firm rejection of the neo-liberalist argument that Europe and the US should participate in the same economic and politico-ideological enterprise, Žižek starts by considering the Habermas-Derrida initiative of summer 2003, which was borne out of the ashes of September 11 and was aimed at reviving the idea of Europe from a leftist position (see Borradori, 2003). In Žižek's words, Habermas and Derrida (who for this occasion overcame their mutual resentment) tried to convey the message that 'faced with the challenge of the new American Empire, Europe should find the strength to reassert its ethico-political legacy' (Žižek, 2004a, 32). However, Žižek asks, is this the correct response to the challenges posed by the post-September 11 geopolitical constellation? More precisely, what does such an ethical injunction actually amount to? If it is merely 'a plea for a little more "radical" democracy, human rights, tolerance, solidarity, welfare state', he avers, 'this is clearly not enough':

> For many years, I have pleaded for a renewed 'leftist Eurocentrism'. To put it bluntly: do we want to live in a world in which the only choice is between the American civilization and the emerging Chinese authoritarian-capitalist one? If the answer is no, then the true alternative is Europe. The Third World cannot generate a strong enough resistance to the ideology of the American Dream; in the present constellation, only Europe can do that (Žižek, 2004a, 32–3).

Our wager here is that, as it transpires from his direct and passionate line of reasoning, Žižek sees contemporary Europe as incarnating the potentialities of the Lacanian act, the psychoanalytic notion that can safely be regarded as the innermost theoretical reference for his political interventions. First of all, it is worth repeating that, in Lacan, the act realises an unconscious desire for which the subject (in clinical terms, the analysand) is enjoined to assume responsibility. To simplify things we could consider a straightforward comparison: while the law is predicated upon the notion of intentionality, psychoanalysis extends its jurisdiction to unintentional actions. However, the key Lacanian claim is that this unintentional or unconscious dimension, which remains utterly impermeable to knowledge, designates nothing less than the kernel of the subject, the structuring core whose repression allows for the formation of our different, historically and symbolically constructed, identities. The centrality of the unconscious, and consequently of the act that links us to its uncharted depths, is emphatically confirmed by Lacan in the second part of his teaching career, despite the fact that the very term 'unconscious' is progressively replaced by 'the Real', the signifier which comes to indicate an all-pervasive dimension occupied by a displaced, disavowed and thus intrinsically traumatic substance. Leaving to Part III of the present book the detailed survey of the complex casuistry of the Lacanian Real, suffice it to recall that, to Žižek, radical socio-political change can only be effected through an act that disturbs the strictly non-symbolisable and yet foundational dimension of the Real:

> Precisely because of this internality of the Real to the Symbolic, it *is* possible to touch the Real through the Symbolic – that is the whole point of Lacan's notion of psychoanalytic treatment; this is what the Lacanian notion of the psychoanalytic *act* is about – the act as a gesture which, by definition, touches the dimension of some impossible Real (in Butler *et al.*, 2000, p. 121).

Here, however, the central Žižekian claim that by touching the Real the act sets itself up as a self-destructive intervention aimed at 'achieving the impossible', needs to be supplemented by the previously exposed strategic logic that fully defines its function. The real object of Žižek's argument is not the suicidal dimension of the act *per se*, but the demarcation of an intervention that 'changes the coordinates of what seems possible':

> The point is not simply that, once we are thoroughly engaged in a political project, we are ready to put everything at stake for it, including our lives; but, more precisely, that *only such an 'impossible' gesture of pure expenditure can change the very co-ordinates of what is strategically possible within a historical constellation*. This is

the key point: an act is neither a strategic intervention *in* the existing order, nor its 'crazy' destructive negation; an act is an 'excessive', trans-strategic intervention which redefines the rules and contours of the existing order (Žižek, 2004a, 81).

One can see here that the act cannot simply be defined as a psychotic leap into the void, for if this is a necessary condition, it is certainly not a sufficient one. Quite differently, whilst the act retains the formal appearance of a self-destructive intervention, it does so against the background of what *is* empirically possible, and yet *appears* impossible.[5] From the vantage point of Žižek's plea for a leftist Eurocentrism, politicising the Third World *today* would amount precisely to a travesty of the act, a psychotic and ultimately impotent *passage à l'acte*, since in his view the Third World is completely co-opted and hegemonised by the American Empire. What this argument proves, ultimately, is that the act is a combination of strategic and non-strategic determinations: its crucial self-destructive core is necessarily structured around a series of equally crucial tactical considerations. If Žižek identifies Europe as the only viable leftist alternative to American hegemony, this choice can only actualise itself as a *trans-strategic* intervention: an antagonistic Europe is both strategically possible (it has strong intellectual and political resources to resist American supremacy) and yet it cannot fail to appear, simultaneously, as a traumatic/impossible event (Europe today is effectively a distorted image of the US, sharing *in toto* its economy, ideology, etc.). Žižek's views on Europe provide a theoretically illuminating and politically significant example of what the act is: an intervention that actualises a disavowed potentiality in order to determine as possible what is perceived as impossible.

According to Žižek's insight, precisely because the true conflict is between the US and Europe rather than between the US and Jihad (since 'Jihad and McWorld are two sides of the same coin; Jihad is already McJihad'), Europe should not follow the 'liberal warriors' who are prepared to give up the ideals of freedom and democracy to fight anti-democratic fundamentalism, otherwise 'we may lose "Europe" through its very defence' (Žižek, 2004a, 33–4). The problem is that Europe has already started adopting the 'new racism of the developed world', which is 'in a way, much more brutal than the previous form' for it is legitimised by 'unabashed economic egotism – the fundamental divide is between those who are included in the sphere of (relative) economic prosperity and those who are excluded from it' (Žižek, 2004a, 35). Žižek touches here on another cardinal theme of his politics, the notion of exclusion as the necessary precondition to authentic antagonism. This point is summed up in the following passage:

> The leftist political gesture *par excellence* (in contrast to the right-ist slogan 'to each his or her own place') is thus to question the concrete existing universal order on behalf of its symptom, of the part which, although inherent to the existing universal order, has no 'proper place' within it (say, illegal immigrants or the home-less in our societies). ... one pathetically asserts (and identifies with) *the point of inherent exception/exclusion, the 'abject', of the concrete positive order, as the only point of true universality* (Žižek, 2000a, 224).

From a different angle it can be argued that Žižek asserts the conflation of exclusion and universality in the attempt to distance himself from what he perceives as the political deadlock of the type of deconstructionist stance embraced by fellow theorists such as, for example, Judith Butler:

> I perceive the shadowy existence of those who are condemned to lead a spectral life outside the domain of the global order, blurred in the background, unmentionable, submerged in the formless mass of 'population', without even a proper particular place of their own, in a slightly different way from Butler. I am tempted to claim that this shadowy existence is *the very site of political universality*: in politics, universality is asserted when such an agent with no proper place, 'out of joint', posits itself as the direct embodiment of universality against all those who do have a place within the global order (in Butler *et al.*, 2000, 313).

This defence of exclusion as the symptom of the properly political dimension does not blind Žižek to the acknowledgment of the various ways in which such a political dimension has often been disavowed in Europe.[6] This acknowledgment, however, leads him to argue that today, differently from the past, we find ourselves in an exceptional situation where the political dimension is not simply repressed, but rather foreclosed, insofar as the very notion of ideological antagonism has been replaced by the joint post-political venture of enlightened technocrats and liberal multiculturalists. The awareness of the enormity of the task ahead leads Žižek to his first conclusion with regards to Eurocentrism:

> Against this end-of-ideology politics, one should insist on the potential of democratic politicization as the true European legacy from ancient Greece onwards. Will we be able to invent a new mode of repoliticization questioning the undisputed reign of global capital? Only such a repoliticization of our predicament can break the vicious cycle of liberal globalization destined to engender the most regressive forms of fundamentalist hatred (Žižek, 1999a, 1000).

If we consider the European legacy, this much-needed repoliticisation hinges, first and foremost, on a gesture of 'thorough self-criticism':

> If the European legacy is to be effectively defended, then the first move should be a thorough self-criticism. What we find reprehensible and dangerous in US policies and civilization is a part of Europe itself, one of the possible outcomes of the European project – so there is no room for self-satisfied arrogance (Žižek, 2004a, 35).

Žižek paraphrases Max Horkheimer's injunction that 'those who do not want to speak (critically) about liberalism should also keep silent about Fascism', in order to claim that 'those who do not want to engage critically with Europe itself should also keep silent about the USA' (Žižek, 2004a, 35). The implicit targets of his criticism here are those European nation-states whose arrogant attachment to the grandeur of their colonial past prevents them from articulating a radically antagonistic position to US global capitalism (since such a stance would imply the drastic problematisation of their own roots).

The second conclusion, which follows logically from the first, provides a more precise indication as to the questions that Europe needs to address if its aim is to reinvent itself: 'in the act of defence, one has to reinvent that which is to be defended. What we need is a ruthless questioning of the very foundations of the European legacy, up to and including those very sacred cows, democracy and human rights' (Žižek, 2004a, 35). Here it becomes apparent that Žižek's Eurocentrism effectively coincides with what we have already defined as an injunction to move beyond liberal democracy in order to 'reinvent that which is to be defended': ultimately, democracy itself. Europe to him represents the only foreseeable opportunity for a drastic and ruthless emptying of a symbolic referent that has become nothing more than the complementary political face of global capitalism. In Žižek's view, therefore, today's European centre-left appeals to freedom and (liberal) democracy as the proper way to combat the excesses of capitalism (including terrorism) will have to be challenged, for the simple reason that 'liberal democracy, in truth, is the political arrangement under which capital thrives best' (Žižek, 2002c, 15).

Žižek may appear to be striking at the wrong enemy here. However, his claim seems justified by its explicit reference to a background which is characterised by the pervasive and seemingly irreversible retreat of the Marxist historico-political project. He argues that given our current political predicament the great majority of those who still declare themselves leftists are caught in a deadlock: on one hand they are profoundly convinced that real alternatives to the existing liberal-democratic capitalist system are no longer possible, but on the other hand they are unable to renounce their passionate attachment to a vision of global change. The result is the objective cynicism typical of melancholy, whereby the *melancholic* link to the lost object (true political passion) is what allows us one to criticise and distance oneself from the global capitalist project while fully participating in it (see Žižek, 2001b, 141–3). In Žižek's view, therefore, the majority of today's leftists end up investing their political energy in the defence of 'an abstract and excessively rigid moralising stance', which effectively coincides with the endorsement of 'global capitalism with a human face' (Žižek, 1999b, 7).

Tarrying with the *no*!

Moving back to Žižek's post-referenda article, it would seem that the primary object of his investigation are not the direct motivations behind the No, including those reflecting an authentic political stance. What his unique combination of Lacanian psychoanalysis and Hegelian dialectics resolutely strives to salvage is the paradox of a 'knowledge that does not know itself', of a 'belief before belief', the crucial passage in the argument being that our choices always signal the disavowed presence of an unconscious desire that cannot be fully integrated in the explicit text of our demands. Why? Because the nature of this desire is traumatic, and as such it generates fear. But whose fear, we may ask? 'When commentators described the no as a message of befuddled fear, they were wrong. The real fear we are dealing with is the fear that the no itself provoked within the new European political elite. It was the fear that people would no longer be so easily convinced by their "post-political" vision' (Žižek, 2005c).

Here is the opening, the potential breaking point in a self-enclosed deterministic universe of causes and effects (our idea of Europe). What if, Žižek asks, our leaders are afraid of what the referenda have finally disclosed as Europe's innermost desire, which strictly speaking corresponds to an instance of shattering negativity secretly aimed at sweeping away the present post-political constellation? Precisely because the true aim of Žižek's article is the negativity of 'Europe's unconscious', he can put forward his central claim that 'the no is a message and expression of hope ... the hope that politics is still alive and possible, that the debate about what the new Europe shall and should be is still open' regardless of the fact that the left has to share the No 'with strange neo-fascist bedfellows' (Žižek, 2005c). Here we have a clear insight into the theoretical matrix of Žižek's thought, which not only functions as the necessary presuppositions to his siding with the No, but more importantly explains the way he relates the categories of hope and agency. The crucial point to note is the strict Hegelian character of Žižek's argumentation. The fact that the No may have also emerged for the wrong reasons does not merely tell us that we have to take risks, but it crucially confirms the very dialectical logic according to which a true change only comes about as a result of a misperception, a distortion in our awareness of what the real goals are.

According to Žižek's reading of it, Hegel's analysis of phrenology in his *Phenomenology of Spirit* lends us an insight into the fundamental condition for revolutionary intervention: in any given situation, the only way for us to reach our declared aim is by making what appears to be the wrong choice, the choice that explicitly contradicts the aim (in our case, the No to the European constitution). According to Žižek's Hegel-indebted social theory, it is impossible to make the right choice directly, to achieve the target in a straight line. What Hegel uncovers is precisely 'this [enigmatic] necessity of making the wrong choice in order to arrive at the proper result' (Žižek, 2003b, 84). More specifically,

> the Fall is *in itself* already its own self-sublation, the wound is *in itself* already its own healing, so that the perception that we are dealing with the Fall is ultimately a misperception, an effect of our distorted perspective. ... We rise again from the Fall not by undoing its effects, but in recognizing the longed-for liberation in the Fall itself (Žižek, 2003b, 86).

If brought down to its essentials, the whole of Žižek's theoretical project, including his attempt to reclaim the militant core of Christianity from a Marxist angle (see Part III), seems articulated around the overwhelming will to assert this paradoxical coincidence of negativity and freedom. Against the neo-Kantian spirit of our times, whereby freedom is conceived as a 'striving for freedom', an intrinsically frustrated opening towards the impossible Thing (in the Levinas-Derrida tradition, the ever-elusive Other), Žižek proposes a radicalisation of the terms in question. He brings together Lacan's theory of lack and Hegel's dialectics to demonstrate that the opening of freedom is always-already included in our predicament. More precisely, he claims that the object of our striving, the other, is not detached and unreachable, but rather it is the very abyssal kernel of the subject (the Unconscious) as well as of what we experience as social reality (Lacan's Real, Hegel's absolute negativity). From this angle the assertion that 'freedom is impossible' (since it implies an endless progress towards its realisation) becomes 'the impossible is freedom', in the precise sense that only by asserting the foundational, strictly speaking non-discursive (impossible) power of the negative, do we activate freedom as a concrete break towards a new beginning.

Ultimately, Žižek's reaction to the recent referenda on the European Constitution is founded upon a coherent theoretical defence of the dialectical power of negativity: the No effectively amounts to a shattering setback in the form of a risky flirting with an uncertain alternative; however, the very emergence of this risk provides us with sufficient evidence that the underlying domain of freedom has been disturbed. As such, the No harbours the Yes to a radically different Europe.

Notes

1. The most important ones are *The Collapse of the Second International* (Lenin, 1960ff, vol. 21, 205–59), *The Defeat of One's Own Government in the Imperialist War* (Lenin, 1960ff, vol. 21, 275–80), *Socialism and War* (Lenin, 1960ff, vol. 21, 295–338), and *Opportunism, and the Collapse of the Second International* (Lenin, 1960ff, vol. 21, 438–54).
2. For a detailed account of the historical background, see Steenson (1991).
3. To substantiate his argument Lenin draws on precise politico-economic analyses revealing the extent to which 'Capital has become international and monopolist': 'The world has been carved up by a handful of Great Powers, i.e., powers successful in the great plunder and oppression of nations. The four Great Powers of Europe – Britain, France, Russia and Germany, with an aggregate population of between 250,000,000 and 300,000,000, and an area of about 7,000,000 square kilometres – possess colonies with a population of *almost 500 million* (494,500,000) and an area of 64,600,000 square kilometres, i.e. almost half the surface of the globe (133,000,000 square kilometres, exclusive of Arctic and Antarctic regions). Add to this the three Asian states – China, Turkey and Persia, now being rent piecemeal by thugs that are waging a war of 'liberation', namely, Japan, Russia, Britain and France. Those three Asian states, which may be called semi-colonies ... have a total population of 360,000,000 and an area of 14,500,000 square kilometres (almost one and a half times the area of all Europe)' (Lenin, 1960ff, vol. 21, 340).
4. Notably Stalin used Lenin's formulation to legitimate his defence of the national dimension of socialism against Trotsky's internationalist vision (see Stalin, 1953, vol. 6, 391).
5. See also the following quotation: 'The act is therefore not "abyssal" in the sense of an irrational gesture that eludes all rational criteria; it can and should be judged by universal rational criteria, the point is only that it changes (re-creates) the very criteria by which it should be judged' (Žižek, 2001b, 170).
6. In his article 'A Plea for Eurocentrism' he claims that '(a)lthough politics proper is thus something specifically "European" the entire history of European political thought is ultimately nothing but a series of disavowals of the political moment, of the proper logic of political antagonism'. He then proceeds to list four main versions of this disavowal (Žižek, 1999a, 990–1).

Part III
Metastases of the Real

One of the ways to approach Žižek's analytics of the Real is by following his reading of Alain Badiou's theory of the Truth-Event. Chapter 14 shows how despite sharing with Badiou a heartfelt critique of deconstruction as well as the philosophical desire to revive the notion of unversality, Žižek parts way with the French philosopher when he insists on the decisive theoretical and political precedence enjoyed by the Lacanian Real over the notion of Truth-Event. Crucial to Žižek's Hegelian argument is the understanding of the Real as an ontological category that cannot be uncoupled from the psychoanalytic notion of death-drive, and appears therefore fundamentally grounded in negativity. In Chapters 15, 16, 17 and 18 the central Žižekian question of the Real in its relation to the socio-symbolic order is discussed from the vantage point of one of Žižek's most recurrent Lacanian references: the theme of sexual difference. By highlighting the formal difference in the sexual economy of masculinity and femininity, Žižek aims to conceptualise two radically incompatible ways in which the Real connects with the Symbolic. While the masculine context of symbolic knowledge depends on the radical exclusion of an object forever lost to fantasy and *jouissance*, the feminine stance of 'not-all' potentially undermines the masculine logic of exclusion by depriving the Symbolic of its vital reference to a non-symbolisable, libidinally-invested excess. According to Žižek, in other words, woman has a chance to demonstrate the consubstantiality of the Symbolic and the Real, in as much as the Real is always-already included in every act of symbolisation, which therefore cannot but appear as fundamenally inconsistent. Ultimately, femininity makes visible how the Real of enjoyment needs to be rearticulated as the very founding feature of ideology itself. In chapter 19, finally, we shift the focus on Žižek's profoundly materialist understanding of love (including Christian love) as an implicitly violent passion for the Real, which allows us to realise that 'the impossible happens'.

14
Žižek Against Badiou: the Real Beyond the Event

Žižek's actualisation of the Lacanian category of the Real would seem to work, first and foremost, as a polemical statement against the condition of contemporary philosophy. Borrowing Badiou's line of argumentation, we could say that Žižek takes issue against the three main orientations of contemporary thought: hermeneutic, analytic/epistemological and postmodern/deconstructionist, insofar as they all remove the reference to universality (see Badiou, 2005, 31–3), and by so doing avoid the question of agency.[1] In effect, contemporary philosophy is characterised by what Jean-Francois Lyotard famously dubbed 'the end of the great narratives' (where the very use of the word 'narrative' implies that a radical paradigm-shift has already taken place), as well as by the consequent passage from the 'search for truth' to the 'search for meaning'. From such a theoretical angle, the reference to truth is replaced by the incontestable belief in the plurality of meanings. Poststructuralism, for instance, typically defines itself by avoiding questions concerning self-identical substances, fixed points of reference and stable notions of objects. More precisely, poststructuralism defines its own ontology by automatically excluding questions which problematise its concealed foundational principle, i.e. the very reference to ontology.

Bringing to full fruition Lacan's psychoanalytic method, Žižek challenges the deadlock of contemporary philosophy by readdressing the question of the relationship between the subject and ontology. Is there a way in which we can conceive and articulate such relationship? Can we merge the domain of ontology with a theory of the subject? Insisting upon these questions, Žižek approaches the

167

two main qualifications of the subject in a new way: identity and agency. As we have seen, the question of agency presents itself as a perfect case in point: if there is no autonomous and self-identical subject, how can we establish the ground for autonomous, self-transparent action? Foucault may be said to have articulated this deadlock in watertight poststructuralist terms by stating that power and resistance to power are inextricably entwined. If it is so, how can the subject generate autonomous and independent resistances? For Foucault, as we have documented, there is no place outside the manifold discourses of power, which implies that the subject can not posit itself effectively as a free agent endowed with the ability to antagonise radically a given power structure. And even if in his later writings Foucault has endeavoured to devise such a subject by assigning to it an aesthetic project of self-authoring, questions related to the origin of this privileged form of agency, as well as to its efficacy, remain largely unexplained.

In *The Ticklish Subject* (first published in 1999) Žižek seems to follow Badiou's path-breaking book on Saint Paul (*Saint Paul. The Foundation of Universalism*, first published in French in 1997) to theorise the connection between politics and universality. In *The Ticklish Subject* he openly endorses Badiou's notion of 'truth-event' (Žižek, 2000a, 161), although, as we shall see, he does not spare the French thinker a heavy dose of criticism. What is immediately appealing to Žižek in Badiou's notion of truth-event is that it provides a direct insight into the question of universality. As we have already suggested in this book, Žižek's crucial starting point in both theoretical and political terms is the Lacanian split subject, the subject defined by its radical alienation caused by the presence of an unconscious desire (see Žižek, 1989, 201–30; Žižek, 1993, 21–7). From the very beginning of his philosophical enterprise, Žižek tries to reformulate the Lacanian conceptualisation of the split subject in Hegelian terms, for Hegel's dialectical thought allows him to corroborate the idea that the self-division of the subject is precisely what opens up the possibility of an intervention in external reality, i.e. it opens up the possibility of agency and change. The fundamental requisite for this passage from subject to substance, however, is that the division of the subject be regarded as universal, as an ontological anchoring point that cannot in any way be eliminated or ignored. If Hegel provides the most convincing argument for the consubstantiality of subject and substance, Žižek eventually returns to Lacan to define this consubstantiality in terms of a foundational split or antagonism. In his latest works, Žižek has tenaciously attempted to theorise this foundational universal through increasingly sophisticated interpretations of the Lacanian notion of the Real – in itself a sophisticated relative of the Freudian unconscious.

We need to be clear on one crucial point here, which takes us directly to Badiou. According to Žižek, the notion of agency does not rely upon the implication that a subject engages in action against the background of some pre-established principles, or as a consequence of a self-transparent, rational choice. Rather, the Žižekian subject emerges in the world through a sudden break with the chain of symbolic conditions delineating the process of subjectivization. The subject is thus correlative to a traumatic encounter that determines, first, the disintegration of the fantasmatic support of subjectivity, and second the setting up of a new chain of interrelated symbolic references allowing for the construction of a radically different procedure of subjectivization.

This would seem to suggest that Žižek is very close to Badiou in defining the subject through a certain fidelity to a traumatic truth-event that suspends its symbolic functioning. Here, however, we should underline the first significant difference between the two thinkers: whilst Badiou's emphasis falls upon the question of *fidelity* to a traumatic chance encounter (the decisions to be taken after the event has intervened), Žižek tends to focus mainly upon a series of questions related to the constitutive nature of the actual event, i.e. the encounter with the Real.[2] If for Žižek the subject essentially *is* (i.e. it is inescapably defined by) the self-annihilating encounter with the Real, for Badiou it is rather the fidelity to this encounter in terms of the performativity it implies, its constructive development into a socially and politically workable set of actions. In other words, if read through the Lacanian lens, Badiou's subject is already projected onto the process of subjectivization determined by the encounter with the truth-event *qua* Real.

In *The Ticklish Subject*, Žižek describes Badiou's theory of the event by emphasising its affinity with the psychoanalytic logic of repression:

From time to time …, in a wholly contingent, unpredictable way, out of reach for Knowledge of Being, an Event takes place that belongs to a wholly different dimension – that, precisely, of non-Being. Let us take the French society in the late eighteenth century: the state of society, its strata, economic, political, ideological conflicts, and so on, are accessible to knowledge. However, no amount of Knowledge will enable us to predict or account for the properly unaccountable Event called the 'French Revolution'. In this precise sense, the Event emerges *ex nihilo*: if it cannot be accounted for in terms of the situation, this does not mean that it is simply an intervention from Outside or Beyond – it attaches itself precisely to the Void of every situation, to its inherent inconsistency and/or excess. The Event is the Truth of the situation that makes visible/legible what the 'official' situation had to 'repress', but it is also always localized – that is to say, the Truth is always the Truth *of* a specific situation. The French Revolution, for example, is the Event which makes visible/legible the excesses and inconsistencies, the 'lie', of the *ancien régime*; and it is the Truth *of* the *ancien régime* situation, localized, attached to it (Žižek, 2000a, 130).

Žižek's response to this theoretical paradigm could be summed up in the following question: how does the subject fare with respect to the Event? For Badiou, the subject is always-already included in the Event, insofar as (1) the subject is defined by its fidelity to the Event, and (2) the Event exists solely for the engaged subject who recognises its traces. In short, the relationship between Event and subject is circular: the Truth-Event constantly presupposes the standpoint of engaged subjectivity, which in turn is legitimised only by its fidelity to the Event. In the Marxist tradition, for example, partiality is the only way one can access Truth (to believe that history is the history of class struggle implies the belief that history can only be accessed from a partial or distorted perspective, and not from the inherently false viewpoint of impartial objectivity). More precisely, the Event is an invisible void (in Badiou's mathematical terms, it is 'supernumerary') which becomes visible – and thus antagonises a given socio-symbolic network – only when it is assumed by the engaged subject. The decision to assume the void of the Event is a retroactive one, in as much as the Event, like the Lacanian Real, is always in its place, always attached to its specific Situation. From this angle, both Žižek and Badiou can be seen as radically opposed to the postmodernist/

deconstructionist notion of the endless postponement of the encounter with Truth: Truth-Events are not only possible, but are absolutely immanent, always-already included in our socio-symbolic horizon.

As we gather from Žižek's reading of Badiou, therefore, the Event can be understood as an encounter with the Real which fulfils its potential only on condition that it is translated into a new set of socio-symbolic references. The Event of the Crucifixion fulfils itself in the engaged community of believers; the revolutionary upheaval fulfils itself in revolutionary consciousness, and so on (see Žižek, 2000a, 140–1).[3] However, as anticipated Žižek disagrees with Badiou on the question of negativity, insofar as Badiou adamantly denies the foundational role of the death-drive in its relation to the unconscious of Lacanian psychoanalysis. Žižek identifies this question by referring to Lacan's notion of the 'domain between the two deaths' (Lacan, 1992, 270–87), i.e. between the Symbolic and the Real, which is precisely where one ends up by endorsing the death-drive. Using one of Badiou's favourite references, Žižek clarifies this point by bringing into contention St Paul. As St Paul put it, anticipating Lacan, the law (prohibition) and desire are intertwined, feeding the various perversions of the superego. From this awareness Žižek argues that

> St Paul's problem is thus not the standard morbid moralistic one (how to crush transgressive impulse, how finally to purify myself of sinful urges), but its exact opposite: how can I break out of this vicious cycle of the Law and desire, of the Prohibition and its transgression, within which I can assert my living passions only in the guise of their opposite, as a morbid death-drive? ... The ultimate result of the rule of the Law thus consists of all the well-known twists and paradoxes of the superego: I can enjoy only if I feel guilty about it, which means that, in a self-reflexive turn, I can take pleasure in feeling guilty; I can find enjoyment in punishing myself for sinful thoughts; and so on (Žižek, 2000a, 149–50).

According to Žižek, the importance of St. Paul (and, as we shall see in Chapter 19, of Christianity as a whole) is that it allows us to conceive the 'rupture with the universe of Law and its transgression'

(Žižek, 2000a, 151) *through the death-drive*, the force which brings one to 'die to the law' and consequently embrace Christian Love. This rupture, the dying to the universe of law (and its transgression), is the crucial step for Žižek – and one which Badiou, in his view, largely neglects, or simply leaves unexplained. Foucault himself, from this angle, may be said to have misperceived the function of psychoanalysis, as well as neglected the political potential stored in Christianity:

> The ironic point not to be missed here is that Foucault conceives of psychoanalysis as the final chain in the link that began with the Christian confessional mode of sexuality, irreducibly linking it to Law and guilt, while – at least in Badiou's reading – St Paul, the founding figure of Christianity, does exactly the opposite: he endeavours to break the morbid link between Law and desire (Žižek, 2000a, 152).

Foucault's final conceptualisation of subjectivity in volumes II and III of the *History of Sexuality*, Žižek argues, aims precisely to 'deliver ourselves of the Christian frame' by postulating an ontology of the present modelled on the ancient Greek (Olympian) attempt to domesticate the 'annoying paradoxes of surplus enjoyment' (Žižek, 2001a, 181, 183) which bedevil the Christian believer. And the logic of confession, in Žižek's view, points to the paradox of this disturbing surplus enjoyment (*jouissance*), in as much as the act of contrition is inevitably eroticised, turned into the very source of enjoyment.

Within this conceptual framework, the dimension of negativity that in Lacan causes the failure of every process of subjectivization *is* the crucial dimension for Žižek:

> Lacan's way is not that of St Paul or Badiou: psychoanalysis is not 'psychosynthesis'; it does not already *posit* a 'new harmony', a new Truth-Event; it – as it were – merely wipes the slate clean for one. ... For Lacan, negativity, a negative gesture of withdrawal, precedes any positive gesture of enthusiastic identification with a Cause ... Lacan implicitly changes the balance between Death and Resurrection in favour of Death .... Here Lacan parts company with St Paul and Badiou: ... after Freud, one cannot directly

have faith in a Truth-Event; every such Event ultimately remains a semblance obfuscating a preceding Void whose Freudian name is *death drive*. So Lacan differs from Badiou in the determination of the exact status of this domain beyond the rule of the Law (Žižek, 2000a, 153–4).

More to the point: Žižek specifies that while for Badiou the domain beyond Knowledge or the Order of Being is an Event which participates in a positively accountable Truth, for Lacan this domain coincides with the *lamella*, the immortal, undead, strictly non-discursive libido at work in death-drive. With regard to the deadlock prohibition/law, Žižek therefore indicates that in Lacan one has a chance to move beyond their morbid interaction: 'Lacan's point is that if one fully exploits the potentials opened up by our existence as *parlêtres* ("beings of language"), one sooner or later finds oneself in this horrifying in-between state – the threatening possibility of this occurrence looms over each of us' (Žižek, 2000a, 156). This is a key passage: one cannot access directly the space between the two deaths, but only diagonally, obliquely, as a consequence of the endorsement of the surplus-enjoyment or *plus-de-jouir* which signals the intervention of the death-drive. From this perspective Badiou would find himself sharing company with profoundly different philosophers such as Althusser, Foucault and Derrida, who effectively denied the possibility that the subject could coincide with its founding negativity. Žižek, on the contrary, posits the subject as the ontological void from which a precarious and risky gesture of subjectivization necessarily emerges.

The difference between Žižek and Badiou is thus at its most visible with regard to the conceptualisation of subjectivity *vis-à-vis* external reality. For Žižek the subject is strictly correlative to the lack in the big Other, to the fundamental inconsistency that characterises the object of knowledge; more precisely, the subject intervenes at the level of external reality's radical inconsistency in order to confer upon it a semblance of consistency. Žižek follows Kant in rejecting as a paralogism the notion that reality exists in itself as an autonomous totality. Instead, he holds that reality achieves some fictional consistency or ontological semblance only through the subject, who 'plugs the hole' with a gesture of radical disavowal (subjectivization, which is equivalent to Lacan's symbolic castration). This is why, ultimately, this gesture of disavowal performed by the subject is eminently political: it decides the ontological viability of external reality. What we should not forget, however, is that the act of subjectivization by which the subject determines the positivity of the external world also fills in the very lack at the heart of the subject itself: by naming reality, the subject simultaneously establishes its place in it, since it disavows its own constitutive emptiness. It is this emptiness, or void, that Žižek reclaims as a political weapon. The key thesis is that by filling in the gap which simultaneously grounds the subject and external reality, the subject inevitably reproduces the conditions of possibility of this gap, it re-inscribes the gap in the symbolic order. This is why subjectivity, to Žižek, is ultimately defined by drive: a circular movement around an inherent deadlock, an irreducible obstacle which is precisely what the subject is. Žižek articulates the difference between Lacan and Badiou in the following terms:

> Lacan insists on the primacy of the (negative) *act* over the (positive) establishment of a 'new harmony' via the intervention of some new Master Signifier; while for Badiou, the different facets of negativity (ethical catastrophes) are reduced to so many versions of the 'betrayal' of (or infidelity to, or denial of) the positive Truth-Event. This difference between Badiou and Lacan concerns precisely the status of the subject: Badiou's main point is to avoid identifying the subject with the constitutive Void of the structure – such an identification already 'ontologizes' the subject, albeit in a purely negative way – that is, it turns the subject into an entity consubstantial with the structure .... To this Lacanian ontologization of the subject, Badiou opposes its 'rarity', the local-contingent-fragile-passing emergence of subjectivity: when, in a contingent and unpredictable way, a Truth-Event takes place, a subject is there to exert fidelity to the Event by discerning its traces in a Situation whose Truth the Event is. ... what Badiou and Laclau describe is the process of subjectivization – the emphatic engagement, the assumption of fidelity to the Event ..., while the subject is the negative gesture of breaking out of the constraints of Being that opens up the space of possible subjectivization (Žižek, 2000a, 159–60).

This definition of the subject in terms of its relationship with the external order of Being is very precise: it is not that the subject *qua* death-drive opens up the gap of freedom within the structure of the universe; rather, it constitutes the universe through an excessive gesture which is not grounded in any symbolic referent. The subject, carrying the weight of that ontological derailment called death-drive, 'is the contingent-excessive gesture that constitutes the very universal order of Being' (Žižek, 2000a, 160). In other words, every order implies a passage through death-drive, the negativity which grounds it. For Žižek and Lacan everything (literally) hinges on the death-drive, or on the minimal distance between the constitutive void of subject/Being, and the positive act through which this void is filled out/sublimated. For all of Žižek's theoretical complexity, his effort eventually boils down to the postulation and defence of those limit-experiences where the subject is suddenly faced by, or caught in, the negativity of the death-drive irrespective of its subsequent sublimation.

Badiou, on the other hand, confines psychoanalysis to the self-enclosed relationship between law and desire/transgression, rejecting it when it comes to assessing the domain between law and Truth-Event. According to Žižek, the Truth-Event can only be conceived as correlative to the death-drive, to negativity at its purest, and therefore should not be confused with its gentrified semblance, since 'in a Truth-Event the void of the death drive ... continues to resonate' (Žižek, 2000a, 162–3). From this angle, therefore, Badiou's error would seem to lie in his naivety, which brings him to conceive participation in the Truth-Event as the immortal dimension of humanity, without recognizing that this immortality is the immortality of the undead lamella, the object-libido which qualifies the death-drive. And the point is that the immortality of the lamella

> can emerge only within the horizon of human finitude, as a formation that stands for and fills the ontological Void, the hole in the texture of reality opened up by the fact that reality is transcendentally constituted by the finite transcendental subject. ... In short, against Badiou, one should insist that only to a finite/mortal being does the act (or Event) appear as a traumatic intrusion of the Real, as something that cannot be named directly: it is the very fact that man is split between mortality (a finite being destined to perish) and the capacity to participate in the Eternity of the Truth-Event which bears witness to the fact that we are dealing with a finite/mortal being (Žižek, 2000a, 164).

In Žižek's speculative system, then, it is as if there was an Event before Badiou's Event, an Event which corresponds to the negativity of the death-drive. This can be put in a different way. As is well known Lacan theorises four discourses: Master, Hysteric, University and Analyst. The Master sutures the symbolic field by producing/ embodying the *point de caption* (the anchoring point in the endless signifying chain producing the illusion of fixed meaning); the Hysteric questions ad infinitum the discourse of the Master, on the grounds that there is always a difference, a distance, between the naming of reality and reality itself; the University is perverse by definition, because it attempts to reduce everything to knowledge. Finally, there is the discourse of the analyst:

> This position, while maintaining the gap between the Event and its symbolization, avoids the hysterical trap and instead of being caught in the vicious cycle of permanent failure, affirms this gap as positive and productive: it asserts the Real of the Event as the 'generator', the generating core to be encircled repeatedly by the subject's symbolic productivity (Žižek, 2000a, 165).

Lacan's 'desire of the analyst', in other words, introduces a modality of desire beyond the law and its superego injunction to transgress it, insofar as it offers the possibility *not* to enjoy, i.e. to opt for the withdrawal from the compulsion to enjoy. Such a position implies the fundamental insight into the inconsistency of desire itself: the desire of the analyst corresponds to the awareness that desire, in its 'amalgamating' function, is utterly superfluous.

From this radical take on desire Žižek goes on to surmise that Badiou's hostility towards psychoanalysis is part of his hidden Kantianism, which emerges more blatantly in his distinction between the positive order of Being (Knowledge) and the order of the Truth-Event (see Žižek, 2000a, 166–7). Despite pledging an explicitly anti-Kantian and radically leftist type of ideological commitment, Badiou gets caught in the Kantian trap, for his central notion of Truth-Event works as *an endless attempt to detect the traces of the Truth-Event*, which is precisely what the Kantian ethical injunction is about. With Badiou, truth cannot be grasped as the truth of the entire situation, as such a hypothesis is immediately blocked out by the reference to catastrophic outcomes such as Stalinism and the Maoist

Cultural Revolution (see Žižek, 2000a, 167). In Lacan, on the other hand, the *innomable* core (Truth) is always-already here with us, in as much as it is rooted in a fundamental fantasy which function as a channel for radical agency.

The same argument is developed in *On Belief*, where Žižek claims that despite Badiou's genuine attempt to revive philosophy, he misses the proper philosophical insight shared for example by Hegel and Nietzsche: 'For an authentic philosopher, *everything has always-already happened*; what is difficult to grasp is how this notion not only does NOT prevent engaged activity, but effectively SUSTAINS it' (Žižek, 2001c, 125). The specific target of Žižek's criticism, here, is Badiou's 'marginal anti-Statism', whereby authentic politics *qua* fidelity to the Truth-Event should reject involvement with state power and limit itself to unconditional demands for *égaliberté*, which makes this politics close to becoming apolitical.

So, how does Žižek understand the Event? The most consistent answer is that he thinks of it as Real, i.e. as *the tension between the impossible Real itself and the Symbolic* (the distortion that constitutes the fundamental nature of the Symbolic) – or, on a different level, as the tension between Eternity and History, which opens up the field of historicity proper. It is evident that Žižek admires Badiou, and especially shares his unabashed critique of deconstruction as well as his philosophical defence and reinstatement of the notion of universality. However, he fundamentally parts ways with him on the key notion of Truth-Event. The difference may seem to be minimal, and yet it is crucial, as it allows us to understand what Žižek means by 'the simultaneity of Symbolic and Real'.

This idea is first deployed by Žižek in *Revolution at the Gates*. Here Badiou is rebuked for over-emphasising the importance of Lenin's *What Is To Be Done?*, where the purely political dimension is elevated above Marx's 'economism', thus breaking with it. Following up from *The Ticklish Subject* (see Žižek, 2000a, 171–239), Žižek proceeds to argue that 'pure politics' (represented here by Badiou, Rancière and Balibar) reduces the domain of the economy to an ontic category, not an ontological one, which implies a downgrading of the Marxian critique of political economy (see also Žižek, 2006a, 327–28). In specific connection with Badiou, Žižek finds that his notion of 'pure politics' as a radically autonomous field is grounded in the erroneous opposition of Being and Event, which suggests precisely that Badiou remains trapped in an essentially idealistic vision (see Žižek, 2002a, 271–2). It is at this stage that Žižek proposes his theory of the correspondence of the Symbolic and the Real. In Badiou's terms, this would imply the consubstantiality of Being and Event: the Event is always-already included in Being, and it emerges via the insistence of death-drive, whose role is legitimised by the Lacanian axiom (rejected by Badiou) that the subject is fundamentally empty. This also permits us to see the difference between Badiou's Event and Žižek's Real from the point of view of the subject: while in Badiou the Event *simply happens* and the subject is called upon to demonstrate fidelity to it, in Žižek the subject demonstrates fidelity to the Real only by (unconsciously) making it happen, by disturbing it through the endorsement of death-drive.[4]

Žižek's critique of Badiou, however, is at its clearest in his book on Deleuze (*Organs Without Bodies*, 2004), where the notion of the simultaneity of the Symbolic and the Real, already outlined in the preceding *The Puppet and the Dwarf* (2003), is fully developed. In *Organs Without Bodies* Žižek insists that Badiou's mistake lies in conceiving the Event as external to Being, whilst it should rather be 'located in the "minimal difference" inherent to the order of Being itself'. The very fact that Badiou defines Evil as the forcing of the Unnameable, i.e. 'the dream of total Nomination', suggests that he is still operating from within the remit of Kant's regulative Idea, as Badiou's ethics of Truth become 'the ethics of the respect for the unnameable Real that cannot be forced' (Žižek, 2004c, 104–5). As we know, Žižek opposes any 'transcendentalisation' of Lacan, and for the same reason he opposes Badiou's risk of transcendentalising the Real: 'does Badiou, *the* anti-Levinas, with this topic of the respect for the unnameable, not come dangerously close precisely to the Levinasian notion of the respect for Otherness – the notion that is, against all appearances, totally inoperative at the political level?' (Žižek, 2004c, 106). Žižek puts his criticism in the clearest possible terms when he claims that

> there is a Kantian problem with Badiou that is grounded in his dualism of Being and Event and that has to be surpassed. The only way out of this predicament is to assert that the unnameable Real is not an external limitation but an *absolutely inherent*

limitation. ... like the Lacanian Real that is not external to the Symbolic but makes it not-all from within ..., the unnameable is inherent to the domain of names. ... *This* and only this is the proper passage from Kant to Hegel: not the passage from limited/incomplete to full/completed nomination ('absolute knowledge') but the passage of the very limit of nomination from the exterior to the interior (Žižek, 2004c, 107).

Žižek's and Lacan's Real can therefore be understood in its 'suturing' function. Rather than a close relative of Heidegger's *Ab-grund*, the Real is *the presence of an absence which is necessary for the presence of a presence*. The word 'site', used by Badiou to circumscribe the intervention of the Event, is quite accurate from this angle. The Real is the presence of an evental-site (*site événementiel*). It does not guarantee that change will take place – that the traumatic encounter will materialise. However, it harbours the potential for an unpredictable and explosive occurrence with no place in the order of the universe as we know it. According to Badiou, it might well be that it happens and nothing changes because nobody recognises its importance, since a political intervention, for him, begins with the initial naming of the Event as an Event. In Žižek, however, *the Real always happens*, since it is glued to, and inseparable from, the symbolic order. As in Lacan's classic example of the sexual relationship, fully expanded in the following chapters, the Real 'does not stop not being written',[5] i.e. *it is written precisely as the impossibility of being written* – the main problem being how to get the subject to face up to the explosive inevitability of the Real.

Žižek's fundamental point with regard to the Lacanian Real is that it can only be approached through the Symbolic, through language and meaning, for in its ultimate configuration it does coincide with language and meaning. More precisely, we become aware of the Real only as an effect, as a consequence of a certain failed symbolisation – as an effect of our being immersed in a distorted framework of meaning. This Real is thus not the pre-symbolic substance that precedes our entrance into knowledge; it is not the immutable and terrifying Other constantly eluding symbolisation; it is not the transcendental Thing, a hard kernel that can only be experienced as trauma or ecstatic plenitude. Žižek does not hesitate to define these characterizations of the Real – which he himself, it must be said, has often flirted with – as obscurantist: 'The Real as the terrifying primordial abyss that swallows everything, dissolving all identities ... is precisely the ultimate lure that, as Richard Kearney was right to emphasise, lends itself easily to New Age appropriation'. The Real, then, is rather the inherent obstacle constitutive of the process of symbolization: 'that invisible obstacle, that distorting screen, which always "falsifies" our access to external reality, that "bone in the throat" which gives a pathological twist to every symbolization, that is to say, on account of which every symbolization ultimately fails' (Žižek, 2003b, 66–7). This Real is also the truth of the psychoanalytic discourse, since in psychoanalysis truth emerges when speech gets disrupted or perturbed by some unconscious symptomatic formation (in dreams, slips of the tongue, etc.). Incidentally, this is the reason why Žižek is profoundly Hegelian and fundamentally anti-Kantian: if Kant holds that the tension between phenomena is determined by the impossibility of reaching the Thing-in-itself (noumena), Hegel accomplishes the passage from externality to internality, whereby the Thing is not conceived as external to phenomena, but rather as the distilled core of their inconsistency, the very gap that qualifies inconsistency as such.

In an attempt to clarify and refine his grasp of the Real, Žižek claims that, essentially, it has to be posited as form rather than content: 'This notion of Form is a properly dialectical one: form is not the neutral frame of particular contents, but the very principle of concretion, that is, the "strange attractor" which distorts, biases, confers a specific colour on every element of the totality' (Žižek, 2002a, 190). Such a view has major political consequences. Against the liberal-multiculturalist notion of form as a neutral frame to be filled with different, replaceable and equally respectable 'narratives', Žižek's dialectical re-elaboration of the notion implies that:

> Form has nothing to do with 'formalism', with the idea of a neutral Form, independent of its contingent particular contents; it stands, rather, for the traumatic kernel of the Real, for the antagonism which 'colours' the entire field in question. In this precise sense, class struggle is the form of the Social: every social phenomenon is over-determined by it, so that it is not possible to remain neutral towards it (Žižek, 2002a, 190).

Žižek is at his most accurate and convincing when he defines the Real as the gravitational pull that shapes the Symbolic and that, ultimately, *is* the Symbolic in its particular, inherently distorted mode of appearance. Here, again, we come upon the Hegelian/Lacanian core of his thinking: the Real belongs to the Symbolic, it is fully and inextricably enmeshed in it, in as much as it is the invisible deadlock whose displacement allows for the (inevitably fragmentary, anamorphotic, distorted) emergence/existence of meaning. As Žižek puts it, 'the Real intervenes through anamorphosis' (Žižek, 2003b, 75), i.e. there is no other way of thinking it except as anamorphosis (distortion). In the final analysis, the Real can only be detected *through* and *in the form of* the various swerves of the Symbolic. Jonathan Lear's analogy seems in this sense truly illuminating: the Real is tantamount to black holes, which can only be accounted for 'by the way light swerves towards them' (in Žižek, 2003b, 73). However, Žižek notes, crucially, that it is in the very swerve that we should recognize the presence of the Real:

> For Lacan, however, the Real (of trauma) is also a 'swerve', a black hole detectable only through its effects, only in the way it 'curves' mental space, bending the line of mental processes. And is not sexuality (this Real of the human animal) also such a swerve? Here one should endorse Freud's fundamental insight according to which sexuality does *not* follow the pleasure principle: its fundamental mode of appearance is that of a break, of the intrusion of some excessive *jouissance* that disturbs the 'normal', balanced functioning of the psychic apparatus. ... the Lacanian Real – the Thing – is not so much the inert presence that 'curves' the symbolic space (introducing breaks in it), but, rather, the effect of these breaks (Žižek, 2003b, 74).

Ultimately, Žižek conflates transcendence and immanence, in a typically Hegelian interpretation: 'The Real is thus *simultaneously* the Thing to which direct access is not possible and the obstacle that prevents this direct access; the Thing that eludes our grasp and the distorting screen that makes us miss the Thing' (Žižek, 2003b, 77). The point being that what we perceive as the gap between ourselves and the Thing is already the Thing itself: Hegel's radicalisation of Kant's crucial insight, a minimal but fundamental shift of perspectives (a parallax view).

On this evidence, Žižek maintains that passion for the Real and passion for semblance are, in their deepest connotation, one and the same thing if analysed through the Lacanian/Hegelian lens. The standard postmodern insight that appearances are more valuable than reality – insofar as reality ultimately does not exist as such – needs therefore to be radicalised: while it is not true that everything is an interplay of appearances, since the Real functions precisely as an anchoring point, at the same time this Real is not a deeper dimension or a traditionally conceived type of truth, but rather the abyssal gap between appearances and our very presupposition that there is a deeper, true reality. The Real is thus homologous to the Hegelian 'appearance qua appearance': we can never access the Thing or truth without a certain perspectival distortion, insofar as the Thing or truth is precisely the ontological appearance of this distortion: 'There is a truth; everything is not relative – but this truth is the truth of the perspectival distortion as such, not the truth distorted by the partial view from a one-sided perspective' (Žižek, 2003b, 79).

15
'There Is No Such Thing as a Sexual Relationship': the Formal Deadlock of Sexuality

One of Žižek's favourite ways to approach and discuss the question of the relationship between the Symbolic and the Real, and thus the key theoretical aspect of his ideology critique, is by referring to one of Lacan's most highly debated and controversial topics, the question of sexual difference (the so called 'formulas of sexuation', see Fig. 15.1). As a rule, Žižek starts with the assertion that sexual difference is Real insofar as it establishes the impossibility of sexual identity as such, i.e. it cuts across both fields of femininity and masculinity:

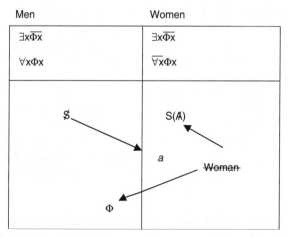

Figure 15.1

Sexual difference is the Real of an antagonism, not the Symbolic of a differential opposition: sexual difference is not the opposition allocating to each of the two sexes its positive identity defined in opposition to the other sex (so that woman is what man is not, and vice versa), but a common Loss on account of which woman is never fully a woman and man is never fully a man – 'masculine' and 'feminine' positions are merely two modes of coping with this inherent obstacle/loss (Žižek, 2000a, 272).

Žižek's reading of Lacan's formulas, therefore, highlights the fact that men and women are plagued by the same structural deadlock which, however, manifests itself in radically incompatible ways. Let us define this claim more closely: both men and women are inherently split, or alienated, by the Real of sexual difference, which traverses both fields; the key point, however, is to grasp how this Real is precisely (literally) *the antagonism which defines the relation of one sex to the other*, preventing each of the sexes to fully realise itself:

… men and women are not incompatible simply because they are 'from different planets', each involving a different psychic economy, and so on, but precisely because there is an inextricably antagonistic link between them – that is to say, because they are from the same planet which is, as it were, split from within. … Lacan … grounds the impossibility of sexual relationship in the fact that the identity of each of the two sexes is hampered from within by the antagonistic relationship to the other sex which prevents its full actualisation. 'There is no sexual relationship' not because the other sex is too far away, totally strange to me, but because *it is too close to me*, the foreign intruder at the very heart of my (impossible) identity. Consequently, each of the two sexes functions as the inherent obstacle on account of which the other sex is never 'fully itself': 'man' is that on account of which woman can never fully realize herself as woman, achieve her feminine self-identity; and, vice versa, 'woman' materializes the obstacle which prevents man's self-fulfilment (Žižek, 2000a, 72–3).

The Real of sexual difference, then, is predicated upon the assumption that the partner is a traumatic other with whom any symbolic/communicative negotiation takes place against the background of a fundamental impossibility, which might be repressed but not eliminated. Sexual difference translates as a kind of uncoordinated embrace between the two sexes: they might think they have locked themselves into each other's arms; however, what they hold tight is never the other, but rather a fantasmatic, inadequate and deeply incompatible symbolisation of the other. One can already see here how Žižek's Lacanian conceptualisation of sexuality could not be more distant from Foucault's. If on the one hand Žižek concedes that sexual difference is not grounded in biology and eventually emerges as a 'complex and contingent socio-symbolic power struggle' (Žižek, 2000a, 275), on the other hand he claims that this historically accountable construction of gendered identities is itself the effect of a more fundamental gesture, which involves the necessary foreclosure of sexual difference *qua* Real. In other words, Žižek argues that the Foucauldian notion of the social construction of gender is secondary to the Lacanian notion of sexual difference.

Let us now start exploring how Žižek reads the specific inconsistencies of the two fields as portrayed by Lacan. As is well known, in Seminar XX feminine sexuality is identified as the inconsistent modality of 'not-all' (*pastout*), whereas masculinity is defined by the phallic function *qua* 'all' (*tout*). In what follows, our main task will be to clarify Žižek's analysis of the significant divergence and uncoordination of these two modalities in connection with his attempt to identify the crucial ideological role played by the Lacanian Real.

As early as in *Tarrying with the Negative* (see Žižek, 1993, 57–8) Žižek claims that there is a standard way to misunderstand Lacan's theory of sexuation, one which applies particularly (but not only) to the various feminist readings on the topic. The basic *faux pas* is that of considering the feminine position as a fully articulated exception or point of resistance to masculine phallocentrism. That is to say: since the masculine field is defined by the phallic function, the feminine bears witness to a position which, no matter how ambiguously, manages to defy the rule; while no woman is fully exempted from the phallic function, at the same time a part of femininity resists it or eludes it.

Žižek insists that there is a more literal and at the same time radical way of reading Lacan's formulas. This is by conceding that, contrary to the previous hypothesis, *no part of woman resists the phallic order*, i.e. woman is fully submitted to the phallus: precisely because of her total identification with what would seem to determine her condition of submission, woman is able to undermine its totalising function. In what is undoubtedly a contentious thesis that many a feminist critic have taken issue against, Žižek resolutely claims that, in Lacan, the authentically subversive dimension of femininity can only be accounted for by acknowledging that woman belongs fully in the symbolic order. As we shall see in the following pages, Žižek's central Lacanian argument is that woman *is immersed in the symbolic order without exception* (see Žižek, 1993, 58; 2000b, 145) – without the crucial exception that allows man to set up the phallic domain as a universalised field. While man can only define and relate to the world by positing a libidinally-invested, fantasised about point of exclusion, woman has a chance to connect with the big Other in a radically different way, one which presupposes no exception to the rule and which, by the same token, demonstrates the consubstantiality of the Symbolic and the Real.

There is, however, a necessary prerequisite to our discussion, which has been clearly highlighted by Bruce Fink in his analysis of Lacan's formulas:

> Lacan's way of defining man and woman has nothing to do with biology. ... From a clinical vantage point, a great many biological females turn out to have masculine structure, and a great many biological males prove to have feminine structure. Part of an analyst's training must thus consist in breaking old habits of thought whereby one immediately assumes that a female is an hysteric and thereby can be characterized as having feminine structure. Each person's relation to the signifier and mode of jouissance has to be examined more carefully; one cannot jump to conclusions on the basis of biological sex (Fink, 1995, 108).

As it will become clear later on, Fink's argument that Lacan's reference to the sexes is of a strictly psychological nature (see also Lacan, 1998b, 80) is implicitly confirmed by Žižek's consistent and deliberate avoidance of content-related definitions of masculinity and femininity. What Žižek aims at is certainly *not* the definition of sexed individuals; rather, he intends to focus on the formal deadlock inherent to sexuality as such: 'What we experience as "sexuality" is precisely the effect of the contingent act of "grafting" the fundamental deadlock of symbolization onto the biological opposition of male and female' (Žižek, 1994a, 155). More precisely, sexual difference for Žižek is functional to demonstrating the impossibility of symbolisation in the following terms: while in the masculine field this impossibility is primordially repressed, in the feminine field it makes itself available as an encounter with the Real.

The implicit foundation of Žižek's view of sexual difference, therefore, is that there is no such thing as 'sexual substance': sexuality in general can only be defined in formal terms and not by way of content-related formulas. This also indicates that the passage from the masculine position to the feminine one (and vice versa) hinges merely on a formal shift. Sexuality is a 'universal surplus' (Žižek, 1994a, 127), the 'Real of the human animal' (Žižek, 2003b, 74) that manifests itself as a deadlock signifying a fundamental structural imbalance. Thus every attempt to define sexuality as a context filled with substantial features, whether in relation to man or woman, completely misses the point.[1] What counts in masculinity is the split introduced by the phallus, with the phallus representing a thoroughly formal category (the signifier of lack). As for femininity, Žižek holds that any prescriptive feminist view regarding positive contents could also as a rule be read as a male patriarchal cliché about women, which implies that the question concerning the substance of feminine sexuality remains thoroughly ambiguous:

> The question that instantly pops up is: what is, then, the feminine 'in itself', obfuscated by male clichés? The problem is that all answers (from the traditional eternal feminine, to Kristeva and Irigaray) can again be discredited as male clichés. Carol Gilligan, for example, opposes to the male values of autonomy, competitiveness, etc., the feminine values of intimacy, attachment, interdependence, care and concern, responsibility and self-sacrifice, etc. Are these authentic feminine features or male clichés about women, features imposed on them in the patriarchal society? The matter is undecidable, so that the only possible answer is, both at the same time (Žižek, 1995).

What woman is 'in herself' remains radically disjointed from what she is 'for the other' (for man, but also 'for herself'); in turn, this gap can only be articulated in terms of a formal/topological split, since differentiating between two sets of contents would simply lead (and does lead) to a normative deadlock.

Here we go back to the initial point: from a formal viewpoint, woman is split in a different way from man, as she represents the possibility of the dissolution of the 'knot' through which the symbolic field is constituted. If masculinity is defined by an intervention that externalises its core into a surplus object (*objet a*), in femininity the surplus is, as it were, *brought back where it originally belongs*: in the very self-fracture of the symbolic order. Žižek reads Lacan's (in)famous thesis that 'Woman does not exist' precisely along these lines: what does not exist in the formal organisation of femininity is the external reference to the 'enigma of femininity' that would confer a (fake) subjective consistency to her being. Consequently, the reference to an ever-elusive, mysterious essence of femininity is unmasked as a deeply delusive masculine strategy (typical, for example, of the tradition of courtly love) through which man ultimately seeks to assert his own symbolic position. In contrast to this masculine logic, and in a way that challenges it profoundly, woman provides evidence for the fact that her presumed essence coincides with void.

The fundamental premise to our discussion is that we can account for sexual difference precisely by doing away with arguments about the specific substantial disparity between men and women (which can be summed up by the popular maxim that 'men are from Mars and women from Venus'). This indicates that the deadlock of sexual difference concerns the two incompatible ways in which masculinity and femininity strive to come to terms with the gap separating subjectivity from subject, i.e. the fictional yet fully-constituted self and its empty frame. Žižek sums up this question – the fundamental question of Lacanian psychoanalysis, if there is one – in the following terms:

> Lacan's point here is that an insurmountable gap forever separates what I am 'in the real' from the symbolic mandate that procures my social identity; the primordial ontological fact is the void, the abyss on account of which I am inaccessible to myself in my capacity as real substance .... Every symbolic identity I acquire is ultimately nothing but a supplementary feature whose function is to fill out this void (Žižek, 1994a, 144).

Bearing in mind that the subject of Lacanian psychoanalysis, in its deepest connotation, is an empty screen retroactively filled with positive content, woman is the subject par excellence insofar as her sexually-specific formal constitution suggests a closer relationship with the inconsistency of the subjective frame, with the 'void called subject' – ultimately, with the unconscious of the Freudian-Lacanian tradition.

16
Objet a, or the Ruse of Masculinity

The first point to discuss, however, is the paradoxical nature of the masculine position. As anticipated, the masculine ground effectively stands on an instance of radical exclusion, which means that the possibility of symbolic knowledge opens up through a kind of founding contradiction: the totalising mode of masculinity (its reliance upon a self-sufficient, consistent symbolic context) depends on the intervention of a cut through which a part of the field is relegated to a non-symbolisable domain accessible only through fantasy. Put differently, the realm of symbolic knowledge coterminous with the phallic function is founded upon its own limit – the fact that, to exist as such, it has to set up a certain boundary beyond which, as it were, 'the word gets stuck in *jouissance*'. The paradox is that it is precisely the self-imposed limit – together with the fantasy of transgression it inevitably engenders – that confers consistency to the masculine economy. Thus, the masculine context of symbolic knowledge depends on an exceptional object lost to *jouissance*, which means that we enter the domain of knowledge the moment we sacrifice this object (*objet petit a*) by handing it over to the Other, who is perceived as having the right to enjoy it to the full.

The central psychoanalytic notion we are dealing with is, of course, that of 'symbolic castration'. It is only insofar as man is defined by what Lacan calls symbolic castration that the masculine field is totalised. The key figure designating the limit-dimension and thus the paradox of the masculine position is that of the Freudian primal father (as introduced in *Totem and Taboo*). By defying castration and reaching out directly for unbridled enjoyment (of all women), the primal father stands for the exception to the logic of symbolic castration which grounds the masculine field. Lacan expresses the paradox of the masculine field with the two formulas $\exists x\overline{\Phi x}$ and $\forall x\Phi x$, in the top left part his sexuation graph (Figure 15.1). While $\forall x\Phi x$ signifies that the whole of man ($\forall x$) is defined by the phallic function (Φx), $\exists x\overline{\Phi x}$ means that the masculine field is simultaneously traversed by an exception ($\exists x$) whose role is to negate the phallic function ($\overline{\Phi x}$). What needs to be added is that if symbolic castration renders perfectly the grounding contradiction inherent to masculinity, a modicum of castration is what every human being necessitates in order to establish a connection with the world through language.

A brief digression needs to be introduced here, especially with regard to the standard postmodern interpretation of Lacan as a thinker who rejects the notion of universality. Žižek insists that to speak about symbolic castration is not the same as to speak about the effective impossibility to achieve universality, on the grounds that a remainder sticks out and regularly prevents the squaring of the circle. Rather, symbolic castration tells us that access to universality *is* possible, albeit at the (heavy) price of a sacrifice that thoroughly alienates the field of masculinity: what is sacrificed, ultimately, is the 'object' that constitutes the very kernel of what we call 'subject'. In other words, masculine universality coincides with the barred subject ($\$$), the neutral, empty, desexualised plane of subjectivity deprived of its innermost sexualised core, which is displaced onto *a*. What we call 'men' are those speaking beings who universalise the symbolic field by submitting themselves to symbolic castration and simultaneously displacing enjoyment onto an external object. The example most frequently deployed by Žižek with regard to the symbolic economy of masculinity in its universalising mode is that of the lady in the tradition of courtly love, already amply discussed by Lacan in *The Ethics of Psychoanalysis* (see Lacan, 1992, 139–54). The effect determined by the positing of the lady as an elusive/impossible object of sexual desire is the opening up of the desexualised symbolic field that defines the masculine economy. The sublimated figure of the lady thus embodies the paradox of the phallic function to perfection: while effectively rendering the masculine subject impotent (since the lady is conceived as inaccessible), it allows him to establish the authority of the phallic domain.

The reference to phallus is of capital importance for our analysis. When Žižek makes the apparently preposterous claim that phallus (Lacan's Φ) is the fundamental category of dialectical materialism (see Žižek, 1994a, 130) his aim is, bluntly said, to demonstrate the overlap of sexuality and ideology. What he actually means is that the essential element responsible for the emergence of ideology (and, concomitantly, politics) is phallus *qua* signifier of castration, i.e. the immaterial, insubstantial formal intervention aimed at creating the structural conditions for the emergence of symbolic space. Phallus is the cut through which the symbolic order materialises, at the same time its limit and condition of possibility. Phallus thus conflates the notions of power and impotence, which define in equal measure the field of masculinity. In the classic case of the political leader, for instance, power proper is in effect constituted through the inscription of a certain indefinable edge which signals the moment where, paradoxically, the political discourse fails and is replaced by what normally goes under the name of charisma, the incalculable libidinal aura that exudes from the leader's persona. This proves that the self-limitation of the phallic function works as its own success: symbolic consistency is established via the inscription of a split through which lack, the domain beyond the nameable, suddenly acquires a positive presence. As in the case of ideology, positing a certain indefinable space beyond the remit of reason appears to be the best way to strengthen one's reasons. Masculine sexuality thus brings to light the logic of ideological symbolisation, for it effectively draws a line of separation between the Symbolic and the Real. The catch is, of course, that such a move amounts to a strategy to avoid the traumatic encounter with the Real, or more precisely to neutralise its impact.

The best way to render the functioning of masculinity is by referring back to symbolic castration. The effect of symbolic castration on man is, literally, the drawing of a line of demarcation between accessible and inaccessible women, which is to be intended at its most radical. As Fink puts it, '[c]astration brings about an exclusion: mom and sis are off-limits' (Fink, 1995, 110). While mother and sister become simply inaccessible, all other women are turned into *objet a*, i.e. they are accessible only insofar as they do not exist as women *tout court* but rather because they are seen as possessing the precious object-cause that sets desire in motion.[1] However, mistaking *objet a* for the Real would amount to missing completely the significance of the mechanism of fundamental displacement upon which the masculine field is structured. *Objet a* is precisely the ruse that allows man to universalise its field – and, concurrently, to fill this field with the veils of 'ideological fantasy'.[2] To replicate Lacan's well-known definition, *a* is the empirical object elevated to the dignity of the impossible Thing *qua* Real. Where, then, should we look for the Real of masculinity? If we refer to the paradigmatic case of symbolic castration, the answer can only be a profoundly traumatic and highly impracticable one: in the deeply-repressed incestuous fantasies that bring the figure of the primal father (Lacan's father-*jouissance*) back into the picture. This would suggest that in each man's unconscious the implicitly traumatic ideal of noncastration (of boundless, unproblematic enjoyment of all women) shadows the necessary intervention of symbolic castration (see Fink, 1995, 111). In conclusion, the masculine field is ill-equipped to disturb the Real of sexual difference. The indispensable presence of *objet a* works as a powerful stratagem through which the Real remains foreclosed.

17
Woman's 'Not-All' and the Paradox of Passive Aggression

Having clarified Žižek's view of the exclusionary logic that sustains the 'all' of the masculine field in Lacan, let us now have a look at his controversial interpretation of Lacan's definition of femininity. The main argument, regularly rehearsed by Žižek, is that in femininity the exclusionary logic is absent. Femininity undermines the masculine logic of the 'exception to the rule' by *fully* identifying with the rule *qua* symbolic law, i.e. by abolishing the fracture between the Symbolic and the Real, thus depriving the Symbolic of its founding excess. In the feminine position of 'not-all' there is simply no exception to the phallic economy, but total identification with it – no part of woman is free from the phallic function:

> ... totalization takes place through its constitutive exception, and since, in the feminine libidinal economy, there is no Outside, no Exception to the phallic function, for that very reason a woman is immersed in the symbolic order more wholly than a man – without restraint, without exception (Žižek, 2003b, 68).[1]

This topic can also be tackled by referring to the status of what Lacan calls *jouissance féminine*, which Žižek considers at various points in his work. According to Lacan's graph of sexuation (figure 15.1), the inconsistency of the feminine field is characterised by woman's bond with two objects: the phallic signifier (Φ) and S($\cancel{A}$). Whilst the phallic signifier designates woman's specific fantasy of man, S($\cancel{A}$) represents none other than woman's relationship with the symbolic field as radically inconsistent, fraught with Real gaps, always-already penetrated by *jouissance*. If in the first case woman constructs her identity and organises her enjoyment through her relationship with the phallic signifier (her own specific fantasy of man), in the second she achieves enjoyment 'beyond the phallus', i.e. *jouissance féminine*.

The fact that woman defines herself through the phallus *as well as* the Other indicates, first and foremost, the peculiarity of her division: 'Woman has a relation with S(Ⱥ), and it is already in that respect that she is doubled, that she is not-whole, since she can also have a relation with Φ' (Lacan, 1998b, 81). It is precisely in the distinctive closeness of her relation to the Other that the distinctiveness of the feminine position comes about. Lacan makes it clear that 'woman [in contrast to man] is that which has a relationship to that Other' – where the term 'Other' is characterised by the fact that 'there is no Other of the Other', which amounts to saying that the big Other ('the locus in which everything that can be articulated on the basis of the signifier comes to be inscribed') is the most radical instance of otherness precisely because it is not sustained by any external point of reference (Lacan, 1998b, 81). Since the big Other (qua Ⱥ, i.e. in all its inconsistency) is only available to femininity (in Lacan's graph it is inscribed in the feminine field), this means that, in Lacan's words, 'she has a supplementary jouissance compared to what the phallic function designates by way of jouissance'. One consequence of this is that, since woman's supplementary *jouissance* cannot be controlled by man as it relates to the inconsistency of the big Other (the Real gaps in the symbolic order), 'we would be wrong not to see that, contrary to what people say, it is nevertheless they [women] who possess men' (Lacan, 1998b, 73).

To put it bluntly, the advantage of the feminine position over the masculine one is that she can reach a jouissance 'beyond the phallus' (Lacan, 1998b, 74): while man is locked in compulsive symbolic identification via its relationship with the excluded and fantasised about *objet a*, woman has a chance to disengage from this masculine compulsion to symbolise and, crucially, 'enjoy' the Real inconsistency of the symbolic field – the fact that, to use one of Žižek's most rehearsed slogans, 'the big Other does not exist'.[2] Man's *jouissance* is by definition 'the jouissance of the idiot' (Lacan, 1998b, 81), the (fundamentally masturbatory) phallic enjoyment which never reaches the Other; woman, on the contrary, has a chance to enjoy the Other.

As described by Lacan, instead of pretending to *have* the phallus (masculine position), woman *is* the phallus: she fully vindicates the negativity contained in the phallus as signifier of lack (see Lacan, 1977, 321). From this angle, the cliché whereby man is split between the domain of instrumental rationality (work, duty, authority, etc.) and sexuality (his relation to women) hits the target, provided we add that the former is entirely dependent on the latter: if we remove the external reference to *jouissance*, the symbolic order suddenly collapses.

It is in this precise sense that, according to Žižek, we should read Lacan's thesis that 'woman is a symptom of man': woman (or whatever speaking being assuming the feminine position) functions as the symptomatic receptacle of *jouissance* that man (or whatever human being assuming the masculine position) has to disavow if he is to lend consistency to his symbolic status: '"Woman is a symptom of man" means that *man himself exists only through woman qua his symptom*; all his ontological consistency hangs on, is suspended from his symptom, is "externalised" in his symptom' (Žižek, 2001a, 155). To fully make sense of this reading, however, we need to consider the difference between the psychoanalytic symptom and the medical symptom. In psychoanalytic terms, a symptom is not merely a sign revealing some deep-seated disorder, but more precisely *a sign of disavowed enjoyment*, a reference to some kernel of libidinal investment that has to be repressed if the field is to function smoothly. In Lacan's later work, symptom becomes *sinthome*, a term intended to capture the purely libidinal status of the psychoanalytic symptom as 'the way in which each subject enjoys the unconscious, in so far as the unconscious determines him' (Lacan, unpublished seminar 1974–5, 18 February 1975).[3] Woman as symptom of man thus confirms the impossibility of the sexual relationship, since man can only confront his symptom by 'gentrifying' it into *objet a*.

Such a view of femininity, however, could still be seen to corroborate the standard feminist critique of phallocentrism. Žižek openly confronts this potential deadlock:

> Feminists are usually repulsed by Lacan's insistence on the feminine 'not-all'. Does it not imply that women are somehow excluded from fully participating in the Symbolic order, unable to wholly integrate themselves into it, condemned to leading a

parasitical existence? And, truly, do not these propositions belong to the best vein of patriarchal ideology, do they not bear witness to a hidden normativity to the detriment of woman? Man is able to find his identity in the Symbolic, to assume fully his symbolic mandate, whereas woman is condemned to hysterical splitting, to wearing masks, to not wanting what she pretends to want. How are we to conceive of this feminine resistance to symbolic identification? (Žižek, 1993, 57).

Žižek replies to these questions with a kind of *reductio ad absurdum*: if every masculine portrayal of femininity is biased, what would the 'proper' feminist one be? In other words, can we really account for a 'feminine substance' pre-existent and opposed to the masculine one? As suggested at the beginning of this section, this is precisely the way to miss the originality of Lacan's formulas of sexuation, since they tells us that:

> woman's exclusion does not mean that some positive entity is prevented from being integrated into the symbolic order: it would be wrong to conclude, from 'not-all woman is submitted to the phallic signifier,' that there is something in her which is not submitted; there is no exception, and 'woman' is this very nonexistent 'nothing' which nonetheless makes the existing elements 'not-all' (Žižek, 1993, 57–8).

Far from plunging us back into the pitfalls of patriarchal domination, the insistence on the radical inconsistency of feminine sexuality allows Žižek, with Lacan, to assert woman's ontological priority over man, *since this inconsistency is also the fundamentally repressed truth of the masculine position.* For instance, when he reminds us that Lacan's answer to Freud's *Was will das Weib* ('What does woman want?') is 'a Master whom she will be able to dominate/manipulate', Žižek is actually asserting the intrinsic superiority of woman over man:

> ... does this mean that woman is structurally, formally, in her very definition, immature, an immature subject? Yes – but not in the simple sense that would oppose her to a 'mature' man who doesn't need a Master to tell him what he wants, who can

autonomously set his own limits. What this condition amounts to is, rather, that woman is a true subject, a subject at its most fundamental, while man is a ridiculous fake, a false pretender (Žižek, 2006a, 91).

The main ambiguity surrounding this discussion can be summarised with the following over-arching question: is *jouissance féminine* Real insofar as it is beyond speech, and thus resists symbolisation, as Fink (see Fink, 1995, 107) and most of Lacan's readers have it? Against this persuasion, Žižek insists that Lacan identifies *jouissance féminine* with the *jouissance* of speech, and not simply with what is beyond speech. Far from betraying a contradiction, this suggests that, from the feminine perspective, to be within speech and outside speech is one and the same thing, provided we radicalise the function of speech beyond its phallic role, i.e. beyond the masculine logic of symbolic totalisation through the exception. Thus, *jouissance* of speech effectively corresponds to the Lacanian *jouissance de l'Autre* – and it is precisely this modality of enjoyment that Žižek defends as intimately subversive. In *The Parallax View*, for instance, he goes as far as to argue that feminine *jouissance* of speech is comparable to a kind of 'endangered species' in our contemporary post-ideological universe, since in such universe 'what addresses us is a direct "desublimated" call of *jouissance*, no longer masked in an ideological narrative proper' (Žižek, 2006a, 188). As a rule, his argument is accompanied by a vivid narrative exemplification:

> Imagine (a real clinical case) two love-partners who excite one another by verbalizing, telling one another their innermost sexual fantasies to such a degree that they reach full orgasm without touching, just as the effect of 'mere talking'. The result of such an excess of intimacy is not difficult to guess: after such a radical exposure, they will no longer be able to maintain their amorous link – too much has been said, or, rather, the spoken word, the big Other, was too directly flooded by *jouissance*, so the two are embarrassed by one another's presence and slowly drift apart, they start to avoid one another's presence. This, not a full perverse orgy, is the true excess: not 'putting your innermost fantasies into practice instead of just talking about them', but, pre-

cisely, talking about them, allowing them to invade the medium of the big Other to such an extent that one can literally "fuck with words", that the elementary, constitutive, barrier between language and *jouissance* breaks down. Measured by this standard, the most extreme 'real orgy' is a poor substitute (Žižek, 2006a, 188–9).

This clinical case functions as a perfect illustration of Žižek's conviction that Lacan's *jouissance féminine* should be located fully within, and not outside, the symbolic field.[4] It is, literally, a case of bringing about the Real dimension (the Real of *jouissance*) inherent to or 'secreted' by the Symbolic (the big Other *qua* language, the desexualised domain of symbolic exchange). It is not a matter of stepping out of the Symbolic so as to identify with what is in excess of it (masculine phallic *jouissance*); but, quite differently, of identifying with the Symbolic (excluding nothing) and yet being able to elicit its Real core.

On the basis of this reading, Žižek contends that, far from working as an anti-feminist stance, Lacan's formulas grant woman a revolutionary role, since it is precisely the absence of the gesture of identification-cum-exclusion that threatens to expose the inconsistency of the big Other.

Looked at from a slightly skewed perspective, however, this key point acquires a different resonance. If we consider the feminine stance today, in an age which, as Lacan had predicted, is threatened more and more with the apocalyptic prospect of 'the impossible saturation of the Symbolic by the Real of *jouissance*' (Žižek, 2006a, 193), does not such a stance signal simultaneously a return to symbolisation, albeit in a radically different modality? Žižek's argument would appear to acquire a truly philosophical ambiguity: the 'openness' of our post-ideological universe is one that can lead us either to a permanent explosion of primitive, unmediated superegoic Real, or to the 'Real with the Symbolic' – to a disintegration of the Symbolic which can only take place after the Symbolic itself has been reinstated in its ideological dignity. However, while the superegoic Real of the masculine position tends by definition to 'confirm the rule' – to strengthen the grip of the law *qua* symbolic order – the feminine not-all dissolves the masculine universal by transforming its external reference to *jouissance* into a mode of enjoyment *that can only manifest itself as a form of symbolisation* – more precisely, *as the minimal difference between symbolisation and its gap*. When Žižek claims that the true revolutionary act implies an intervention in the obscene underground domain of the Real ('Acheronta movebo') in order to change it (see Žižek, 2006a, 366), what he has in mind is the feminine not-all, where the Symbolic emerges as always-already impregnated with the explosive inconsistency of the Real. Transforming the Real means precisely passing from masculine *jouissance* to feminine not-all: the obscene, externalised reference to enjoyment which fortifies ideology is rearticulated as the founding feature of ideology itself. In yet another way: while the masculine field accounts for the tension between a series and its exception, the feminine one shows how 'a series and an exception *directly coincide*: the series is always a series of "exceptions", of entities which display a certain exceptional quality that qualifies them to belong to the series' (Žižek, 2000b, 115). Thus, the political potential that Žižek inscribes in feminine sexuality becomes a useful theoretical tool to demonstrate the consubstantiality of the Symbolic and the Real, and consequently the changeability of the big Other.

In his most recent books, Žižek seems to advance the following parallel apropos of the feminine not-all and the struggle against global capitalism. Firstly, all attempts to locate and politicise the multiplicity of flaws within capitalist ideology effectively end up reinforcing the grip of capitalism, since, as we have seen, the peculiar strength of the capitalist machine lies in 'its constant self-revolutionizing ... the constant overcoming of its own limit' (Žižek, 2006a, 318). This indicates that we only need a slight shift in perspective to realise that 'all the activity of "resistance", of bombarding those in power with impossible "subversive" (ecological, feminist, antiracist, antiglobalist...) demands, looks like an internal process of feeding the machine of power, providing the material to keep it in motion' (Žižek, 2006a, 334). From the viewpoint of Lacan's formulas, these demands correspond to 'masculine' endeavours to symbolise a given (anti-capitalist) field, and are therefore inevitably sustained by a secret liaison with what they seem to contest. The classic Žižekian example here, as we have seen in Chapter 6, is that of the anti-racist struggle as inherently sustained by illicit fantasies. In contrast to this attitude, Žižek proposes a new 'ethics of passive aggression', whose ultimate function would be that of eluding the urge to 'symbolise' and, instead – in line with the logic of the feminine not-all – force the dominant symbolic field to open up to its inconsistent (Real) gaps, where symbolisation proves impossible:

> The threat today is not passivity but pseudo-activity, the urge to 'be active', to 'participate', to mask the Nothingness of what goes on. People intervene all the time, 'do something'; academics participate in meaningless 'debates', and so forth, and the truly difficult thing is to step back, to withdraw from all this. Those in power often prefer even a 'critical' participation, a dialogue, to silence – just to engage us in a 'dialogue', to make sure our ominous passivity is broken (Žižek, 2006a, 335).

It is in this context that we should place Žižek's rejection of the ideology of human rights: the problem with the universalisation of humanism is the abandonment of the only point from which a given symbolic context could be reconfigured, i.e. the perspective of the abyssal, 'inhuman' remainder that resists symbolisation and thus silently sabotages the system. The contemplation of the 'attitude of passive aggression as a proper radical political gesture' is, for Žižek, 'the necessary first step which, as it were, clears the ground, opens up the place, for true activity, for an act that will actually change the coordinates of the constellation' (Žižek, 2006a, 342). The violent character of this gesture should not be missed; conceived as the exact opposite of those irrational outbursts of aimless violence (*passages à l'acte*) which speak for impotent passivity, the inactivity theorised by Žižek is meant as a violent gesture that threatens the very foundations of the status quo:

> Violence is needed – but *what* violence? There is violence and violence: there are violent *passages à l'acte* which merely bear witness to the agent's impotence; there is a violence the true aim of which is to make sure that nothing will change – in a Fascist display of violence, something spectacular should happen all the time so that, precisely, nothing will really happen; and there is the violent act of actually changing the basic coordinates of a constellation. In order for the last kind of violence to take place, *this very place should be opened up* through a gesture which is thoroughly violent in its impassive refusal, through a gesture of pure

withdrawal in which – to quote Mallarmé – *rien n'aura eu lieu que le lieu*, nothing will have taken place but the place itself (Žižek, 2006a, 381).[5]

The place, of course, is ontologically empty, and the feminine stance ultimately relies on the awareness that the void of the Real is simply the Symbolic in the modality of not-all. The paradox of passive aggression is clearly representative of the feminine stance: in such a condition there would be no big Other to guarantee the stability of our symbolic space, but only a series of extremely fragile symptoms preceding the catastrophic collapse of our universe of sense. One can see how the shift from masculine to feminine accompanies the shift, in Lacan, from the notion of symptom to that of *sinthome*: with the latter we have definitely entered the feminine universe described in *Seminar XX*, a universe permanently penetrated by *jouissance*, where no a priori law is able to generate a minimum of symbolic identification, since there is no external symptom onto which to anchor meaning. In a way, then, we are back to the defence of masochism discussed in Part II: we can only accomplish a truly political act after we have 'died to ourselves'; only if grounded in symbolic death can our activity lead to political change.

18
The Zero-level of Femininity: the Real as Symbolic Failure

By re-opening the debate on Lacan's theorisation of feminine sexuality, which had characterised the 70s and 80s, Žižek urges us to recognise the outstanding attribute of femininity in woman's privileged relationship with the ontological void of the subject. To strengthen his point he often draws on Lacan's notion of masquerade: it is the radical contingency and open artificiality of the positive features assumed by woman that speak for her closeness to the zero level of subjectivity, since in Žižek's view the outcome of this typically feminine masquerade of 'shifting identities' is the appearance of the fundamental gap, or lack, that *is* the subject:

> The loss a woman has to assume to become one is not the renunciation of masculinity but, paradoxically, the loss of something which, precisely, forever prevents her from fully becoming a woman – 'femininity' is a masquerade, a mask supplementing a failure to become a woman (Žižek, 2000a, 272).

Above all, this indicates that femininity, much more readily than masculinity, can be conceptualised as the minimal formal difference between what the subject is 'in herself' and what she is 'for the other': the latter will never coincide with the former precisely because the former stands for a reference to the empty framework that grounds subjectivity:

> Woman can never be caught, one can never come up with her, one can either endlessly approach her or overtake her, for the

very reason that 'woman in herself' designates no substantial content but just a purely formal cut, a limit that is always missed – this purely formal cut is the subject qua $ (Žižek, 1995).

We can put this in more straightforward Lacanian terms: woman is split in such a way that her consciousness (the masquerade which makes up what she is 'for the other') does not hinge upon exclusion, but exclusively upon itself – upon the very inconsistency/artificiality of the mask. Contrary to man, then, woman displays a propensity to reveal that behind appearances there is nothing but the quintessential core of appearance, the very gap that 'unlocks' the space for the materialization of appearance itself. This emerges in the different way each sex relates to the other. While man is convinced that he should be loved for what he really is (his positive characteristics, the 'social mandate' he ascribes to himself), woman, as Lacan puts it, wants to be loved for what she is not,[1] for the contingent masks she wears:

> A man stupidly believes that, beyond his symbolic title, there is deep in himself some substantial content, some hidden treasure which makes him worthy of love, whereas a woman knows that there is nothing beneath the mask – her strategy is precisely to preserve this 'nothing' of her freedom ... (Žižek, 1995)

It is fairly evident that the notion of masquerade works on the same level as that of hysteria. The dread of feminine hysteria, which at the turn of the last century marked the advent of psychoanalysis, essentially coincides with the dread of void, as Žižek illustrates in his analysis of Otto Weininger's *Sex and Character* (see Žižek, 1994a, 137–64). What frightens and frustrates man (and as it is particularly evident in the works of fin-de-siècle male artists such as Edvard Munch, August Strindberg and Franz Kafka – but the list could be endless!) is not so much the opacity of woman as such but the trouble in locating a stable subject behind the masks of femininity. The very notion of *femme fatale* in *film noir*, a modern version of the lady in courtly love, is predicated upon the delusive supposition that femininity exists as a positive series of features. However cold, cruel, mysterious and manipulative, *femme fatale* is still an identifiable entity, and as such *a desirable one* for man. Thus, she belongs entirely in the masculine symbolic economy, where it functions as a compromise formation, a stopgap, a fantasy projection, in short a desperate strategy through which man endeavours to avoid the Real *qua* empty kernel of the subject – ultimately, the empty kernel of his own being reflected in that of woman. At the same time, however, bringing to light *femme fatale* as part and parcel of the 'obscene' fantasmatic support to patriarchy, implies that patriarchy itself is undermined.

On the strength of this argument, Žižek claims that each masculine definition of femininity is to be regarded as a patriarchal stratagem aimed at establishing and underpinning the domain of the phallus. However, by converse, this also means that all feminist attempts to define a 'feminine discourse' beyond, outside or against the phallic function are doomed to fail, since they inexorably end up validating the masculine logic of the exception. Much more productive, he argues, would be to stick to the Lacanian insight that woman stages the ontological limit of the subject, rather than the epistemological one. That is to say: while the 'beyond' of man is structured as a plausible and transgressive fiction (*objet a*), the 'beyond' of woman is 'a fiction of the fiction' (Hegel's appearance *qua* appearance), i.e. the pure formal essence of fictionality that can only be rendered as a connection with void. And this void is none other than the kernel of the symbolic order, the traumatic break in the causal link on account of which 'the big Other does not exist'.

What we should not forget is that the status of this Other accessible to woman is, in its deepest connotation, that of the peculiar combination of the Symbolic and the Real. In a manner which proves to be consistent with his overall project, in his analysis of sexual difference Žižek emphasises the anti-humanistic equation subject-void as well the non-existence of the big Other *qua* ideological fantasy.[2] His resolve in bringing the question of femininity back into the equation is therefore functional to his political attempt to theorise a break with the crucial philosophical presupposition of the Enlightenment. Choosing as distinguished allies both Hegel and Lacan, Žižek maintains that 'the subject is no longer the Light of Reason opposed to the non-transparent, impenetrable Stuff (of Nature, Tradition...); his very kernel, the gesture which opens up the space for the Light of *Logos*, is absolute negativity *qua* 'night of the world' (Žižek, 1994a, 145). Hence the prominence accorded to the Lacanian Real as the traumatic point of absolute freedom where the subject, in its negativity, meets the non-existence of the big Other. As previously discussed, in his latest works Žižek has moved more and more resolutely towards conceptualising the Real as a dimension which is fully consubstantial with the symbolic order:

> the Real is not external to the Symbolic: the Real is the Symbolic itself in the modality of not-all, lacking an external Limit/ Dimension. In this precise sense, the line of separation between the Symbolic and the Real is not only a symbolic gesture par excellence, but the very founding gesture of the Symbolic and to step into the Real does not entail abandoning language, throwing oneself into the abyss of the chaotic Real, but, on the contrary, dropping the very allusion to some external point of reference which eludes the Symbolic (Žižek, 2003b, 69–70).[3]

Unquestionably, this is one of the most accurate definitions of the Real delivered by Žižek, one that substantiates his insight that the Real can only be expressed in the form of the very void-experience generated by the radically fragmented character of our symbolic existence.

This brings us back to the deadlock of the sexual relationship – to Lacan's thesis that 'every relationship between the sexes can take place only against the background of a fundamental impossibility' (Žižek, 1994a, 155). Or, more pointedly:

> In so far as sexual difference is a Real that resists symbolization, the sexual relationship is condemned to remain an asymmetrical non-relationship in which the Other, our partner, prior to being a subject, is a Thing, an 'inhuman partner'; as such, the sexual relationship cannot be transposed into a symmetrical relation- ship between pure subjects (Žižek, 1994a, 108–9).

The point to re-emphasise is that the terms 'masculine' and 'femi- nine' do not designate two positive sets of properties (active vs. passive, reason vs. emotion, etc.), but instead two asymmetrical or uncoordinated ways in which the subject *fails* in his or her bid for identity. On this account, 'masculine' and 'feminine' should not be regarded as two opposite parts of a whole; quite differently, they express two completely unrelated failures to attain this whole (see Žižek, 1994a, 159–60).

The analysis of the specific nature of sexual failure allows us to make further ground on the question of the rapport between the Symbolic and the Real. To recapitulate the argument so far: every symbolic order produces an excessive, 'supernumerary' element that eludes the logic of the signifying system and yet, precisely through its elusiveness, secretly supports its functioning. Meaning operates, literally, through an elusive/fantasmatic obstacle that allows for some kind of disavowed anchoring. We 'make sense' by secretly relying on an excessive element that needs to be repressed if sense is to emerge; we hang on to meaning by excluding a disturbing surplus of meaning. When, then, do we encounter the Real? From the privileged viewpoint of Lacan's formulas of sexuation, precisely the moment we dissolve the masculine logic of the exception and, adopting the feminine position, force the Symbolic *to fully become itself*, i.e. to overlap with its traumatic structuring deadlock. Meaning dissolves into the Real the moment our symbolic existence in thought, language and communication extends over to the unconscious structuring kernel of our being. The feminine Real (the radical inconsistency of woman's desire) is the Symbolic in the guise of 'not-all'.

What we have here is an exemplification of the paradox embodied by Hegelian universality. As suggested in Part II, Žižek follows Hegel in considering universality a radically divided field perpetually attempting to conceal its founding division by presenting itself as a neutral container of a multitude of particular struggles. What is truly universal, therefore, is the very 'crack' that pertains to what presents itself as neutral universality. The same with Lacan's formulas of sexuation: while masculinity stands for universality *qua* phallic function, what is truly universal is the fracture that structures this function. The masculine 'all' is in effect nothing but a stratagem to obfuscate the underlying presence of the non-symbolisable universal limit/antagonism through which masculinity is able to emerge and claim, spuriously, its universal reliability. Ultimately, only through the feminine 'not-all' can one vindicate the universal divide that tacitly structures the masculine bid for (phallic) universality.

In Žižek's Hegelian method, an identical mechanism defines the relationship between immanence and transcendence. On the one hand, masculinity relies on the disavowed tension between the two terms, since symbolic/phallic immanence is achieved through the gesture of 'transcendentalising' the Real, positing it as radically external to any possible process of symbolisation. On the other hand, femininity has a chance to show that what was made to appear as a transcendental gap was always-already 'included in the picture', part of the very symbolic/immanent texture of masculinity. In short, woman's role is a profoundly sobering one: it makes us aware that, as a power-related strategy, transcendence corresponds to a perspective illusion binding us to the symbolic field, for any transcendental gesture is merely a way to disavow the divide that originally brands the Symbolic itself.

From a Lacanian standpoint, this (implicitly false) gesture of 'transcendentalisation', which brings about the symbolic order, is by definition masculine. The main problem with it is, strictly speaking, that of abstraction, for the masculine strategy responsible for symbolisation displaces the structural, concrete antagonism of its field into two main forms of secondary antagonism. Firstly, the antagonism between two radically opposed poles, which leads us straight into the deadlock of our geopolitical constellation: the dualism of Us vs. Them (civilisation vs. terror, tolerance vs. fundamentalism, good vs. evil, etc.), which is always the result of a perspective illusion whose deepest function is to externalise (and thus neutralise) the unbearable weight of the split within Us, the fact that 'we never coincide with ourselves'. Secondly, the masculine reliance on a transcendental gesture opens up the symbolic field itself to the struggle for hegemony between a multitude of different actors/signifiers. Against these two gentrified modes of antagonism, Žižek holds on to the Lacanian 'monist' insight that there is only a (radically split) One, whose antagonistic core is the difference between itself and the original void that marks its place of inscription.[4] The Symbolic is never in its place, for this original place is a void that can never be fully filled up; consequently, the Symbolic can only be given as a distortion generated by the disproportionate relationship between itself and the lack that always-already subtends it. This minimal difference between the element and its place – the 'bone in the throat' that structures the symbolic field as its internal limit/inconsistency – is of course none other than the Real. And the key point is that ideology relies precisely upon the ambiguity of this Real, upon its mobilisation into *objet petit a*, the sublime/obscene object targeted by fantasy.

Stricto sensu, we achieve ideological symbolisation through the fantasy we invest in *objet a qua* elusive residue or excess that surreptitiously gives body to the gap between ideology and its empty place of inscription. From the masculine standpoint, the symbolic field totalises itself through a secret libidinal liaison with *objet a*. Against this mechanism, femininity activates the logic of 'not-all', whereby the secret liaison with *objet a* is rearticulated as a fundamentally intractable relationship that defines the symbolic field itself, since *objet a* is exposed as an inconsistent object through which the trauma of void is simply camouflaged, or gentrified. Femininity thus holds the potential to bring to light the truth of the rapport between *objet a* and Real *qua* structuring empty core of the symbolic field. Ultimately, then, the Real of sexual difference relates to the incompatibility of the masculine and feminine ways to deal with the excess generated by symbolisation. While masculinity turns this excess into *objet a*, femininity restores it as Real – as the explosive nucleus of negativity consubstantial with every symbolisation.

19
The Miracle of Love and the Real of Christianity

At this stage we should introduce the Žižekian differentiation between sexuality and love. To put it simply: while desire is on the side of the Symbolic, love manages to disturb the Real. In order to understand this differentiation we shall first look at Žižek's assessment of love as a contingent inter-subjective event; in a second step, the concept will be examined in connection with Žižek's political evaluation of Christianity.

To Žižek, who here repeats Lacan almost verbatim, love between two individuals coincides, essentially, with a miraculous 'transferential' encounter whereby we exchange what we do not possess (see Žižek, 1994a, 103–4),[1] an encounter predicated upon our being 'subjects of lack'. Let us try to unravel the meaning of this statement. As we have seen, the relationship always takes place against the background of a fundamental impossibility. The cause of this impossibility is the asymmetrical way in which the sexes relate to the Real, the very obstacle to their full assertion as subjects. This incompatibility simultaneously manifests itself in the way the sexes relate to each other, that is to say: since they symbolise the world in radically asymmetrical ways, this asymmetry also emerges in the way they symbolise each other. The way woman tries (and fails) to make sense of man is incompatible with the way man tries (and fails) to make sense of woman. Put in yet another way, man and woman fantasise about each other in profoundly unco-ordinated manners, as Žižek illustrates by commenting on a TV advert for a beer:

> The first part stages the well-known fairy-tale anecdote: a girl
> walks along a stream, sees a frog, takes it gently into her lap,

kisses it, and, of course, the ugly frog miraculously turns into a beautiful young man. However, the story isn't over yet: the young man casts a covetous glance at the girl, draws her towards him, kisses her – and she turns into a bottle of beer, which the man holds triumphantly in his hand. ... For the woman, the point is that her love and affection (symbolized by the kiss) turn a frog into a beautiful man, a full phallic presence (in Lacan's mathems, big Phi [Φ]); for the man, it is to reduce the woman to a partial object, the cause of his desire (in Lacan's mathemes, the *objet petit a*). Because of this asymmetry, 'there is no sexual relationship': we have either a woman with a frog or a man with a bottle of beer – what we can never obtain is the 'natural' couple of the beautiful woman and man. ... Why not? Because the phantasmic support of this 'ideal couple' would have been the inconsistent figure of *a frog embracing a bottle of beer* (Žižek, 1997, 74).

The main obstacle to a fully harmonious relationship is that we connect with the loved one through an object which is neither directly related to the other nor the same one for the two sexes. While man desires woman as *objet a*, woman desires man as the signifier of the phallic function of symbolisation (Φ). What should be noted is that, despite their incompatibility, both desires are sustained by an ontological lack filled out by different fantasmatic features: woman *qua objet a* conceals the empty kernel of the feminine subject; man *qua* phallus corresponds to an empty, desexualised field. We are now in a better position to understand the meaning of love as 'the exchange of what we do not possess'. The paradox is that the loved one owes its status to 'something' that he/she does not actually possess. Given this deadlock, Žižek's point is that love can only emerge as a kind of de-potentiation of our subjective status as objects of desire. That is to say: we become 'worthy of love' when we abdicate the privileged position of object of desire and make manifest to the other that the feature(s) that made us 'special and unique' in fact coincide with a missing link in our subjective configuration. In this sense love is, literally, an 'answer of the Real': we engage in a loving relationship by acknowledging that our status as object of desire is Real. Love therefore involves a risky passage from object to subject, insofar as the loved one, self-assured in his/her position as object of desire, suddenly appears in the eyes of the loving one as lacking it, as frail and vulnerable – which is precisely what always-already characterises the position of the loving one:

> Therein consists, according to Lacan, love's most sublime moment: in this inversion when the beloved object endeavours to deliver himself from the impasse of his position, from the impossibility of complying with the lover's demand, by assuming himself the position of the lover, by reaching his hand back to the lover and thus answering the lover's lack/desire with his own lack (Žižek, 2001a, 58).

The conclusion to draw is that love *qua* answer of the Real is on the side of 'not-all', for it can only be experienced by a subject aware of its radical inconsistency: 'Only a lacking, vulnerable being is capable of love: the ultimate mystery of love, therefore, is that incompleteness is, in a way, higher than completion' (Žižek, 2003b, 115); or, along the same lines, 'true love is precisely the ... move of *forsaking the promise of Eternity itself for an imperfect individual*' (Žižek, 2003b, 13). At this stage in the discussion, the difference between sex and love should appear fairly obvious: while in sexuality pure and simple we get stuck in the dialectics of desire and symbolic fantasy – since, strictly speaking, the partner 'functions as a prop for our indulging in fantasies' – 'it is only through love that we can reach the Real (of the) Other' (Žižek, 2003b, 116), for in love we are forced to exchange what we do not have, i.e. we can only experience ourselves as subjects of lack (not-all). However, despite the fact that the disparity between the loving and the loved one can be dissolved through the 'answer of the Real', what needs to be added is that 'the asymmetry persists' (Žižek, 1994a, 104), which explains the status of love as a miraculous event that permits us to endure the very deadlock of the sexual relationship.

Together with sexuality, and in direct connection with the theorisation of love, the context in which the question of the Real in Žižek returns without fail is religion, and more specifically Christianity. Žižek essentially brandishes Christianity as the religion that, more than any other, embodies the potential ethico-political impact of the Real. In his defence of Christianity, Žižek has drawn upon himself a heavy dose of criticism from different quarters, particularly – as one might expect – from leftist and generally Marxist or post-Marxist positions (see for example Parker, 2004). In our opinion Žižek's stance is too often taken at face value. What risks going amiss is the theoretical focus of his argument, which changes radically the very standard perception of Christianity itself – as usual with Žižek, we are dealing with a 'symptomatic reading'.

Fully aware that in modernity religion cannot function as a 'binding force of social substance' (Žižek, 2003b, 5), he aims to restore the subversive kernel of Christianity by claiming that 'this kernel is accessible *only* to a materialist approach – and vice versa: to become a true dialectical materialist, one should go through the Christian experience' (Žižek, 2003b, 6). It is, first and foremost, a question of belief. Although in the enlightened West nobody 'really believes' anymore, this attitude of cynical distance from direct belief (as we have seen in Part I) is symptomatic of our secret immersion, enjoyment and identification with the values expressed by our symbolic universe.[2] By shunning direct belief as an old-fashioned stance practiced only by the 'primitive other' we actually consign ourselves wholly to the merciless rule of capitalist ideology – which, of course, demands unwavering belief! Against the disavowed and opportunistic functioning of today's belief, Žižek fully endorses the Christian narrative of death and resurrection by reading it through Saint Paul, i.e. as a powerful injunction to undergo 'symbolic death' so as to generate the conditions for an institutional reconfiguration of symbolic space. No wonder Žižek sees Saint Paul as a Leninist: what matters to Saint Paul is the 'true Leninist business ... of organizing the new party called the Christian community' (Žižek, 2003b, 9). The whole point of Žižek's insisted reference to 'Pauline militancy' is that it allows him to set up a powerful connection between Saint Paul and Christ. The aim is to demonstrate that the subversive core of Christianity lies in the structural coincidence of Fall and Redemption, insofar as the Fall popularised by Christ's 'narrative' represents a shattering encounter with abstract negativity that signals the intervention of the Real, thus prompting the birth of the new symbolic community (the Holy Spirit) via Saint Paul.

To put it another way, we could say that Žižek conflates the Christian narrative with the Lacanian logic of the identification with the symptom. The symptom here is explicitly connoted as the 'excremental remainder' of the very process of symbolisation that defines the Christian doctrine:

> Christianity's entire theological edifice relies on such an excremental identification – on the identification with the poor figure of the suffering Christ dying in pain between the two thieves. The artifice by means of which Christianity became the ruling ideology was to combine this radical excremental identification with full endorsement of the existing hierarchical social order (Žižek, 2000a, 229).

Christ as excremental remainder, therefore, functions both as closure and potential breaking point of the symbolic order it belongs to. For that reason he represents a thoroughly ambiguous figure.

In *The Fragile Absolute*, however, Žižek reassesses this ambiguity by asserting the core of the Christian legacy as a fully-blown militant attitude of a strictly speaking non-humanist kind, one beginning with a radical, traumatic gesture of 'uncoupling'. By uncoupling Žižek means the arduous work of disengaging from the logic that enjoins us to our particular symbolic order. This intervention is best epitomised by Pauline *agape*, the work of love, which involves the suspension of superego pressure and, consequently, of the link between the law and its transgression: '*the proper Christian uncoupling suspends not so much the explicit laws but, rather, their implicit spectral obscene supplement*' (Žižek, 2000b, 130). In other words, Christianity disturbs the balance of the masculine position, where the totalised field is sustained by the exception. The proper difference introduced by Christianity, Žižek argues, is that the exception is always-already embedded in universality: the inconsistency normally neutralised by the exception is inscribed as the very foundational feature of Christianity. This feature is of course Pauline *agape*, love, defined by Saint Paul in *Corinthians* as a dimension accessible only by incomplete beings, beings aware of the fundamental incompleteness of their knowledge: 'love is not an exception to the All of knowledge, but precisely that "nothing" which makes even the complete series/field of knowledge incomplete' (Žižek, 2000b, 146).

As a predictable result, Žižek maintains that the dimension of Christian love, in its feminine guise of not-all, erodes and subverts the given order by ignoring the masculine logic of retribution/transgression and situating itself fully within such order. The most unequivocal example of this logic is perhaps the famous phrase from Jesus' 'Sermon on the Mount' in the Gospel of Saint Matthew: 'If someone strikes you on the right cheek, turn to him the other also' (Matthew 5:39). As Žižek notes (see Žižek, 2000b, 125), what is at stake here is not stupid (potentially perverse) masochism, but rather an attempt to interrupt the vicious cycle of the logic of retribution and, simultaneously, cause a kind of 'unplugging' from social substance. The implication is that obeying the law thoroughly proves to be much more subversive than transgressing it, since complete identification allows one to perceive and bring to the surface the very inconsistency that grounds the law itself. From a sociopolitical perspective, then, what does Christian love *qua* feminine position tell us? In Žižek's words, 'that in order effectively to liberate oneself from the grip of existing social reality, one should first renounce the transgressive fantasmatic supplement that attaches us to it' (Žižek, 2000b, 149). To Žižek, such a renunciation is not only ethical, but also eminently political, as it is aimed at redefining the very framework of the social.

In the final analysis, it is according to the above reasoning that we should also read the mystery of the Crucifixion. Žižek insists that Christ's death should be read as a political event signalling the suspension of meaning through the dissolution of the symptom *qua* grounding exception. The Crucifixion is therefore, *stricto sensu*, a feminine event, where 'the very structure of sacrifice, as it were, sublates itself, giving birth to a new subject no longer rooted in a particular substance, redeemed of all particular links (the "Holy Spirit")' (Žižek, 2000b, 158). The specific modality of sacrifice under scrutiny here is a sacrifice 'without object', that is to say an empty gesture which is not tied to any kind of (no matter how unconscious) opportunistic logic, but rather aimed at the very inconsistency of the symbolic edifice. This sacrifice is typically feminine: 'While men sacrifice themselves for a *Thing* (country, freedom, honor), only women are able to sacrifice themselves for *nothing*. (Or: men are moral, while only women are properly ethical)' (Žižek, 2001c, 78). With regard to the connection between femininity and Christianity, then, Žižek's wager is that both fields are, in their deepest connotations, defined by the implicitly revolutionary gesture of the 'empty sacrifice'. It is precisely this empty, non-symbolisable gesture that sets up the connection with the Real breaking point of a particular order, since the Real can only be accounted for in terms of an imperceptible and ultimately illusory appearance *stripped of any symbolic reference*, an evanescent and utterly substance-less *Schein*. Among the three dimensions of the Real referred to in Chapter 5, then, the crucial one for Žižek's approach to Christianity is the 'imaginary Real', which he links to the figure of Christ as the miserable, abject body on the cross bathed in a sublime light.

As Žižek regularly acknowledges, his reading is heavily influenced by Hegel's interpretation of Christ's demise. In his *Lectures on the Philosophy of Religion*, Hegel comments on the Christian narrative of 'rebirth through radical self-contraction': Christ's sacrifice is a gesture of sublation (*Aufhebung*) whereby the divine, as it were, 'traverses its own fantasy' (identifies with its own lack) for the birth of a new subject, the new community bound together by the Holy Spirit. Rather than breeding disenchantment, cynicism and resignation, the knowledge that 'the king is naked' – that God is the empty recipient of an impossible demand – works, in Žižek's reading, as an exhortation to reconfigure the status of a given social totality. Let us not forget that Hegel defines Christ as 'the God-Man' whose 'absolute finitude' is reflected in the fact that he died 'the aggravated death of the evil-doer', which implies that 'in Him humanity was carried to its furthest point'. The 'divine finitude' that Hegel reads into the death of Christ, however, implies that the latter be intended 'in its polemical attitude towards outward things', rather than as a celebration of religion *per se*:

> Not only is the act [Christ's death] whereby the natural will yields itself up here represented in a sensible form, but all that is peculiar to the individual, all those interests and personal ends with which the natural will can occupy itself, all that is great and counted in the world, is at the same time buried in the grave of the Spirit. This is the revolutionary element by means of which the world is given a totally new form. And yet in this yielding up of the natural will, the finite, the Other-Being or otherness, is at the same time transfigured (Hegel, 1962, 89).

The passage is highly significant as it suggests how any radical transformation depends on the 'yielding up of the natural will', insofar
as this intrinsically divine 'passage through the zero (or lowest)
point of humanity' is 'the revolutionary element' that gives the
world 'a totally new form'. The self-effacement performed by the
'contingent divine', in other words, is the fundamental condition
for its return in the form of a new symbolic configuration:

> Now, however, a further determination comes into play – God
> has died, God is dead – this is the most frightful of all thoughts,
> that all that is eternal, all that is true is not, *that negation itself is*
> *found in God*; ... The course of thought does not, however, stop
> short here; on the contrary, thought begins to retrace its steps:
> God, that is to say, maintains Himself in this process, and the
> latter is only the death of death. God comes to life again, and
> thus things are reversed (Hegel, 1962, 91 our emphasis).

Hegel asserts the shameful death of the God-Man as the intervention of an instance of shattering negativity through which Spirit
enacts its conversion, its movement from 'negation' to 'negation of
negation' (the death of death). It is this traumatic encounter that
Žižek aims to salvage in his defence of the Christian legacy, insofar
as he sees in it a revolutionary potential, a powerful narrative telling
us that the void of the Real can be reached – that the impossible can
be accomplished. Put differently, Christ's subjective trajectory from
son of God to a miserable human being who dies on the cross abandoned by his Father, epitomises the workings of death-drive. At the
end of *The Puppet and the Dwarf*, his second book explicitly devoted
to Christianity, Žižek writes:

> The point of this book is that, at the very core of Christianity,
> there is another dimension. When Christ dies, what dies with
> him is the secret hope discernible in 'Father, why hast thou for-
> saken me?': the hope that there *is* a father who has abandoned
> me. The 'Holy Spirit' is the community deprived of its support in
> the big Other. ... Christianity ... attacks the religious hard core
> that survives even in humanism, even up to Stalinism, with its
> belief in History as the 'big Other' that decides on the 'objective
> meaning' of our deeds (Žižek, 2003b, 171).

Žižek's defence of Christianity is perfectly consistent with his attestation of atheism, in as much as it deploys as its central referent the abyss of our existential experience deprived of any support in the big Other. If taken to its extreme, this implies that 'in the figure of Christ dying on the cross, God himself turns into an atheist, experiencing himself as abandoned by God-the-Father' (Žižek, 2004c, 61). This position is modelled on Lacan's own paradoxical claim that those who are normally regarded or regard themselves as atheists (those who boldly/heroically refuse to consider the truth-potential embodied in religious faiths) are exactly the opposite of what they claim to be, i.e. the staunchest of believers (in history, science, love, human solidarity, etc.). In a typical Lacanian move, Žižek turns around the standard Marxian view of religion as the 'opium of the people' and locates in it its symptom, the thoroughly alienated and disaffected core that opens up the opposite path, which we might call 'the practice of atheism through Christianity'.[3] From this angle, Žižek remains profoundly anti-clerical and generally hostile to any form of organised religious faith. His appraisal of Christianity is a militant one, strictly in line with his symptomatic reading of Lenin. In both cases what is at stake is *freedom*, intended as the power to break with the seductive lure of symbolic efficiency. For Žižek, Christ and Lenin represent two crucial examples of an intervention that successfully politicises the constitutive excess inherent to humanity, that specific 'undead' quality known as death-drive.

Ultimately, it is this traumatic abyss of freedom which is at issue in Žižek's reading of 'Christian love'. One the best way to epitomise this paradox is by referring to the deeper meaning of the word 'betrayal'. In *The Puppet and the Dwarf*, Žižek claims that the real (Real) hero of the New Testament is Judas, since the divine plan could only be executed through his readiness to betray Christ and accept eternal damnation (see Žižek, 2003b, 16). What we are encouraged to do, therefore, is to interpret Judas' gesture of betrayal and consequent acceptance of sacrifice as *the highest expression of love*, precisely because the path to universality (inclusive of its founding negativity) necessarily implies a terrifying act of infidelity. More precisely: to 'betray out of love' entails a crucial reflexive movement whereby the loved object (Christ) is perceived as split between its empirical persona and the (empty) place it occupies, the

Real void it gives body to. In his betrayal, therefore, Judas remains faithful to what Christ represents, the Real abyss of freedom/negativity that underscores his intervention. This means that 'Christian love is a violent passion to introduce a Difference, a gap in the order of being', and simultaneously that 'violence is already the love choice as such, which tears its object out of its context, elevating it to the Thing' (Žižek, 2003b, 33). Similarly, true fidelity is always fidelity to the abyss of freedom embodied by a hero or loved person, and it is in the 'cruelty' of such a paradox that one can discern the militant edge of Žižek's understanding of love.

At the same time Žižek claims that while fidelity to the Real of freedom (the implicitly violent inscription of negativity that disturbs a given balance) is always higher than our love/fidelity to an empirical individual, the latter can emerge in all its categorical power only as a kind of side-effect:

> The message of true love is thus: even if you are everything to me, I can survive without you, I am ready to forsake you for my mission .... The underlying paradox is that love, precisely as the Absolute, should not be posited as a direct goal – it should retain the status of a byproduct, of something we get as undeserved grace. Perhaps there is no greater love than that of a revolutionary couple, where each of the two lovers is ready to abandon the other at any moment if revolution demands it. It is along these lines that we should look for the nonperverse reading of Christ's sacrifice, of his message to Judas: 'Prove to me that I am everything to you, so betray me for the sake of the revolutionary mission of both of us!' (Žižek, 2003b, 19–20).

Notes

14 Žižek Against Badiou: the Real Beyond the Event

1. Badiou maintains that 'what is proper to philosophy is not the production of universal truth, but rather the organization of their synthetic reception by forging and reformulating the category of Truth. Auguste Comte defined the philosopher as one who "specialized in generalities"' (Badiou, 2003, 108).
2. As noted by Oliver Feltham and Justin Clemens, for Badiou 'the subject ... is not limited to the recognition of an event, but extends into the prolonged investigation of the consequences of such an event. This investigation is not a passive, scholarly affair; it entails not only the active transformation of the situation in which the event occurs but also the active transformation of the human being. Thus in Badiou's philosophy there is no such thing as a subject without such a process of subjectivization' (Badiou, 2005, 5).
3. Žižek's analysis of Badiou's Event in its circular relation to the subject brings him to suggest its closeness to Althusser's notion of interpellation, as in his view Badiou (particularly in his book on St Paul) aims to describe the process of 'an individual interpellated into a subject by a Cause' (Žižek, 2000a, 145), with the consequence that Badiou's opposition of knowledge and truth turns around Althusser's opposition of ideology and science.
4. Incidentally, this is what Rex Butler's account of Žižek's Badiou misses (see Butler, 2005, 86–94).
5. 'The "doesn't stop being written" ... is the impossible, as I define it on the basis of the fact that it cannot in any case be written, and it is with this that I characterise the sexual relationship – the sexual relationship doesn't stop not being written' (Lacan, 1998b, 94).

15 'There Is No Such Thing as a Sexual Relationship': the Formal Deadlock of Sexuality

1. Žižek often plays the Real of sexual antagonism against the aseptic tolerance of sexuality typical of today's postmodern universe, which deprives sex of its disturbing yet constitutional surplus. He reminds us that sexuality is by definition violent and antagonistic, and as such it involves a certain unplugging, an instance of (psychotic) separation from what we think we are – in other words, it involves an encounter with the Real. Žižek is thus firmly against today's biopolitics of the 'sacredness of life', precisely because they contain a (political) lure: enjoy without excess,

which does not simply mean 'renounce life' (as Žižek often puts it), but more pointedly renounce the reference to the disavowed excess which holds together the symbolic configuration and which, at the same time, stands for the only way out of it. To this renunciation, he opposes his well-known formula: enjoy your symptoms! The critical point to consider here is that the very renunciation is itself sexualised, or eroticised: we enjoy precisely by restraining ourselves – as in the classic example of the ascetic monk who practices flagellation – which provides more evidence to the Lacanian thesis that there is simply no way we can get rid of the Real of *jouissance*. In fact, the main Žižekian question is not how to free ourselves from the burden of the Real but rather how to confront it.

16   *Objet a*, or the Ruse of Masculinity

1. Lacan claims that 'this $ [man *qua* barred subject] never deals with anything by way of a partner but object *a* inscribed on the other side of the bar. He is unable to attain his sexual partner, who is the Other, except inasmuch as his patner is the cause of his desire. In this respect ... this is nothing but fantasy. This fantasy, in which the subject is caught up, is as such the basis of what is expressly called the "reality principle" in Freudian theory' (Lacan,1998b, 80).
2. See the first chapter of Žižek's *The Plague of Fantasy* entitled 'The seven veils of fantasy' (Žižek, 1997, 3–44). What should not be missed is the double role of fantasy: on one hand it is directed at *objet a qua* other, on the other it refers to the interplay of ideological positions that fill the empty frame opened up by *objet a*.

17   Woman's 'Not-All' and the Paradox of Passive Aggression

1. In terms of sexual pleasure pure and simple, *feminine jouissance*, according to Žižek, is articulated around the inconsistency of woman's desire, which implies that, while masculine sexuality is centred on the teleological principle of 'phallic orgasm *qua* pleasure *par excellence*', feminine pleasure 'involves a dispersed network of particular pleasures that are not organized around some teleological central principle' (Žižek, 1994a, 160).
2. Here is how Lacan describes the feminine *jouissance* beyond the phallus: 'There is a jouissance that is hers, that belongs to the "she" that doesn't exist and doesn't signify anything. There is a jouissance that is hers about which she herself perhaps knows nothing if not that she experiences it – that much she knows' (Lacan, 1998b, 74).
3. On this evidence, it comes as no surprise that Lacan devotes so much of his unpublished seminar *Le sinthome* (1975–76) to James Joyce, whose art he regards as a perfect example of a successful answer to the failure of the paternal metaphor. To Lacan, who in the later stage of his teachings

became increasingly fond of linguistic puns, Joyce exemplifies precisely the position of a writer who *jouis*, who enjoys – or, even better, *il Joyce trop*, he enjoys too much. Lacan admired Joyce's most cryptic works such as *Ulysses* and, particularly, *Finnegans Wake*, for he saw them as attempts to bring the Real of enjoyment within the symbolic order of language as a strategy to compensate for the absence of the paternal function. More specifically, Joyce's famous epiphanies are regarded by Lacan as examples of how the subject organises its relation to the Other *without* the mediation of fantasy, *objet a*, and the neurotic loop: in the later Joyce language unties its knot to the phallic function and assumes a thoroughly 'suspended' position with regard to the big Other in all its enigmatic inconsistency. And does this position not exemplify Lacan's definition of feminine *jouissance* beyond the phallus? Amongst other things, this reference to Joyce proves the non-biological character of Lacan's formulas of sexuation.

4. A similar example is provided in *The Parallax View*: 'a promiscuous teenager may engage in extreme orgies with group sex and drugs, but what he cannot bear is the idea that his mother could be doing something similar – his orgies rely on the supposed purity of his mother, which serves as the point of exception, the external guarantee: I can do whatever I like, since I know that my mother keeps her place pure for me. ... The most difficult thing is not to violate the prohibition in a wild orgy of enjoyment, but to do this without relying on someone else who is presupposed not to enjoy so that I can enjoy: *to assume my own enjoyment directly, without mediation through another's supposed purity*' (Žižek, 2006a, 91). It is clear that this second proposition designates the feminine position.

5. This is Žižek's latest position on violence. Only a couple of years ago, however, he seemed much less certain about the classification of violent *passages à l'acte*:

    'However, ... I would emphasize that nonetheless the two dimensions – the violent *passage à l'acte* and the act proper – cannot always be clearly distinguished. Sometimes, when you are in a certain symbolical ideological deadlock, you have to explode in a violent *passage à l'acte* and then, a second time, this opens up to you a certain emancipatory perspective of passing to the act proper. ... I think that the only way an oppressed people or individual can react initially to such a situation is through some kind of irrational violent outburst which simply allows them to acquire a distance towards it. In this sense, I think that we should return to the problematic of Franz Fanon – which is now rather neglected by most postmodern theorists – and the question of at what level some kind of violence is necessary. I am not thinking about legitimizing street gangs or violence against others. What we need more is a certain violence against ourselves. In order to break out of an ideological, double-bind predicament, you need a kind of violent outburst. It is something shattering. Even if it is not physical violence, it is extreme symbolic violence, and we have to accept it. At this level I think that in order to change the existing society, this will not come about in the terms of this liberal tolerance. It will explode as a more shattering experience. And this is, I think, what is needed today: this awareness that true changes are painful' (Žižek and Daly, 2004, 120–21).

18   The Zero-level of Femininity: the Real as Symbolic Failure

1. 'It is for that which she is not that she wishes to be desired as well as loved' (Lacan, 1977, 321)
2. '(T)he supreme illusion consists precisely in this reliance on the consistency of the "big Other". The "big Other doesn't exist", as Lacan puts it: it is just a subject's presupposition – the (presup)position of an immaterial, ideal order, i.e. of Another Place that guarantees the ultimate meaning and consistency of the subject's experience. ... This "big Other" is retroactively posited, i.e., presupposed, by the subject in the very act by means of which he is caught in the cobweb of an ideology. ... This act of (presup)position is perhaps the elementary gesture of ideology ...' (Žižek, 2001a, 58–9).
3. Or, as he put it in *Organs without Bodies*, 'the Real is not simply external to the Symbolic but, rather, the Symbolic itself deprived of its externality, of its founding exception' (Žižek, 2004c, 54).
4. This is the obverse of Lacan's thesis, often asserted in Seminar XX, that 'y'a de l'un' (there is something of the one). This phrase allows us to make sense of the non existence of the sexual relationship in a more direct way, with reference to sexuality: *y'a de l'un* means that 'the two partners are never alone, since their activity has to involve a fantasmatic supplement that sustains their desire (and that can ultimately be just an imagined gaze observing them while they are engaged in sexual intercourse) ... every erotic couple is a couple of three: 1 + 1 + *a*, the "pathological" stain that disturbs the pure immersion of the couple' (Žižek, 2004c, 99). In *The Parallax View*, Žižek attempts an audacious Hegelian translation of this principle by conceptualising it as a triadic movement: we begin with copulation *a tergo*, where we have a kind of animalistic immediacy which does not need the fantasmatic supplement; then we move on to the abstract negation of the first movement, represented by masturbation as fully supported by fantasy; and finally we get the synthesis of the two positions: 'the sexual act proper in a missionary position, in which face-to-face contact guarantees that full bodily contact (penetration) remains supplemented by fantasizing. This means that the "normal" human sexual act has the structure of double masturbation: each participant is masturbating with a real partner. However, the gap between the raw reality of copulation and its fantasmatic supplement can no longer be closed; all variations and displacements of sexual practices to follow are so many desperate attempts to restore the balance of the two' (Žižek, 2006a, 12).

19 The Miracle of Love and the Real of Christianity

1. Žižek refers specifically to chapters 4 and 5 of Lacan's *Seminar VIII, Le Transfert* (1960–61).
2. The classic Žižekian reference here is 'Western Buddhism' and, generally, Oriental spirituality, which he describes as a pop-cultural phenomenon completely integral to the logic of late capitalism, since 'preaching inner distance and indifference toward the frantic pace of market competition, is arguably the most efficient way for us fully to participate in capitalist dynamics while retain the appearance of mental sanity – in short, the paradigmatic logic of late capitalism' (Žižek, 2003b, 26).
3. This is also the reason for the difference between standard atheism and Žižek's version: '"Atheism" (in the sense of deciding not to believe in God) is a miserable pathetic stance of those who long for God but cannot find him (or who "rebel against God"...). A true atheist does not choose atheism: for him, the question itself is irrelevant' (Žižek, 2006a, 97).

Epilogue: *Maradona in Mexico*

The highlight of the 1986 football world cup in Mexico was undoubtedly the quarter-final between Argentina and England, with the 2–1 victory of the South Americans who, from then, went on to lift the most prestigious trophy in the world. The reason why this particular game is often remembered as the game of the championship is very simple: the two extraordinary goals scored by Diego Armando Maradona, Argentina's captain and, according to most commentators, the best footballer to have ever played the 'beautiful game'. Now, what is the relationship between Maradona's goals in Mexico 1986 and the theoretical ruminations that fill the pages of our book? Everything. One of the most exciting and valuable lessons of Žižek's ideology critique is that we are encouraged to apply it to every field of human activity, including those where we would least expect to get some philosophical joy from (such as a football pitch). If this 'exhortation to dare' is not entirely original in method (1960s semiotics had already excelled in this kind of enquiries), it is certainly so in ambition, since from a Žižekian angle the lower and normally neglected manifestations of the human spirit allow us an insight into nothing other than the object of all philosophical investigations from time immemorial: truth, or rather universality.

What is it, then, that makes Maradona's goals so enlightening, so worthy of theoretical praise, and, ultimately, so exemplary for our analysis of Žižek's writing? For want of a better expression, their *shameful monstrosity*. Let us do what every football commentator should do: examine goals in detail. First, at the beginning of the second half, comes the infamous *mano de Dios*, the hand of God. A sliced clearance by the England defence balloons up into the air, Maradona darts through and jumps towards the ball together with England goalkeeper Peter Shilton; a second later, the ball slowly, mockingly bounces into the empty net.... What was imperceptible to the naked eye is revealed by the slow-motion replay: Maradona had raised his left hand positioning it between his head and the ball, thus crucially anticipating and eluding the goalkeeper's intervention. The truly uncanny aspect of this well known passage of play is that Maradona's hand started working as what Žižek, borrowing the expression from Gilles Deleuze, would call 'an organ without body', i.e. 'the virtuality of the pure affect extracted from its embeddedness in a body' (Žižek, 2004c, 30). The aim of Žižek's revisitation of Deleuze's metaphor of the organ detached from the body is to radicalise the significance of Lacan's notion of partial object (*objet a*). The first and crucial step towards this radicalisation is by conceiving the partial object as invested by the *jouissance* of drive, a *jouissance* that turns the object into a desubjectivized organ which, as if by magic, 'starts to speak', i.e. acquires an autonomous life of its own (drive), irrespective of central bodily commands. Žižek's array of bracing examples, here, range from the literary tradition of the 'talking vagina' (in Diderot's 1748 novel *Les Bijoux indiscrets*; in Frederic Lansac and Francis Leroi's 1975 cult film *Le sexe qui parle*; in Eve Ensler's contemporary melodrama *The Vagina Monologues*), to the Grimms brothers' fairy tale *The Willful Child*, Marx's insight into the commodity who starts to speak, circus clowns, pornography as well as the usual series of Hollywood films (see Žižek, 2004c, 170–6).

The fundamental Lacanian theme that runs through all these examples is that of the primacy of the acephalous (desubjectivized, objectal) drive over the dialectic of desire that sustains the symbolic order of language and meaning (and therefore football as a circumscribed micro-system of inter-related symbolic references). The proper Lacanian term for this drive *qua* organ is *lamella*, as Žižek suggests, for instance, in the following excerpt on Kafka's short story 'The Cares of a Family Man' (1919), which is about a strange creature called Odradek:

> Odradek is thus simply what Lacan, in his seminar 11 and in his seminal *écrit* 'Positions de l'inconscient', developed as *lamella*, libido as an organ, the inhuman-human 'undead' organ without a body, the mythical pre-subjective 'undead' life-substance, or, rather, the remainder of life-substance which has escaped the symbolic colonization, the horrible palpitation of the 'acephal' drive which persists beyond ordinary death, outside the scope of paternal authority, nomadic, with no fixed domicile. ... life as such.... The disgust at Life is disgust with *drive* at its purest (Žižek, 2006b, 166–7).

The key point to note here is the emphasis on Odradek's split between the human and the inhuman. Perhaps the most scandalous dimension of Žižek's thought lies in its endeavour to restore the inhuman as an ethical and political category. This endeavour is best epitomised by Žižek's reading of the central concept of postmodern ethics: the other. To him, the only true 'otherness' – against today's prevailing tendencies to gentrify the other as either a different narrative (standard postmodern position) or an unanswerable question that makes my ethical commitment both impossible and a matter of infinite responsibility (Levinas) – is the repulsive excess inherent to the very fact of 'being human', insofar as 'every normative determination of the "human" is only possible against an impenetrable ground of "inhuman", of something which remains opaque and resists inclusion into any narrative reconstitution of what counts as "human"' (Žižek, 2006b, 158). True otherness corresponds to the inhuman, 'undead' kernel of indestructible libido that inhabits every human being, to the extent that it constitutes its traumatic disavowed substance. No wonder Maradona's hand was received with such disgust by every self-righteous football lover! If we read it with Žižek, what we get with it is, effectively, the shameful disclosure of *jouissance*, whereby football is suddenly stripped of its symbolic dignity, uncovering the scandal of its Real core.

This, incidentally, is the exact obverse of today's fashionable theme of 'football fantasy'. While in today's global capitalist frenzy fantasy is ruthlessly exploited as a vehicle for the universalisation of football as a commodity (from the endless array of videogames to the omnipresent injunction to 'enjoy football' as a totalizing symbolic/virtual experience), Maradona's hand allows us, at least from a theoretical angle, to dispel this fantasmatic mist and claim the primacy of Lacan's 'fundamental fantasy', the most disavowed fantasmatic screen where the subject exposes himself to an unbearable shame.[1] This reference to shame is particularly instructive. The strength of Maradona's position was that of not retreating from the shameful Real of *jouissance* back into symbolic closure. What remained exposed was the non-castrated surplus (his hand) which caused scandal precisely because, later, it was not 'covered up'. Instead of admitting that the goal came as a result of a deliberate act of cheating, Maradona broke what Žižek calls 'the vicious circle of ethics and sacrifice' (Žižek, 2006b, 152) by giving the most succinct definition of the Lacanian act: God (the other par excellence) acted through me, for a few second this hand of mine became God's hand, an organ whose deeds my conscious being does not/cannot control nor recognise. Had Maradona made public amend for his misconduct, he would have 'escaped into guilt', thus endorsing a logic of sacrifice that plugs the hole in the Symbolic and strengthens its texture (recall, for instance, Bill Clinton's public contrition after his sexual affair with Monica Lewinsky). Instead, Maradona opted *not* to cover his 'dirty' hand through guilt. Rather, he shamelessly and provocatively accentuated its embarrassingly excessive dimension by calling God into question (just imagine Clinton doing the same: this cigar that I inserted into Ms. Lewinsky's vagina was actually God's cigar ...). In such circumstances, what is difficult to do is not to repent, doing what the big Other wants you to do, but precisely to hold on to the contingency of one's shameful choice, since this type of fidelity cannot but bring division and conflict. Apropos of organs without a body, Žižek writes: 'When a man exposes his distorted limb to his neighbor, his true target is not to expose himself, but the neighbor: to put the neighbor to shame by confronting him with his own ambiguous repulsion/fascination with the spectacle he is forced to witness' (Žižek, 2006b, 171). The same with the Argentine star: what if the ultimate aim of his gesture was to confront us with the ambiguity of shame, forcing us to acknowledge that true fascination is only the flipside of repulsion (and vice versa)? More insightfully, we could argue that since shame necessarily relies on the mortifying gaze of others (ultimately, the big Other), Maradona's brazen fidelity to his 'organ without body' presupposes what is perhaps the most crucial political consequence of Žižek's Lacanianism: the insight into the non existence (and changeability) of the big Other.

There is therefore more truth than we think in Maradona's postmatch claim that the goal was scored by the hand of God: 'Even if there was a hand, it must have been the hand of God'. The strictly speaking psychotic nature of this infamous statement should be taken literally: 'although it is obvious that I did it, somebody else for a moment took over my bodily functions and acted through me'. Does not such claim fit perfectly Žižek's definition of the act as 'an intervention in the course of which the agent's identity itself is radically changed' (Žižek, 2001c, 85)? What legitimises an authentic act is its ability to surprise the agent itself, who is unable to reduce it to a conscious choice. The paradox at stake is that in the act 'the highest freedom coincides with the utmost passivity, with a reduction to a lifeless automaton who blindly performs its gestures' (Žižek, 2000a, 375): from this angle, true freedom does not reside in the liberal notion of 'freedom of choice' – in the active evaluation of all possible outcome – but in 'being driven' by an unintelligible cause, in the compelling and startled realisation that 'we cannot do otherwise'. The most difficult thing to accept, according to Žižek, is precisely the human potential for such radical freedom, since this freedom, which truly liberates us, depends on the momentary (and traumatic) suspension of the familiar horizon of consciousness.

Back to Maradona. The miracle of his goal involves precisely the sudden activation of an 'undead' drive that insists in us irrespective of our conscious bodily functions, the decisive proof that we are 'in us more than ourselves'. The following passage could easily be read as a defence of Maradona's claim:

> To put it in somewhat pathetic terms, this is how the 'divine' dimension is present in our lives, and the different modalities of ethical betrayal relate precisely to the different ways of betraying the act-event: the true source of Evil is not a finite mortal man who acts like God, but a man who denies that divine miracles occur and reduces himself to just another finite mortal being (Žižek, 2000a, 376).

Although it is easy and tempting to bemoan his goal as the ultimate piece of evidence against the proverbial Latin penchant for dodging the law, theoretically much more fruitful would be to discover in the 'hand of God' the emancipating dimension of drive. Maradona's invisible/virtual hand stands for the alien 'object in the subject' that gives body to 'the impossible equivalent of the subject itself' (Žižek, 2004c, 175), the subject at its purest.

As we hope to have demonstrated in our book, Žižek's philosophy is aggressively anti-biopolitical. For Žižek, the moment we conceptualise life as a self-regulating deployment of the human potential to enjoy, what we miss is life in its self-defining excess (Lacan's *jouissance*, Freud's 'beyond the pleasure principle'). This is how Lacanian psychoanalysis, according to Žižek, turns around the standard scientific opposition of life and death: on the one hand, we are dead when we are colonised by the symbolic order of language and communication (i.e. when we pursue our everyday existence in the big Other); on the other hand, we are properly alive only when our existence is taken over by the 'undead' substance of drive, the palpitating, sickening compulsion to repeat a certain gesture that leads us into the domain of the 'living dead', threatening to sever our vital social link with the symbolic order.

What we should not overlook is the connection between the two dimensions. One of the crucial political claims of Žižek's philosophy rests on his Lacanian persuasion that '*lamella*, the "undead" object, is not a remainder of castration in the sense of a little part which somehow escaped unhurt the swipe of castration, but, literally, the *product* of the cut of castration, the *surplus* generated by it'. This means that 'what appears as obstacle is a positive condition of possibility' (Žižek, 2006b, 174 and 176). In other words, the elusive object of desire/drive plays a key role in the process of subjectivation, since it gives body to the disturbing surplus *secreted during that process itself*, which, for that reason, needs to be disavowed if the subject is to achieve a modicum of consistency. The subject emerges as an individual endowed with a wealth of specific inner features only by disavowing its own partial object *qua* 'most personal' feature, i.e. by renouncing its direct eroticisation. In a similar way, the symbolic order is constantly engaged in a battle to eliminate its own excess, the reprehensible 'part of no part' that would undermine its totalising scope.[2] By contrast, full libidinal investment in the partial object (*objet a*) holds the potential to bring about an implicitly traumatic break, from which the field can be resignified. In this precise sense, drive is the endless circulation around (fixation on) the obstacle (*objet a*) *which becomes the obstacle itself*, the excessive feature on account of which reality loses its unproblematic, smooth, spontaneous character to become a curved space, a distorted screen where identification is impossible.

A different way of putting this is by suggesting that Maradona's hand functions as a fetish, insofar as the fetish always obfuscates the inconsistency of the symbolic order; in this case, however, what is required is the theoretical 'leap' from fetish to drive, which unmasks the object as a mere stand-in for the lack in the Other. The previously mentioned Grimms brothers' story *The Willful Child* provides a surprisingly similar parallel with the 1986 'hand of God' tale. The child's disobedience to his mother is such that it enrages none other than God, who causes him to fall ill and die. The dead child's body is lowered in a grave and covered with earth, but then something odd happens: his little arm sticks out, as if in defiance of death itself. All attempts to bury the arm prove futile, as it keeps popping up. Eventually, the mother herself goes to the grave and beats the arm down, until it completely disappears underground. Žižek's comment on the metaphorical significance of the story could work well, again, as a comment on Maradona's hand: 'Is this obstinacy that persists even beyond death not freedom – death drive – at its most elementary? Instead of condemning it, should we not celebrate it as the ultimate resort of our resistance?' (Žižek, 2004c, 176).

What emerges from each of Žižek's books (especially the latest ones) is the celebration of drive as *the* key concept for the politicisation of Lacanian theory. This conviction leads him to reject completely any transcendental understanding of Lacan's psychoanalytic theory. To Žižek, transcendentalising Lacan amounts to gentrifying his lesson. The Lacanian Real is not akin to Kant's noumenal Thing-in-itself, the impossible Absolute which, due to its very impossibility, opens up the possibility of meaning, or rather the conceptual framework of the endless, frustrating search for Meaning – with, as an ethical corollary, the 'respect for Otherness' theme, never so flaunted and yet hypocritically ignored as today. The moment we endorse this transcendental logic, which spares us the encounter with the abyssal dizziness of freedom and the ensuing anxiety (see Žižek, 2006a, 88), we get caught in the quicksand of watertight immanence, in as much as we effectively deny ourselves any workable 'crack'/opening from which to reconfigure our symbolic experience. The foreclosure of the break results in the acceptance of the perverse logic of desire/transgression, with the accompanying illusion that the Real of freedom can be accessed by way of simply transgressing a given prohibition. Thus, transcendence for Žižek is merely the result of a perspectival illusion, and as such it should be avoided. If there is a gap where freedom can be found, this gap should not be predicated upon a notion of unreacheable 'otherness', since it actually designates the minimal distance between the One and its empty foundation, between immanence and the void that makes it radically inconsistent, between

Maradona and his 'hand of God'. It is this minimal gap that drive feeds on and, ultimately, coincides with. Žižek's Lacan is therefore the Lacan of the drives, where the subject is defined by a libidinal excess that is directly linked to (overlaps with, activates) the gap within immanence, the foundational inconsistency of the symbolic order.

It is here that the Hegelian character of Lacanian theory reveals itself with utmost clarity. The Hegelian equivalence between Substance and Subject, in Žižek, is tantamount to the Lacanian equivalence between 'the big Other does not exist' and 'the primacy of drive'. Going back to our example, this implies that Maradona's 'hand of God' ultimately discloses the non-existence of God as a transcendental universal entity; on the contrary, it tells us that God can only be posited as a thoroughly immanent notion insofar as it coincides with a disturbing partial object that suddenly becomes the site of an unbearable/explosive antagonistic tension. In somewhat inadequate football terms, this antagonism emerges as the dispute between England and Argentina over the legal status of the goal – which, of course, one is tempted to relate to the then still open wound of the dispute between the two countries over the Falkland/Malvinas islands. Such antagonism is truly irreducible: despite the fact that the goal was allowed to stand and the final result settled forever, Maradona's hand marks the 'ethical suspension of the symbolic status of the game' which, one must add, is *football at its purest.* Just like any other symbolic context (subjectivity, family, sexuality, politics, history, society, etc.), football is traversed by its own Real impossibility, i.e., paraphrasing Lacan's quip on the subject, 'there is no football without aphanisis of football'. And, again, the significance of drive, of the partial object that suddenly, and not without a traumatic impact, acquires a disturbing autonomy within a system of interrelated signs, is that it circumscribes the limited space of freedom. Simultaneously, it uncovers the true meaning of universality. Žižek's often rehearsed point with regard to universality (including Christian universality) is that it should not be conceived as a neutral encompassing framework filled by a variety of particular contents, but instead as the hard kernel of struggling antagonism that embodies the limit and disavowed foundation of every totalising function.

On this evidence, it comes as no surprise that in recent years Žižek's writing has increasingly focused on religion, with a specific interest in Christianity. In Christian terms, this struggling universality cannot but make us aware of the strange overlapping of Christ as the highest point of humanity and Christ as the incarnation of the strictly speaking inhuman excess/monstrosity that is the subject. This is one of the many examples of the Hegelian 'infinite judgement' deployed by Žižek. As he states in *The Parallax View*, Christ is essentially '*diabolos* (to separate, to tear apart the One into Two)' as opposed to '*symbolos* (to gather and unify)' ... the ultimate diabolic figure, insofar as he brings "the sword, not peace", disturbing the existing harmonious unity' (Žižek, 2006a, 99). Not surprisingly, Žižek's favourite Christian quotation is the following passage from Luke's Gospel: 'if anyone comes to me and does not hate his father and his mother, his wife and children, his brother and sister – yes even his own life – he cannot be my disciple' (Luke 14: 26). Christ's divine status thus overlaps with the monstrosity of his presence as a singular universal who, precisely as the excluded 'part of no part', speaks through the innermost kernel of subjectivity, the inhuman core of a human being. As such, his existential stance cannot fail to appear consubstantial with that of figures of evil such as the Devil and Judas, without whom he would never have been able to accomplish the works of love (see for example Žižek, 2003b, 15–18). Consequently, Christian love is defined in unfashionable militant terms: not as an all-inclusive stance of unconditional, all-forgiving care, but as an excessive and thereby deeply divisive attachment to the Cause, 'a biased commitment which disturbs the balance of the Whole' (Žižek, 2006a, 103).

It is crucial to stress that this is the commitment of drive, i.e. the type of attachment legitimised only by its turning into dis-attachment, into the awareness that there is in us an 'indivisible remainder' which cannot be domesticated, symbolised, subsumed into the wealth of our subjective position(s). All Žižekian heroes are driven. What links figures as diverse as Christ, Lenin, Saint Paul, Antigone, Sygne de Coûfontaine and many more is the fact that, at some point, in relation to key events or choices, they start to 'speak the language of drive', that is to say, they are taken over by the subject of the unconscious.

Our final thoughts as impenitent football lovers cannot but go to Maradona's virtuoso second goal in the Mexico 1986 match against England, which is known as 'the goal of the century'. Nine minutes into the second half, Maradona receives the ball some ten metres inside his own half and, with an impromptu pirouette, begins his deservedly famous dash towards the English goal. On the way he skips past five English players, eluding challenge after challenge while miraculously retaining his balance. Finally, in an outrageous display of arrogance, he rounds the goalkeeper and slots the ball into the empty net. If the first goal signals the intervention of drive, the second emphatically confirms it through repetition. More precisely, what is confirmed in this ten-second sixty-meter run is the insistence of *lamella*, the indomitable excess of life that refuses domestication. Against its standard interpretation, Maradona's 'goal of the century' is not merely the ultimate expression of a creative genius, it is more properly *monstrous*: it shows us a body invaded by the alien substance of drive.

Having said that, it is once again crucial to reflect on Maradona's own account of his goal. In his biography, he claims that, when he started his run, the idea was to set up his team-mate Jorge Valdano, who was in a better position to score; however, as he saw himself surrounded by English players, he suddenly felt that he had no choice but go all the way and try to score himself (see Maradona, 2004, 128–9). This account provides a perfect exemplification of how drive and freedom are linked. First, as in the case of the opening goal, it tells us that drive materialises as a kind of malfunctioning, a self-sabotaging deracination from full immersion in the pacified symbolic network: the subject breaks the deterministic/utilitarian chain of being by 'following a certain automatism which ignores the demands of adaptation' (Žižek, 2006a, 231). As anticipated, we experience freedom through drive precisely as a 'no choice' situation (the paradox being that I am truly free when, confronted by a given dilemma, I experience my freedom to choose as a forced choice: 'I cannot do otherwise'). More significantly, however, Maradona's account of his second goal can be said to betray the radically self-reflexive dimension of every human act, since it reveals that his extraordinary feat came about as a consequence of a certain impasse, or blockage, at the level of consciousness. As Žižek repeatedly claims, (self-)consciousness begins with my awareness that I am not in control, that my untroubled immersion in the symbolic network is suddenly perturbed by some obstacle (in psychoanalytic terms, this obstacle is of course the 'desire of the Other'). The first implication here is that I encounter the core of my self when I endorse the deadlock of 'cogito', the radical contingency of consciousness. The second is that 'the only way effectively to account for the status of (self-)consciousness is to assert the ontological incompleteness of "reality" itself: there is "reality" only insofar as there is an ontological gap, a crack, in its very heart, that is to say, a traumatic excess, a foreign body which cannot be integrated into it' (Žižek, 2006a, 242). We are therefore back to Žižek's favourite Hegelian motto 'Substance is Subject', which implies the overlapping of two lacks brought about by drive.

If Maradona's second goal qualifies as drive, thereby opening up the space of freedom, it does so *against* the (New-Age-*cum*-capitalist) commonplace of the footballer/sportsman who 'just plays without thinking', simply unleashing the potential of his/her natural talent (recall the well known sports advert catch-phrase 'Just do it!'). Drive emerges as a libidinal fixation on a negative instance, as a forced choice *not* to carry out a seemingly free-willed desire (Maradona's 'free decision' to pass the ball to his team-mate). As Žižek puts it, 'the elementary act of freedom, the manifestation of free will, is that of saying no, of stopping the execution of a decision ... freedom is not the freedom to do as you like (that is, to follow your inclinations without any externally imposed constraints), but to do what you do not want to do, to thwart the "spontaneous" realization of an impetus' (Žižek, 2006a, 202). This means that freedom operates retroactively: freedom is 'my ability to choose/determine retroactively which causes will determine me' (Žižek, 2006a, 203). It is clear that such an understanding of freedom can only be predicated upon the primacy of drive as the very embodiment of unconscious/Real negativity. In other words, there can be no such retroactive self-determination (with all its crucial political consequences) without the intervention of the specific negativity that Žižek associates with drive. The ultimate message to be read into Maradona's two goals at the Azteca Stadium in Mexico City, then, is: 'although I did not intend to score such goals, I now choose to have scored them'. In Žižek's terms, Maradona's goals can be said to have the structure of a revolutionary act.

Notes

1. One of Žižek's most convincing explanations of the link between shame and the excessive 'organ without body' comes from his reading of a scene from Chaplin's *City Lights*, when the tramp swallows a whistle by mistake, gets a fit of hiccups and as a result starts emitting strange and embarrassing sounds: 'Does this scene not stage shame at its purest? I am

ashamed when I am confronted with the excess in my body. It is significant that the source of shame in this scene is sound: a spectral sound emanating from within the Tramp's body, sound as an autonomous "organ without body", located in the very heart of his body and at the same time uncontrollable, like a kind of parasite. A foreign intruder – in short, what Lacan called the voice-object, one of the incarnations of *objet petit a*, of the *agalma*, that which is "in me more than myself"' (Žižek, 2006b, 169).

2. Once again, the analogy is tempting: is not Maradona precisely this excess that the system (football as a capitalistic enterprise) needs to (or tries to) eliminate? Is not Maradona's cocaine addiction and consequent exclusion from football (which culminated in his falling into a coma) a clear example of how a given symbolic system produces a surplus that it then has to get rid of? In contrast to Maradona, Pelè (Edson Arantes do Nascimento), his eternal rival in every poll for 'best footballer of the century', would seem to stand for the excessive element that has been successfully integrated into the system: despite being involved in a number of scandals (drugs, corruption, etc.), Pelè has been Minister of Sports in Brazil and currently is UNESCO Goodwill Ambassador.

References

Abu-Lughod, L. and Lutz, C. (1990) 'Introduction: Emotion, Discourse, and the Politics of Everyday Life', in idem (eds), *Language and the Politics of Emotion*, Cambridge: Cambridge University Press.

Allen, A. (1999) *The Power of Feminist Theory: Domination, Resistance, Solidarity*, Boulder, Colo., Westview.

Allen, A. (2000) 'The Anti-Subjective Hypothesis: Michel Foucault and the Death of the Subject', in *Philosophical Forum*, vol. 31, no. 2, pp. 113–30.

Althusser, L. (1970) 'Ideology and Ideological State Apparatuses (Notes towards an Investigation)', in Žižek (ed.), *Mapping Ideology*, pp. 100–40.

Andersen, N. A. (2003) *Discursive Analytical Strategies: Understanding Foucault, Koselleck, Laclau, Luhmann*, Bristol: Policy Press.

Armstrong, A. (2006) 'Foucault and Feminism', in *The Internet Encyclopaedia of Philosophy*, ed. by James Fieser and Bradley Dowden, http://www.iep.utm.edu/, accessed: 16/07/2006.

Ashenden, S. and Owen, D. (eds) (1999) *Foucault contra Habermas: Recasting the Dialogue between Genealogy and Critical Theory*, London: Sage.

Badiou, A. (2003) *Saint Paul. The Foundation of Universalism*. Standford, CA: Standford University Press.

Badiou, A. (2005) *Infinite Thought: Truth and the Return of Philosophy* (London and New York: Continuum).

Balibar, É. (1992) 'Foucault and Marx: the Question of Nominalism', in Armstrong, T. J. (ed.), *Michel Foucault: Philosopher*, New York: Harvester Wheatsheaf, pp. 38–56.

Barrett, M. (1991) *The Politics of Truth: From Marx to Foucault*, Cambridge: Polity.

Barry, A., Osborne, T. and Rose, N. (eds) (1996) *Foucault and Political Reason: Liberalism, Neo-Liberalism, and Rationalities of Government*, Chicago: University of Chicago Press.

Baudrillard, J. (1987) 'Forget Foucault' [1977], in *Forget Foucault and Forget Baudrillard: Interview with Sylvère Lotringer*, trans. by Nicole Dufresne, New York: Semiotext(e), pp. 7–64.

Beaumont, M. and Jenkins, M. (2000) 'An Interview with Slavoj Žižek', in *Historical Materialism*, 7, pp. 181–97.

Benveniste, E. (1971) *Problems of General Linguistics* [1966], trans. by Mary E. Meek, Miami: Miami University Press.

Berger, S. (2003) *The Search for Normality: National Identity and Historical Consciousness in Germany since 1800*, 2nd edn, Oxford: Berghahn.

Bernauer, J. (1990) *Michel Foucault's Force of Flight: Towards and Ethics for Thought*, Atlantic Highlands, NJ: Humanities Press.

Bernauer, J. and Mahon, M. (2005) 'The Ethics of Michel Foucault', in G. Gutting (ed.), *The Cambridge Companion to Foucault*, 2nd edn., Cambridge, Cambridge University Press, pp. 149–75.

Bernstein, R. (1989) 'Foucault: Critique as a Philosophical Ethos', in Axel Honneth (ed.), *Zwischenbetrachtungen im Prozess der Aufklärung*, Frankfurt/Main: Suhrkamp, pp. 395–417.

Biebricher, T. (2005) 'Habermas, Foucault and Nietzsche: A double Misunderstanding', in *Foucault Studies*, no. 3, pp. 1–26.

Black, J. (1997) 'Taking Sex out of Sexuality: Foucault's Failed History', in David H. J. Larmour, Paul Allen Milller, and Charles Platter (eds), *Rethinking Sexuality: Foucault and Classsical Antiquity*, Princeton, NY: Princeton University Press, pp. 42–60.

Borradori, G. (2003) *Philosophy in a Time of Terror: Dialogues with Jürgen Habermas and Jacques Derrida*. Chicago: University of Chicago Press.

Boucher, G., Glynos, J. and Sharpe, M. (eds) (2005) *Traversing the Fantasy: Critical Responses to Slavoj Žižek*, Aldershot: Ashgate.

Boynton, R. (1998) 'Enjoy your Žižek', *Linguafranca: the Review of Academic Life*, 7, http://www.linguafranca.com/9810/Žižek.html (accessed: 08/02/February 2005).

Bratich, J., Packer, J. and McCarthy, C. (eds), *Foucault, Cultural Studies, and Governmentality*. Albany, NY: State University of New York Press, 2003.

Brecht, B. (1967) *Gesammelte Werke*, vol. 9, Frankfurt on the Main: Suhrkamp.

Brieler, U. (1998) *Die Unerbittlichkeit der Historizität: Foucault als Historiker*, Cologne, Weimar and Vienna, Böhlau.

Brieler, U. (2003) 'Blind Date: Michel Foucault in der deutschen Geschichtswissenschaft', in Honneth, A. and Saar M. (eds), *Michel Foucault: Zwischenbilanz einer Rezeption*, Frankfurt/Main: Suhrkamp, pp. 311–34.

Bröckling, U., Krasmann, S. and Lemke T. (eds) (2000) *Gouvernementalität der Gegenwart: Studien zur Ökonomisierung des Sozialen*, Frankfurt-on-Main, Surhkamp.

Brown, W. (1995) *States of Injury: Power and Freedom in Late Modernity*, Princeton, NJ: Princeton University Press.

Buchanan, I. (ed.) (1999) *A Deleuzian Century?*, Durham, NC: Duke University Press.

Burchell, G. *et al.* (eds) (1991) *The Foucault Effect: Studies in Governmentality*. Chicago: University of Chicago Press.

Butler, J. (1990) *Gender Trouble: Feminism and the Subversion of Identity*, New York and London: Routledge.

Butler, J. (1993) *Bodies that Matter: On the Discursive Limits of 'Sex'*, New York and London: Routledge.

Butler, J. (1997) *The Psychic Life of Power: Theories in Subjection*, Stanford: Stanford University Press.

Butler, J. (2003) 'Noch einmal: Körper und Macht', in Honneth, A. and Saar M. (eds), *Michel Foucault: Zwischenbilanz einer Rezeption*, Frankfurt/Main: Suhrkamp, pp. 52–76.

Butler, J. Laclau, E. and Žižek, S. (2000) *Contingency, Hegemony, Universality. Contemporary Dialogues on the Left*. London: Verso.

Butler, R. (2005) *Slavoj Žižek: Live Theory*. London, New York: Continuum.

Butler, R. and Stephens, S. (2006) 'Slavoj Žižek's Third Way', in Slavoj Žižek, *The Universal Exception*, ed. by R. Bulter and S. Stephens, London and New York: Continuum, pp. 1–11.

Cohen, D. and Saller, R. (1994) 'Foucault on Sexuality in Greco-Roman Antiquity', in Jan Goldstein (ed.), *Foucault and the Writing of History*, Oxford: Blackwell, pp. 35–59.

Conrad, J. (2002) 'Lenin and the United States of Europe', in *Weekly Worker*, n. 431, www.cpgb.org.uk/worker/431.lenin_use.html, accessed: 16/07/2005.

Copjec, J. (1994) *Read My Desire: Lacan Against the Historicists*, Cambridge, MA: MIT Press.

Daly, G. (2004) 'Introduction: Risking the Impossible', in Žižek, S. and Daly, G. (eds), *Conversations with Žižek*, Cambridge, Oxford and Malden, MA: Cambridge University Press, pp. 1–22.

Danaher, G. (2002) 'Foucault, Ideology and Social Contract in Australian History', in Clare O'Farrell (ed.), *Foucault: The Legacy*, CD-ROM edition, Queensland University of Technology, pp. 105–10.

Daston, L. (1992) 'Objectivity and the Escape from Perspective', in *Social Studies of Science*, vol. 22, pp. 597–618.

Daston, L. (ed.) (2000) *Biographies of Scientific Objects*, Chicago: University of Chicago Press.

Daston, L. and K. Park (1998) *Wonders and the Order of Nature, 1150–1750*, New York: Zone Books.

Davidson, A. I. (2005) 'Ethics and Ascetics: Foucault, the History of Ethics, and Ancient Thought' [1994], in Gary Gutting (ed.), *The Cambridge Companion to Foucault*, 2nd. edn, Cambridge, Cambridge University Press, pp. 123–48.

Davies, M. (2006) *Historics: Why History Dominates Contemporary Society*, London and New York: Routledge.

Dean, J. (2006) *Žižek's Politics*, New York and London: Routledge.

Dean, M. (1994) *Critical and Effective Histories: Foucault's Methods and Historical Sociology*, London and New York: Routledge.

Dean, M. (1999) *Governmentality, Power and Rule in Modern Society*, London and New York: Routledge.

Deary, V. (2004) 'News from Elsewhere', *Times Literary Supplement*, 16 July 2004, p. 25.

Deleuze, G. (1991) *Masochism*. New York: Zone Books.

Deleuze, G. (1999) *Foucault* [1986], trans. and ed. by S. Hand, London and New York, Continuum.

Dews, P. (1989) 'The Return of the Subject in the Late Foucault', in *Radical Philosophy*, no. 51, pp. 37–41.

Diamond, I. and Quinby, L. (eds) (1988) *Foucault and Feminism: Reflections on Resistance*, Boston, MA: Northeastern University Press.

Dreyfus, H. and Rabinow, P. (1982) *Michel Foucault: Beyond Hermeneutics and Structuralism*. Chicago: University of Chicago Press.

Eagleton, T. (1990) *Ideology of the Aesthetic*, Oxford: Basil Blackwell.

Eagleton, T. (1991) *Ideology: An Introduction*, London and New York: Verso.

Eagleton, T. (2005) *Figures of Dissent*, London and New York: Verso.

240 *References*

Evans, R. J. (2001) *In Defence of History*, new edn, with an extensive afterword, London: Granta.
Ewald, F. (1992) 'A Power Without an Exterior' in Armstrong T. J. (ed.), *Michel Foucault: Philosopher*, New York: Harvester Wheatsheaf, pp. 169–75.
O'Farrell, C. (2005) *Michel Foucault*, London: Sage.
Fink, B. (1995) *The Lacanian Subject Between Language and Jouissance*, Princeton: Princeton University Press.
Flynn, T. (2005a) *Sartre, Foucault and Historical Reason*, 2 vols, Chicago: University of Chicago Press.
Flynn, T. (2005b) 'Foucault's Mapping of History', in Gary Gutting (ed.), *The Cambridge Companion to Foucault*, Cambridge, 2nd edn, Cambridge University Press, pp. 29–48.
Forrester, J. (1990) *The Seductions of Psychoanalysis: Freud, Lacan and Derrida*, Cambridge: Cambridge University Press.
Foucault, M. (1963) *Raymond Roussel*, Paris: Gallimard.
Foucault, M. (1965) *Madness and Civilization* [1961], New York: Vintage.
Foucault, M. (1970) *The Order of Things* [1966], London and New York: Routledge.
Foucault, M. (1977) 'The Political Function of the Intellectual', in *Radical Philosophy* 17, pp. 12–14.
Foucault, M. (1980) 'The Confession of the Flesh' [1977], in *Michel Foucault, Power/Kowledge: Selected Interviews and Other Writings 1972–1977*, ed. by C. Gordon, Brighton: The Harvester Press, pp. 194–228.
Foucault, M. (1981) 'The Order of Discourse', Inaugural Lecture at the Collège de France' [1970], in *Untying the Text: A Poststructuralist Reader*, ed. by Robert Young, London: Routledge and Kegan Paul, pp. 48–77.
Foucault, M. (1984) 'Preface to *The History of Sexuality*, Volume II', in *The Foucault Reader*, ed. by Paul Rabinow, New York: Pantheon, pp. 333–9.
Foucault, M. (1985) *The History of Sexuality*, vol. 2: *The Use of Pleasure* [1984], New York: Pantheon.
Foucault, M. (1986a) *The History of Sexuality*, vol. 3: *The Care of the Self* [1984], New York: Pantheon.
Foucault, M. (1986b) 'Dream, Imagination and Existence' [1954], in Michel Foucault and Ludwig Binswanger, *Dream and Existence*, ed. by Keith Hoeller, Seattle: Humanities Press, pp. 31–78.
Foucault, M. (1988) 'Power and Sex' [1977], in *Politics, Philosophy, Culture: Interviews and Other Writings, 1977–1984*; trans. by Alan Sheridan *et al.*, ed. with an introduction by Laurence D. Kritzman, New York and London: Routledge, 110–24.
Foucault, M. (1989) 'Rituals of Exclusion' [1971], in *Foucault Live: Interviews, 1966–84*, ed. by Sylvere Lotringer, New York: Semiotext(e), pp. 63–72.
Foucault, M. (1990) *The History of Sexuality*, vol. 1: *An Introduction* [1976], London: Penguin.
Foucault, M. (1991) *Discipline and Punish* [1975], London: Penguin.

Foucault, M. (1994a) 'Dialogue sur la pouvoir', ['Dialogue on Power' 1978], in *Dits et Écrits*, ed. by Daniel Defert and François Ewald, Paris: Éditions Gallimard, vol. 3, no. 221, pp. 464–77.

Foucault, M. (1994b) 'Lacan, le "libérateur" de la psychanalyse', ['Lacan, il liberatore della psicanalisi' 1981], in *Dits et Écrits*, ed. by Daniel Defert and François Ewald, Paris: Éditions Gallimard, vol. 4, no. 299, pp. 204–5.

Foucault, M. (1994c) 'Espace, savoir et pouvoir', ['Space, Knowledge and Power' 1982], in *Dits et Écrits*, ed. by Daniel Defert and François Ewald, Paris: Éditions Gallimard, vol. 4, no. 310, pp. 270–85.

Foucault, M. (1994d) 'Qu'est-ce qu'un philosophe?' [1966], in *Dits et Écrits*, ed. by Daniel Defert and François Ewald, Paris: Éditions Gallimard, vol. 1, no. 42, pp. 552–3.

Foucault, M. (2000a) 'Structuralism and Poststructuralism' [1983], in *Aesthetics: Essential Works of Foucault 1954–1984*, vol. 2, ed. by James D. Faubion, trans. by Robert Hurley and others, London: Penguin, pp. 433–59.

Foucault, M. (2000b) 'Subjectivity and Truth' [1981], in *Ethics, Subjectivity and Truth: Essential Works of Foucault 1954–1984*, vol. 1, ed. by Paul Rabinow, trans. by Robert Hurley and others, London: Penguin, pp. 87–92.

Foucault, M. (2000c) 'Theatrum Philosophicum' [1970], in *Aesthetics: Essential Works of Foucault 1954–1984*, vol. 2, ed. by James D. Faubion, trans. by Robert Hurley and others, London: Penguin, pp. 343–68.

Foucault, M. (2000e) 'Return to History' [1972], in *Aesthetics: Essential Works of Foucault 1954–1984*, vol. 2, ed. by James D. Faubion, trans. by Robert Hurley and others, London: Penguin, pp. 419–32.

Foucault, M. (2000f) 'A Preface to Transgression' [1963], in *Aesthetics: Essential Works of Foucault 1954–1984*, vol. 2, ed. by James D. Faubion, trans. by Robert Hurley and others, London: Penguin, pp. 53–68.

Foucault, M. (2000g) 'The Order of Things' [1966], in *Aesthetics: Essential Works of Foucault 1954–1984*, vol. 2, ed. by James D. Faubion, trans. by Robert Hurley and others, London: Penguin, pp. 261–7.

Foucault, M. (2002a) *The Archaeology of Knowledge* [1969], London and New York: Routledge.

Foucault, M. (2002b) 'The Subject and Power' [1982], in *Power: Essential Works of Foucault 1954–1984*, vol. 3, ed. by James D. Faubion, trans. by Robert Hurley and others, London: Penguin, pp. 326–49.

Foucault, M. (2002c) 'Truth and Power' [1977], in *Power: Essential Works of Foucault 1954–1984*, vol. 3, ed. by James D. Faubion, trans. by Robert Hurley and others, London: Penguin, pp. 111–33.

Foucault, M. (2002d) 'Preface to Anti-Oedipus' [1976], in *Power: Essential Works of Foucault 1954–1984*, vol. 3, ed. by James D. Faubion, trans. by Robert Hurley and others, London: Penguin, pp. 106–10.

Foucault, M. (2003a) 'What Is Enlightenment?' [1984], in *The Essential Foucault: Selections from Essential Works of Foucault 1954–1984*, ed. by P. Rabinow and N. Rose, New York and London: The New Press, pp. 43–57.

Foucault, M. (2003b) 'Technologies of the Self' [1982], in *The Essential Foucault: Selections from Essential Works of Foucault 1954–1984*, ed. by P. Rabinow and N. Rose, New York and London: The New Press, pp. 145–69.

Foucault, M. (2003c) 'Nietzsche, Genealogy, History' [1971], in *The Essential Foucault: Selections from Essential Works of Foucault 1954–1984*, ed. by P. Rabinow and N. Rose, New York and London: The New Press, pp. 351–69.

Foucault, M. (2003d) *'Society Must Be Defended': Lectures at the Collège de France, 1975–76*, ed. by Mauro Bertani and Alessandro Fontana, trans. by David Macey, London: Allen Lane/Penguin.

Foucault, M. (2003e) *The Birth of the Clinic: An Archaeology of Medical Perception* [1963], trans. by Alan Sheridan, London and New York: Routledge.

Foucault, M. (2004) *Geschichte der Gouvernementalität: Vorlesungen am Collège de France, 1977–79*, vol. 1: *Sicherheit, Territorium, Bevölkerung (1977–78)*, ed. by Michel Sennelart, Frankfurt, Main: Suhrkamp.

Foucault, M. (2006) *The Hermeneutics of the Subject: Lectures at the Collège de France, 1981–1982*, ed. by Frédéric Gros, English edn. ed. by Arnold I. Davidson, trans. by Graham Burchell, New York: Picador.

Fraser, N. (1989) 'Foucault on Modern Power: Empirical Insights and Normative Confusions', in idem, *Unruly Practices: Power, Discourse and Gender in Contemporary Social Theory*, Cambridge: Polity, pp. 17–34.

Fraser, N. (2003) 'Von der Disziplin zur Flexibilisierung? Foucault im Spiegel der Globalisierung', in Axel Honneth and Martin Saar (eds), *Michel Foucault: Eine Zwischenbilanz*, Frankfurt, Main: Suhrkamp, 239–58.

Freeden, M. (1996) *Ideologies and Political Theory: A Conceptual Approach*, Oxford: Clarendon.

Freeden, M. (2003) *Ideology*. Oxford, New York: Oxford University Press.

Freud, S. (1961) *The Ego and the Id and other works, The Standard Edition 19.* London: Hogarth Press.

Gallagher, C. and S. Greenblatt (2000) *Practicing New Historicism*, Chicago: University of Chicago Press

Goldstein, J. (ed.) (1994) *Foucault and the Writing of History*, Oxford: Blackwell.

Gordon, C. (2002) 'Introduction', in *Power: Essential Works of Foucault 1954–1984*, vol. 3, ed. by James D. Faubion, trans. by Robert Hurley and others, London: Penguin, pp. xi–xli.

Gramsci, A. (1975) *Quaderni del Carcere*, Historical-critical edition, ed. by V. Gerratana, Turin: Einaudi.

Gros, F. (2006) 'Course Context', in Michel Foucault, The Hermeneutics of the Subject: Lectures at the Collège de France 1981–1982, ed. by Frédéric Gros, Engl. edn. ed. by Arnold I. Davidson, trans. by Graham Burchell, New York: Picador, pp. 507–50.

Gutting, G. (1989) *Michel Foucault's Archaeology of Scientific Reason*, Cambridge, New York, Melbourne: Cambridge University Press.

Gutting, G. (2005a) *Foucault*, Oxford, New York: Oxford University Press.

Gutting, G., ed. (2005b) *The Cambridge Companion to Foucault*, 2nd edn, Cambridge: Cambridge University Press.

Habermas, J. (1985) *Der philosophische Diskurs der Moderne*, Frankfurt, Main: Suhrkamp.

Hacking, I. (2002) *Historical Ontology*, Cambridge, MA, London: Harvard University Press.

Hallward, P. (2003) *Badiou: A Subject To Truth*. Minnesota: University of Minnesota Pres.

Halperin, D. (1995) *Saint Foucault: Towards a Gay Hagiography*, Oxford: Oxford University Press.

Hamilton, P. (2003) *Historicism*, 2nd edn, London, New York: Routledge.

Han, B. (2002) *Foucault's Critical Project*, Stanford: Stanford University Press.

Hartsock, N. (1990) 'Foucault on Power: A Theory for Women?' in Linda Nicholson (ed.), *Feminism/Postmodernism*, London, New York: Routledge, pp. 157–75.

Hegel, G. W. F. (1962) *Lectures on the Philosophy of Religion – Together with a Work on the Proofs of the Existence of God*. London: Routledge & Kegan Paul.

Hegel, G. W. F. (1977) *Phenomenology of Spirit*. Oxford: Clarendon Press.

Hekman, S., ed. (1996) *Feminist Interpretations of Michel Foucault*, Pennsylvania: Pennsylvania University Press.

Hindess, B. (1996) *Discourses of Power: From Hobbes To Foucault*, Oxford, Cambridge, MA: Blackwell

Honneth, A. (1991) *The Critique of Power: Reflective Stages in a Critical Social Theory*, trans. by Kenneth Baynes, Cambridge, MA: MIT Press.

Honneth, A. and Saar, M. (eds) (2003) *Michel Foucault: Zwischenbilanz einer Rezeption*, Frankfurt, Main: Suhrkamp.

Hoy, D. C. (ed.) (1986) *Foucault: A Critical Reader*, Oxford, New York: Blackwell.

Husserl, E. (1970) *The Crisis of the European Sciences and Transcendental Phenomenology: An Introduction to Phenomenological Philosophy* [1954], trans. d. Carr, Evanston: Northwestern University Press.

Howarth, D. (2000) *Discourse,* Buchkingham: Open University Press.

Howarth, D. (2001) *An Archaeology of Political Discourse? Evaluating Foucault's Explanation and Critique of Ideology*, Colchester: University of Essex.

Iggers, G. G. (2005) 'Historicism' [1973], in: *Dictionary of the History of Ideas*, ed. by Ph. P. Wiener, 4 vols, New York: Charles Scribner's Sons, vol 2, pp. 456–64 (http://etext.virginia.edu/DicHist/dict.html; date of accessed: 05/05/2006).

Ingram, D. (2005) 'Foucault and Habermas', in Gary Gutting (ed.), *The Cambridge Companion to Foucault*, 2nd edn, Cambridge: Cambridge University Press, pp. 240–83.

Jameson, F. (1991) *Postmodernism: or the Cultural Logic of Late Capitalism*, London: Verso.

Jones, C. and Porter, Roy (eds) (1994) *Reassessing Foucault: Power, Medicine, and the Body*, London, New York: Routledge.

Kay, S. (2003) *Žižek: A Critical Introduction*, Cambridge: Polity.

Kelly, M. (ed.) (1994) *Critique and Power: Recasting the Foucault/Habermas Debate*, Cambridge, MA: MIT Press.

Kögler, H.-H. (2004) *Michel Foucault*, 2nd edn, Stuttgart and Weimar: Metzler.

Lacan, J. (1977) *Écrits: A Selection*, translated by Alan Sheridan, London: Routledge.

Lacan, J. (1988) *The Seminar. Book I. Freud's Paper on Technique, 1953–54*. New York: Norton; Cambridge: Cambridge University Press.

Lacan, J. (1989) 'Kant with Sade' [1962], trans. James B. Swenson Jr, in *October*, 51, pp. 55–75.

Lacan, J. (1992) *Seminar VII: The Ethics of Psychoanalysis, 1959–1960*, ed. by Jacques-Alain Miller, trans. by Dennis Porter, London: Routledge.

Lacan, J. (1998a) *The Seminar. Book XI. The Four Fundamental Concepts of Psychoanalysis*, New York, London: W. W. Norton.

Lacan, J. (1998b) The Seminar. Book XX. *On Feminine Sexuality. The Limits of Love and Knowledge*. New York, London: W.W. Norton.

Lagrange, J. (1990) 'Lesarten der Psychoanalyse im Foucaultschen Text', in Marcelo Marques, ed., *Foucault und die Psychoanalyse: Zur Geschichte einer Auseinandersetzung*, Tübingen: Edition Diskord, pp. 72–97.

Larmour, D. H. J., Milller, P.A. and Platter C. (eds) (1997) *Rethinking Sexuality: Foucault and Classsical Antiquity*, Princeton, NY:, Princeton University Press.

Laugstien, T. (1995) 'Diskursanalyse', in *Historisch-Kritisches Wörterbuch des Marxismus*, ed. by Wolfgang Fritz Haug, vol. 2, Hamburg: Argument, col. 727–43.

Lemke, T. (1997) *Eine Kritik der politischen Vernunft: Foucault's Analyse der modernen Gouvernemantalität*, Berlin and Hamburg: Argument.

Lemke, T. (2003) 'Foucault, Governmentality, and Critique', in *Rethinking Marxism* 14, pp. 49–64.

Lenin, V. I. (1960ff) *Collected Works*, 4th English edn, Moscow: Progress Publishers.

Luxemburg, R. (2000) *Die Krise der Sozialdemokratie (Die 'Junius'-Broschüre)*, Zürich, 1916, in *Gesammelte Werke*, 6th rev. edn, vol. 4., Berlin: Dietz, pp. 51–164.

Macdonnell, D. (1986) *Theories of Discourse*, Blackwell: Oxford.

Macey, D. (1995) *The Lives of Michel Foucault*, London: Vintage.

Macherey, P. (1992) 'Towards a Natural History of Norms', in Armstrong T. J. (ed.), *Michel Foucault: Philosopher*, New York: Harvester Wheatsheaf, pp. 176–91.

McCarthy, T. (1991) 'The Critique of Impure Reason: Foucault and the Frankfurt School', in idem, *Ideals and Illusions: On Reconstruction and Deconstruction in Contemporary Critical Theory*, Cambridge, MA: MIT Press, pp. 43–75.

McKinlay, A. and Starkey, K. (eds), *Foucault, Management and Organization Theory*, London: Sage, 2004.

Mannoni, O. (1969) 'Je sais bien, mais quand-même', in *Clefs pour l'imaginaire ou l'Autre Scène*, Paris: Seuil, pp. 9–33.

Maradona, D. (2004) *El Diego*. London: Yellow Yersey Press.

Marques, M. (ed.) (1990) *Foucault und die Psychoanalyse: Zur Geschichte einer Auseinandersetzung*, Tübingen: Edition Diskord.

Marx, K. (1970ff) *Marx–Engels–Gesamtausgabe*, Berlin: Dietz.

Marx, K. (1975–2005) *Marx/Engels Collected Work*. London: Lawrence and Wishart.

Marx, K. (1977) *The Communist Manifesto*, in *Selected Writings*, ed. by D. McLellan, Oxford: Oxford University Press, pp. 221–47.

Maset, M. (2002) *Diskurs, Macht und Geschichte. Foucaults Analysetechniken und die historische Forschung*, Frankfurt, Main: Campus.

McNay, L. (1992) *Foucault and Feminism*, Boston: Northeastern Press.

McWhorter, L. (1999) *Bodies and Pleasures: Foucault and the Politics of Sexual Normalisation*, Bloomington: Indiana University Press.

McWhorter, L. (2001) 'Foucault', in *A Companion to the Philosophers*, ed. by Robert Arrington, Oxford and Malden, MA: Blackwell, pp. 249–53.

Megill, A. (1987) 'The Reception of Foucault by Historians', in *Journal of the History of Ideas*, 48, pp. 117–32.

Meinecke, F. (1972) *Historicism: The Rise of the New Historical Outlook* [1936], trans. J.E. Anderson, London: Routledge.

Miller, J.-A. (1992) 'Michel Foucault and Psychoanalysis', in Armstrong T. J. (ed.), *Michel Foucault: Philosopher*, New York: Harvester Wheatsheaf, pp. 58–63.

Miller, P.A. (1997) 'Catullan Consciousness, the "Care of the Self", and the Force of the Negative in History', in David H. J. Larmour, Paul Allen Milller, and Charles Platter (eds), *Rethinking Sexuality: Foucault and Classsical Antiquity*, Princeton, NY: Princeton University Press, pp. 171–203.

Mills, S. (2003) *Michel Foucault*, London, New York: Routledge.

Mills, S. (2004) *Discourse*, 2nd edn, London, New York: Routledge.

Moss, J., ed. (1998) *The Later Foucault: Politics and Philosophy*, London, Thousand Oaks: Sage.

Müller, C. (2003) 'Neoliberalismus als Selbstführung: Anmerkungen zu den "Gouvernmentality Studies', in *Das Argument*, 249, pp. 98–106.

Murray, O. (1992) 'Introduction', in P. Veyne, *Bread and Circuses: Historical Sociology and Political Pluralism*, London: Penguin.

Myers, T. (2004) *Slavoj Žižek* (London: Routledge).

Nietzsche, F. (2000) *On the Genealogy of Morals* [1887], in *Basic Writings of Nietzsche*, ed. and trans. by Walter Kaufmann, New York: Modern Library.

Nobus, D. (2000) *Jacques Lacan and the Freudian Practice of Psychoanalysis*, London: Routledge.

Olssen, M. (2004) 'Foucault and Marxism: Rewriting the Theory of Historical Materialism', in *Policy Futures in Education*, vol. 2, nos 3 & 4, pp. 454–82.

Paras, E. (2006) *Foucault 2.0: Beyond Power and Knowledge*, New York: Other Press.

Parker, I. (2004) *Slavoj Žižek: A Critical Introduction*, London, Sterling, VA: Pluto Press.

Passmore, K. (2003) 'Poststructuralism and History', in Berger, S., Feldner, H. and Passmore, K. (eds), *Writing History: Theory and Practice*, London, New York: Arnold, 2003, pp. 118–40.

Pêcheux, M. (1975) *Language, Semantics and Ideology*, trans. by Harbans Nagpal, London, Basingstoke: Macmillan.

Pêcheux, M. *et al.* (1995) *Automatic Discourse Analysis,* ed. by Tony Hak and Niels Helsloot, trans. by David Macey, Amsterdam, Atlanta, GA: Rodopi.

Pfaller, R. (2005) 'Where Is Your Hamster? The Concept of Ideology in Žižek's Cultural Theory', in Boucher, G., Glynos, J. and Sharpe, M. (eds) (2005), *Traversing the Fantasy: Critical Responses to Slavoj Žižek*, Aldershot: Ashgate, 105–124.

Popper, K. (1957) *The Poverty of Historicism*, London: Routledge.

Porter, Robert (2006) *Ideology: Contemporary Social, Political and Cultural Theory*, Cardiff: University of Wales Press.

Porter, Roy (2003) *Madness: A Brief History*, Oxford: Oxford University Press.

Poster, M. (1984) *Foucault, Marxism, History*, Oxford: Blackwell.

Rabinow, P. and Rose, N. (2003) 'Introduction: Foucault Today', in idem (eds), *The Essential Foucault*, New York, London: The New Press.

Rajchman, J. (1991) *Truth and Eros: Foucault, Lacan, and the Question of Ethics*, London, New York: Routledge.

Ramazanoglu, C. (ed.) (1993) *Up Against Foucault: Explorations of Some Tensions Between Foucault and Feminism*, London, New York: Routledge.

Rée, J. (2004) 'No Good Reason', in *Times Literary Supplement*, 13 August.

Reill, P. H. (1975) *The German Enlightenment and the Rise of Historicism*, Berkeley.

Reitz, T. (2003) 'Die Sorge um sich und niemand anderen: Foucault als Vordenker der Neoliberalen Vergesellschaftung', in *Das Argument*, 249 (vii), pp. 82–97.

Resch, P. R. (2001) 'The Sound of Sci(l)ence: Žižek's Concept of Ideology-Critique', in *Journal for the Psychoanalysis of Culture and Society*, vol. 6, no. 1, pp. 6–20.

Resch, R. P. (2005) 'What If God Is One of Us – Žižek Ontology', in Boucher, G., Glynos, J. and Sharpe, M. (eds) (2005), *Traversing the Fantasy: Critical Responses to Slavoj Žižek*, Aldershot: Ashgate, pp. 89–104.

Roth, M. S. (2004) 'On Keith Jenkins's "Refiguring History": New Thoughts on the Old Discipline', in *History and Theory*, 43 (2004), no. 3.

Rouse, J. (2005) 'Power/Knowledge', in Gary Gutting (ed.), *The Cambridge Companion to Foucault*, 2nd edn, Cambridge: Cambridge University Press, pp. 95–122.

Rüsen, J. (1993) *Konfigurationen des Historismus*, Frankfurt, Main: Suhrkamp.

Sarasin, P. (2001) *Reizbare Maschinen: Eine Geschichte des Körpers 1765–1914*, Frankfurt, Main: Suhrkamp.

Sarasin, P. (2003) *Geschichtswissenschaft und Diskursanalyse*, Frankfurt, Main: Suhrkamp.

Sarasin, P. (2004) *Anthrax*, Frankfurt, Main: Suhrkamp.

Sarasin, P. (2005) *Michel Foucault*, Hamburg: Junius.

Sawyer, R. K. (2003) 'Archäologie des Diskursbegriffs', in *Das Argument: Zeitschrift für Philosphie und Sozialwissenschaften*, vol. 45, no. 1, pp. 48–63.

Sawicki, J. (2005) 'Foucault, Feminism, and the Question of Identity', in Gary Gutting (ed.), *The Cambridge Companion to Foucault*, 2nd edn., Cambridge: Cambridge University Press, pp. 379–400.

Sawicki, J. (1998) 'Feminism, Foucault and "Subjects" of Power and Freedom', in J. Moss (ed.), *The Later Foucault: Politics and Philosophy*, London, Thousand Oaks: Sage, pp. 52–75.

Scholtz, G. (1989) 'Das Historismusproblem und die Geisteswissenschaften im 20. Jahrhundert', in *Archiv fur Kulturgeschichte*, 71, 463–86.

Scott, J. W. (2006) 'History as Critique', public lecture delivered on the Sixth European Social Science History Conference on 23 March 2006 in

Amsterdam; abstract at http://www.iisg.nl/esshc/specialevents2.html, last accessed: 20/04/2006.

Scull, A. (ed.) (1981) *Madhouses, Mad Doctors, and Madmen: The Social History of Psychiatry in the Victorian Era*, London: Athlone.

Scull, A. (1990) Michel Foucault's History of Madness', in *History of the Human Sciences*, 3, 57–69.

Scull, A. (2007) 'Scholarship of Fools: The Frail Foundations of Foucault's Monument', in *Times Literary Supplement*, 23 March 2007, pp. 3f.

Shepherdson, C. (2000) *Vital Signs: Nature, Culture, Psychoanalysis*, New York, London: Routledge.

Smart, B. (1983) *Foucault, Marxism and Critique*, London, New York: Routledge.

Stalin, J. V. (1953) *Works*. Moscow: Foreign Languages Publishing House.

Steenson, G. P. (1991) *After Marx, Before Lenin: Marxism and Socialist Working Class Parties in Europe*, Pittsburgh: University of Pittsburgh Press.

Taylor, C. (1986) 'Foucault on Freedom and Truth', in Hoy, D. C. (ed.), *Foucault: A Critical Reader*, Oxford, New York: Blackwell, pp. 69–102.

Trotsky, L. D. (1926) *Europe and America*, Trotsky Internet Archive, www.marxists.org/archive/trotsky/works/1926/1926-europe.htm, accessed: 17/07/2005.

Veeser, A., ed. (1994) *The New Historicism Reader*, New York, Routledge.

Verhaeghe, P. (1990) 'Causation and Destitution of a Pre-Ontological Non-Entity: On the Lacanian Subject', in Dany Nobus, (ed.), *Key Concepts of Lacanian Psychoanalysis*, London: Rebus Press, pp. 164–98.

Veyne, P. (1997) 'Foucault Revolutionizes History', in Arnold Davidson (ed.), *Foucault and His Interlocutors*, Chicago: Chicago University Press, pp. 146–82.

Veyne, P. (2003) 'Michel Foucault's Denken', in Honneth, A., and Saar M. (eds), *Michel Foucault: Zwischenbilanz einer Rezeption*, Frankfurt, Main: Suhrkamp, pp. 27–51.

Vighi, F. and H. Feldner, eds (2007) *Did Somebody Say Ideology? On Slavoj Žižek and Consequences*, Cambridge Scholars Publishing.

Walzer, M. (1986) 'The Politics of Michel Foucault', in Hoy, D. C. (ed.), *Foucault: A Critical Reader*, Oxford, New York: Blackwell, pp. 51–68.

Weber, M. (1949) '"Objectivity" in the Social Sciences and Social Policy' [1904], in *Max Weber on the Methodology of the Social Sciences*, ed. by E. H. Shils and H. A. Finch, New York: The Free Press, pp. 49–112.

Weedon, C. (1997) *Feminist Practice and Poststructuralist Theory*, 2nd edn, Oxford, Cambridge, MA: Blackwell.

Weedon, C. (1999) *Feminism, Theory and the Politics of Difference*, Oxford, Malden, MA: Blackwell.

Wehler, H.-U. (1998) 'Die "Diszipinargesellschaft" als Geschöpf der Diskurse, der Machttechniken und der "Bio-Politik"', in idem, *Die Herausforderung der Kulturgeschichte*, Munich: Beck, pp. 45–95.

Whitebook, J. (2005) 'Against Interiority: Foucault's Struggle with Psychoanalysis', in G. Gutting, (ed.), *The Cambridge Companion to Foucault*, 2nd edn, Cambridge: Cambridge University Press, pp. 312–47.

Žižek, S. (1989) *The Sublime Object of Ideology*, London: Verso.

Žižek, S. (1993) *Tarrying with the Negative*. Durham: Duke University Press.

Žižek, S. (1994a) *Metastases of Enjoyment: Six Essays on Women and Causality*, London, New York: Verso.
Žižek, S. (1994b) 'The Spectre of Ideology', in idem (ed.), *Mapping Ideology*, London: Verso, pp. 1–33.
Žižek, S. (1995) 'Woman is one of the Names-of-the-Father, or how Not to misread Lacan's formulas of sexuation' in *Lacanian Ink*, 10, pp. 24–39. All quotations from http://www.lacan.com/zizwoman.htm, accessed: 09/04/2006.
Žižek, S. (1997) *The Plague of Fantasies*, London: Verso.
Žižek, S. (1999a) 'A leftist plea for "eurocentrism"', in *Critical Inquiry*, vol. 24 (4), pp. 988–1000.
Žižek, S. (1999b) 'Attempts to Escape the Logic of Capitalism', *London Review of Books*, vol. 21 (21), pp. 3–7.
Žižek, S. (2000a) *The Ticklish Subject*, London, New York: Verso.
Žižek, S. (2000b) *The Fragile Absolute*, London, New York: Verso.
Žižek, S. (2001a) *Enjoy Your Symptom: Jacques Lacan In Hollywood and Out*, 2nd edn, London, New York: Routledge.
Žižek, S. (2001b) *Did Somebody Say Totalitarianism?*, London, New York: Verso.
Žižek, S. (2001c) *On Belief*, London: Routledge.
Žižek, S. (2002a) *Revolution at the Gates*, London: Verso.
Žižek, S. (2002b) *For They Know Not What They Do: Enjoyment as a Political Factor*, London: Verso.
Žižek, S. (2002c) 'Revolution must strike twice', in *London Review of Books*, vol. 24 (14), pp. 13–15.
Žižek, S. (2002d) 'I Am a Fighting Atheist: Interview with Slavoj Žižek' *Bad Subjects*, n. 59, February 2002.
Žižek, S. (2003a) 'Will You Laugh For Me, Please?', *In These Times*, 18 July 2003.
Žižek, S. (2003b) *The Puppet and the Dwarf*, Cambridge, MA, London: MIT.
Žižek, S. (2004a) *Iraq: The Borrowed Kettle*, London: Verso.
Žižek, S. (2004b) 'Over the Rainbow', in *London Review of Books*, 4 November 2004, p. 20.
Žižek, S. (2004c) *Organs Without Bodies: On Deleuze and Consequences*, New York, London: Routledge.
Žižek S. (2005a) 'Žižek Live', in R. Butler, *Slavoj Žižek: Live Theory*, London, New York: Continuum.
Žižek, S. (2005b) 'The Subject Supposed to Loot and Rape. Reality and Fantasy in New Orleans', in *In These Times*, 20 October 2005.
Žižek, S. (2005c) 'The Constitution Is Dead. Long Live Proper Politics', in *Guardian*, 4 June 2005.
Žižek, S. (2006a) *The Parallax View*, Cambridge, MA, London: MIT.
Žižek, S. (2006b) 'Neighbors and Other Monsters: a Plea for Ethical Violence', in S. Žižek, E. Santner and K. Reinhard (eds), *The Neighbor*, Chicago, London: The University of Chicago Press.
Žižek, S. (2006c) *How to Read Lacan*, London: Granta.
Žižek, S. and Daly, G. (2004) *Conversations with Žižek*, Cambridge, Oxford, Malden, MA: Cambridge University Press.

Index